THE LANGUAGE BUILDER

Volume 94

Claude Hagège

The Language Builder

THE
LANGUAGE BUILDER

AN ESSAY ON THE HUMAN SIGNATURE
IN LINGUISTIC MORPHOGENESIS

CLAUDE HAGÈGE
Collège de France

JOHN BENJAMINS PUBLISHING COMPANY
AMSTERDAM/PHILADELPHIA

1993

By the same author

1970. *La langue mbum de Nganha (Cameroun)*. Paris: Klincksieck (Société d'Etudes Linguistiques et Anthropologiques de France), 2. vol.

1973. *Profil d'un parler arabe du Tchad*. Paris: Geuthner.

1975. *Le problème linguistique des prépositions et la solution chinoise (avec un essai de typologie à travers plusieurs groupes de langues)*. (Collection linguistique publiée par la Société de Linguistique de Paris) Paris-Louvain: Peeters.

1978. *La phonologie panchronique* (with André Haudricourt). Paris: Presses Universitaires de France.

1981. *Critical Reflections on Generative Grammar*. (Edward Sapir Monograph Series in Language, Culture and Cognition, 10) Lake Bluff (Ill.): Jupiter Press.

1981. *Le comox lhaamen de Colombie britannique: présentation d'une langue amérindienne*. (Amerindia, numéro spécial 2) Paris: Association d'Ethnolinguistique Amérindienne.

1982. *La structure des langues*. (Que sais-je?, 2006) Paris: Presses Universitaires de France. (2nd ed. 1986).

1983-1990. *Language Reform: History and Future* (with István Fodor). Hamburg: Buske, 5 vol.

1986. *Les catégories de la langue palau (Micronésie): une curiosité typologique*. (Forms of Language Structure, 1) Munich: Wilhelm Fink Verlag.

1987. *Le français et les siècles*. Paris: Odile Jacob.

1990. *The Dialogic Species, A linguistic Contribution to the Social Sciences*. (European Perspectives) New York: Columbia University Press.

1992. *Le souffle de la langue, Voies et destins des parlers d'Europe*. Paris: Odile Jacob.

Library of Congress Cataloging-in-Publication Data

Hagège, Claude, 1936-
    The language builder : an essay on the human signature in linguistic morphogenesis / Claude Hagège.
        p.   cm. -- (Amsterdam studies in the theory and history of linguistic science. Series IV, Current issues in linguistic theory, ISSN 0304-0763; v. 94)
    Includes bibliographical references and indexes.
    1. Linguistics. 2. Language and languages. I. Title. II. Series.
P121.H25   1993
410--dc20   92-42077
ISBN 90 272 3594 5 (Eur.) / 1-55619-155-3 (US) (Hb, alk. paper)   CIP
ISBN 90 272 3596 1 Eur.) / 1-55619-157-X (US) (Pb, alk. paper)

John Benjamins Publishing Co. · P.O. Box 75577 · 1070 AN Amsterdam · Netherlands
John Benjamins North America · 821 Bethlehem Pike · Philadelphia, PA 19118 · USA

Contents

Preface

Linguistics, to the extent that it is a social science, should have something to teach us about humans as social beings. Contemporary linguistics, however, has not really met this need. The insistence of Generative Grammar on processes by which so-called surface structures are derived from deep structures by a series of transformations seemed to announce a renewed interest in the human beings whose mental activity is implied by these operations. But this model regards languages as autonomous systems, and is therefore little concerned with speakers and hearers, their interactions, and their relationships to the world around them. Furthermore, the algorithms and formulas which this model uses on a large scale have much more to do with methodology and the properties of linguistic theories than with languages themselves and those who use them in everyday life.

The enthusiasm with which many linguists formerly trained in Generative Grammar have embraced cognitive approaches to language in recent years seems to promise new insights into the functioning of the human brain, and to lead to a more adequate understanding of language. Yet, exciting though this prospect may be, there remains the need for a thorough study of another, hardly less important, aspect of language; this aspect is by no means contradictory to cognitive investigations: it shows us the users of language within a framework that accounts for the social activity by which speakers build linguistic structures in order to meet the requirements of communication.

The present book is an attempt at a treatment which, based on a wide range of languages of the world, hopes to shed light on language building activity. Humans are therefore defined here as language builders. Certain aspects of language building are conscious, especially those which are related to lexical creativity, commonly referred to as neologization. Within the domains of morphology and syntax, however, this activity is largely unconscious. And yet the striking phenomenon which is stressed here is that by initiating language change, humans leave their signature everywhere, even if they do it unconsciously in most instances. In other words, it is maintained here that human presence is manifest at all levels of consciousness, whether it be total, partial or nonexisting. Therefore, studying humans as language builders is a way of complying with one of the main tasks of linguists as social scientists: to reveal some basic characteristics of human beings as reflected in languages and the way they are used in regular speech activity.

It is my conviction that the human presence in language building deserves much more attention than it has received so far on the part of linguists. Indeed, the time has come to re-humanize linguistics, and to show that this can be done in full accordance with scientific standards. The effort made here in order to restore the human presence in linguistics relies on well-established methods, though it puts into question the opposition between synchrony and diachrony advocated by many linguists, and stresses instead the importance of language as a dynamic activity (speech), as opposed to language as a self-contained system which has been the main, if not the exclusive, concern of most modern linguists.

I would like to express my gratitude to Konrad Koerner for his precious help with the manuscript and his editorial care. My thanks also go to the two anonymous readers of an earlier version of the study, each of whom has made interesting remarks. I have considered many of their suggestions. I am also indebted to Andrée Dufour, Anne Szulmajster, Steve Hewitt and Steven Schaefer, for typing the text and helping me with the proofreading. Any shortcomings, however, must remain my responsibility.

Paris, 14 July 1992
Claude Hagège

List of abbreviations used in glosses

ABL	Ablative	DEM	Demonstrative
ABS	Absolutive	DESID	Desiderative
ACC	Accusative	DET	Determiner
ADJ	Adjectival, Adjective	DIR	Directional
		DISC.M	Discourse modal
AG	Agent	DX	Deixis
AGR	Agreement marker	ERG	Ergative
		EXCL	Exclusive
ALL	Allative	FACT	Factual
ANAPH	Anaphoric	FEM	Feminine
ANISOPH	Anisophoric	FOC	Focalizer
AO	Aorist	FUT	Future
ART	Article	GEN	Genitive
ASP	Aspect	IMM.FUT	Imminent future
ASS	Assertive	IMP	Imperative
AUX	Auxiliary	IMPERF	Imperfective
AV	Aversive	INC.OBJ	Incorporated object
BEN	Benefactive		
CAUS	Causative	INCH	Inchoative
CIT	Citation	INCL	Inclusive
CLSF	Classifier	INDEF	Indefinite
COMP	Complementizer	IND.C	Indirect case
CON	Conative	INDIC	Indicative
COND	Conditional	INF	Infinitive
CONN	Connective	INGR	Ingressive
COP	Copula	INSTR	Instrumental
CORR	Correlative morpheme	INTERR	Interrogative
		INTRANS	Intransitive
DAT	Dative	ISOPH	Isophoric
DECL	Declarative mood	IT	Itive
		LOC	Locative

LOG	Logophoric	PRED.RED	Predicativity
LV	Link vowel		reducer
M	Marker	PRES	Present
MASC	Masculine	PRIV	Privative
N	Noun	PROGR	Progressive
NARR	Narrative	REDUP	Reduplication
NEG	Negation	REFL	Reflexive
NMLZ	Nominalizer	REL	Relator
NMN	Nominalizing	RESUMPT	Resumptive
NOMIN	Nominative	SBJC	Subjunctive
NP	Noun-phrase	SBJCTV	Subjective con-
NUM	Numeral		jugation
OBJ	Object	SG	Singular
OBJCTV	Objective	SOV	Subject-object-
	conjugation		verb
OBL	Oblique	SPEC	Specifier
OPTION	Optional	SUB	Subordinating
PART	Partitive		morpheme
PARTCP	Participle	SUBJ	Subject
PASS	Passive	SUFF	Suffix
PAT	Patient	SVO	Subject-verb-
PER	Personal		object
	index	TERM	Terminative
PERF	Perfective	TOP	Topic
PL	Plural	TRANS	Transitive
POL	Politeness	UND	Undergoer
	marker	V	Verb
POSS	Possessive	VP	Verb-phrase
POT	Potential		

Introduction

In the history of modern linguistics, a striking coincidence deserves to be pointed out: exactly one century after the publication of Bopp's *Conjugationssystem* (1816), which laid the foundation of comparative grammar, there appeared another ground-breaking book, i.e., Saussure's *Cours* (1916), whose main concepts continue today, through various adaptations, to inspire most schools of linguistics. However, if we agree – and few people would disagree – that one of the main tasks of language specialists should be to shed light on the properties which define human beings as a dialogic species (cf. Hagège 1990b), then we must recognize that contemporary research in linguistics still leaves much to be desired. It is true that the various versions of Generative Grammar and the models derived from it have provided interesting interpretations of the relation between language and psychology, and have as well aroused interest in a number of syntactic problems (cf., for instance, Chomsky 1981). But explaining linguistic behavior in terms of the capacity of the human mind to generate an infinite number of sentences is not sufficient, whatever findings such an approach makes possible. Another significant field of study is the building of linguistic forms, a process reflecting a fundamental human activity, whose framework is speech interaction.

In such a perspective, linguistics is explicitly viewed as a branch of anthropology, and linguists are expected to contribute a deeper knowledge of the properties that define mankind and of the place our species occupies in nature. This point calls for further consideration. Given the importance of the interpersonal relationship, through which semantic contents are communicated in everyday life, the social dimension of language is one of the most fundamental. Linguistics can be considered a cognitive science in view of the role played by language in such cognitive faculties and phenomena as memory, acquisition of knowledge, reasoning, decision making, etc. However, we should never forget that *linguistics is the only cognitive science which is also a social science.* This suffices to distinguish it sharply from other cognitive sciences, such as research on artificial intelligence, cognitive anthropology, cognitive psychology, computer theory,

cybernetics, mathematics, neuro-sciences (including neuro-psychology), etc.
I do not deny the importance of the contribution of linguistics to the pro
gram of cognitive science, which aims, as recalled in Anderson (1989:810),
at "providing a new and explicit science of the mind". I simply want to
stress that language is also a social phenomenon, since the building of
linguistic forms is the human answer to the inescapable need to commu-
nicate. In the present book it will appear that studying the genesis of
linguistic forms is one of the properly linguistic tasks which only linguists
can undertake. In this respect, the following point of view, even if it calls
for some qualification, is worth pondering:

> The crisis of autonomy of the late 19th century is being replayed in the
> waning years of the 20th, as linguistics departments find themselves being
> swallowed up by more inclusive cognitive science programs, or bitten into
> by computer scientists, or both at once. The discipline's survival depends
> upon continual reassertion that language can and must be studied in itself,
> along with a recognition that data, models, and metaphors from contingent
> areas can be enlightening, provided that they are not mistaken for linguistics.
> (Joseph 1989: 601).

Another problem is formalization. The choice of a precise and consistent
terminology is a prerequisite for all scientific study. Using tables and
graphs often makes things much clearer. If, on the other hand, formalization is conceived of as the quasi-obligatory, large scale use of
algebraic formulas, algorithms and various systems of calculi, then this
book cannot be counted among those which reflect such a conception. Let
it be stated clearly: although formalization may have some intrinsic value
for theories that try to give linear representation to certain linguistic, and
perhaps even mental, structures, and although it is true that synthetic
formulas help one to catch at a glance the data of a given problem, *formalization must not be mistaken for explanation.*

It is not my purpose here to add yet another polemic enterprise to the
various, not always felicitous, and sometimes superficial criticisms that
have been leveled in the last fifteen years against the proliferation of
formal models in linguistics (an interesting one can be found, for example,
in Gross 1979). I wish only to consider three simple points.

First, linguistics deals with the faculty of language, as manifested by
languages, i.e., by historical, cultural and social "objects". Consequently,
linguistics cannot, at least not primarily, be an axiomatic discipline in

which the best result is that arrived at by the best and most refined reasoning. The method of argumentation, here, is applied to real phenomena, not to abstract entities.

Second, when considering the present state of linguistics, one cannot help thinking that things would be different if language were studied not only in deductive, but also in inductive terms. Many languages are on the brink of extinction. Those which are not may provide interesting contributions to our knowledge of linguistic structures, thus helping to make our theoretical foundations less shaky, and to cast out some of the imaginary formal puzzles that bedevil certain aspects of contemporary linguistics. The collection of a wide variety of languages, far from reflecting a stubborn attachment to simplistic taxonomies, is one of our main tasks if we are to understand some of the mechanisms which underlie speech activity, and thereby characterize human beings as language builders. It may be useful, in that respect, to cite an opinion put forward by an unbiased linguist, who, while doing spadework on little-known languages, is well aware of present theoretical issues:

> I am appalled at the number of man-hours spent in trying to defend one theoretical approach over another when both are usually doomed to be consigned to the waste-bin of linguistic theory within an amazingly short space of time, especially as there remains so much still to be discovered about all sorts of languages. (Hewitt 1988).

However, by stressing the importance of studying as many individual languages as possible, I do not mean that a deductive strategy is worthless. Some of the theoretical issues raised by Generative Grammar, for instance, have provided a basis for the investigation of little-known phenomena. There can be cross-fertilization if we recognize the advantage of doing not only theory-oriented theoretical linguistics, but also data-oriented theoretical linguistics (I prefer this formulation over the somewhat stale "theory-oriented" / "data-oriented" couple, since every linguistics is theoretical, whether or not it claims to be). Realizing that linguistics is both a cognitive and a natural science (the one implies the other) may persuade us not to shy away from data provided by typologically different languages. We thus recognize the importance of typology in linguistic research: it both gives access to material and provides tests of the adequacy of theoretical models. Hence the significance of what I propose to designate as *revealing languages*. Largely by virtue of their atypical character, such languages are likely to show explicit correlations between structures seemingly unrelated in most other systems, and thus to reveal significant properties of human language, and indicate the limits beyond which no grammar can go. It will appear that several among the languages drawn upon in the present book are revealing languages.

Third, I would like to emphasize a point which, as far as I can see, has not received the attention it deserves, despite its importance for the destiny of contemporary linguistics. We know (cf. Kuhn 1970:17) that the initial divergences which are characteristic of the early stages of development of any science soon disappear. Why is linguistics so different in this respect? Most schools of theoretical linguistics today seem to go on working each along its own lines, only rarely paying attention to research within other frameworks, especially that of so-called 'descriptive linguists'. The reason is not far to seek: each school soon develops its own symbols and formal representations, which put off other researchers, who are loath to invest the time and effort necessary to master such a complex apparatus for the often meagre dividends it affords. The result is to make an even more intensive use of this apparatus, and to write increasingly for restricted circles of initiates rather than for a broader audience. To some extent, this helps to explain the present state of linguistics, broken up as it is into many self-sufficient theories which often ignore each other and seem from outside to be addressing radically different objects of study, whereas in fact they are all concerned with language.

Studying the making of linguistic forms can give us an opportunity to go beyond the controversies between various brands of formal research. I will therefore try to characterize languages in both an explicit and accessible way, on the basis of data taken from many different geographical zones and representing a broad diversity of typological features. There is much to gain in examining such data as carefully as possible, instead of cultivating self-contained and self-sustaining paradigms. In this way, we can both test hypotheses arrived at through a hypothetico-deductive strategy and discover general tendencies through a more inductive strategy.

The present book is based on the assumption that linguistics must deal with human presence in language. The book makes use of the notion of consciousness. This word refers here to the intellectual attitude of language users in cases where they know what they are doing when they speak, although they express this knowledge in non-technical terms. For instance, they may comment on the fact that they are using a particular word rather than another one, or that they are meeting a certain communicative need when giving up a formulation in favor of another. Of course, linguistic consciousness in this sense is rarely complete, but it is not always non-existent. This is why I speak of levels of consciousness. The notion of consciousness is important: it is because language users are not always totally unconscious with regard to what they are doing when speaking, that any linguistic theory concerned with human beings as language users must examine their levels of linguistic consciousness. Therefore, it is necessary to study the relationship between human presence in language and levels of consciousness.

The main organizing principle is that *human presence is manifest at all levels of consciousness* - full, partial, and zero. Hence, PART I, **Levels of linguistic consciousness and human intervention in language,** studies cases of full and partial human consciousness in Language building, respectively in chapter 1: "The problem of consciousness in Language building" and chapter 2: "Adaptation of linguistic systems to meet Language Builders' needs". PART II, **The place of humans in language morphogenesis,** examines cases of unconscious Language building, which reveal the human imprint, to no less an extent but in different ways, as compared with the cases studied in PART I. It is divided into three chapters: chapter 3 studies "Languages as anthropocentric systems", chapter 4 examines "The presence of Language Builders in creologenesis", and chapter 5, "Language Builders and the linguistic cycle", shows that language morphogenesis follows cycles related to the human search for expressiveness. PART III, **Two aspects of language morphogenesis,** shows that two important processes of Language building, called "Lexicalization" (chapter 6) and "Grammaticalization" (chapter 7), testify, even if at a very low or zero degree of consciousness in most cases, to the permanent shaping activity of Language Builders, as related to psychosocial requirements.

Throughout these chapters, my purpose is to highlight the aptitude Language Builders have for shaping the linguistic tools they need in their psychosocial life. Therefore the conception which underlies the present work can be clearly stated: one of the functions of linguistics is to characterize human beings as a species whose vocation is to put the world into words, sentences (combinations of words), and texts (combinations of sentences). They do it in the natural environment of interpersonal, i.e., social, communication. In such an environment, their activity can be characterized as operative: they build words, sentences, and texts by applying various and changing operations, which define the different stages of every language.

As a consequence, the framework in which the present book studies morphogenesis can be called *socio-operative linguistics* (Hagège 1990b: chapter 10). It aims at characterizing human beings by their linguistic behavior, thus deepening our knowledge of human nature.

Modern linguistics has attained "scientific" status largely by means of ignoring precisely those aspects of human consciousness, will, and linguistic presence which I target in this book. An orientation of linguistic theory toward the human dimension, then, seems necessary. I hope this book will be taken as a contribution, however modest, to that aim.

PART I

LEVELS OF

LINGUISTIC CONSCIOUSNESS

AND HUMAN INTERVENTION

IN LANGUAGE

Human presence in language is manifest at all levels of consciousness. The first part of this book will show that there are manifestations of human presence at the levels of full consciousness and low consciousness. The former are observable in certain cases of direct intervention in the lexicon, but also in phonology, and even in some domains of morphosyntax (chapter 1). The latter are observable through the constant effort by which humans try to adapt linguistic systems to meet the needs of everyday linguistic communication (chapter 2).

CHAPTER 1

The problem of consciousness
in Language building

After some preliminary definitions (1.1), the present chapter will examine certain impulses that characterize Language Builders' linguistic behavior (1.2); it will then show that there are, in Language building, manifestations of human presence at various degrees of consciousness, including many types of full consciousness; this will appear not only in the lexicon (standardization and neological activities among other manifestations), but also in phonology, and even in certain types of intentional morphosyntactic building (1.3); the conclusion (1.4) will draw some consequences with respect to the properties which define human beings as Language Builders.

1.1 Defining the concept of Language Builder

I have chosen to introduce the concept of Language Builder (LB) as defining, in a linguistic perspective, *all human beings*, and to say that LBs are characterized by the activity of Language building (Lb). I could just as well have introduced, if I had retained a learned Greek terminology, the concept of *glossogenetes*, from *glossa*, "language" and *genetês* "the one who engenders or creates" (distinct from *genêtos* "born in"). Both Language Builder and *glossogenetes* imply that Language building is a panchronic and pantopic activity: it corresponds to an ongoing and continuously renewed process of generation of languages, and it takes place in all of them. LBs "glotticize" by nature, both putting the world into language and building/reshaping languages. LBs are defined, and have always been defined, by this activity.

I will leave aside here the implications of the concept of Lb with regard to the history of language as a faculty and its evolution since its putative "beginnings", of which we know little. Nor will I consider, other than occasionally, the ontogenetic implications, in other words, the important process by which children acquire language and may even thereby contribute to its evolution. I would like to stress, on the other hand, that "LB" refers to the listener as well as the speaker, and should by no means be interpreted as applying, in a reductive way, to the speaker alone. Lb could not have occurred, and is inconceivable, without the constant bond of the interpersonal relationship which arises within the framework of communication. Humans try out new forms and modify old ones; but at the same time, they react to new or modified forms which they may hear. These two activities cannot be kept separate. They serve to define humans as an *articulate species*, where *articulate* covers both production and reception. Consequently, one should not lose sight of the phonological aspect. Phonology has often played a crucial role in the recent history of linguistics. Thus, the Prague School, following from Saussure, laid the foundations of structuralism by stressing a phenomenon which, simple and obvious though it may appear today, had gone almost unnoticed: meaning is carried by the association of distinctive sounds. Facts relevant to phonology will appear everywhere in this study.

These two interrelated points, i.e., the role of the listener and the importance of phonology, have quite rightly been stressed in the eighties by various authors (cf., among others, Ohala 1981). I would like to point out, however, a particular feature of the present book. What is at stake here is not so much language change *per se* as the building of language. Instead of saying that a language changes, it seems more appropriate to say that *it is produced,* and this to the very extent that language is not an independent entity or a natural organism of the same type as the objects studied by physics. Language is a method of expression built by, and meant for, the human species. Thus, language has no phenomenal reality outside the human mind and social exchange. This amounts to saying that permanent glossogenesis and speaker-listener interaction are two fundamental dimensions of language. As a consequence, the search for the causes of linguistic change is partly misleading, unless we mean thereby two of the Aristotelian types of causes, i.e., efficient causes (human motivations) and final causes (meeting human needs). It so happens that both those causes lie in human activity and nowhere else.

Therefore, the only rewarding work is not a metaphysical quest for the deep reasons, but the attempt to bring the building processes to light. This will not result in stating rules without exceptions, but in discovering general tendencies. Such a result is not surprising, since linguistics is a science which deals with a cultural phenomenon. LB-governed efficient causes, including contact-induced influences and propelling forces, are examined here, rather than rule-governed phenomena viewed as reflecting an inborn competence. Such phenomena have already been studied in an abundant literature. It may be useful to explore other paths.

1.2 The LBs' impulses

Interesting dynamic processes can be observed in the linguistic behavior of LBs. Two such processes will be examined here, which I propose to call Homonymic Assimilation (HA) and Allonymic Dissimilation (AD). Although apparent opposites, they represent two aspects of the same tendency.

HA prompts a loanword to be given the form of one or more similar sounding native words, even though the meanings have nothing in common. Thus, in English (Buyssens 1965:26-27),

(1)

OFr	*moisseron*	became	*mushroom*	(*mush + room*)
Fr	*lustrine*	"	*lutestring*	(*lute + string*)
It	*marzapane*	"	*marchpane*	(*March + pane*)
Port	*garoupa*	"	*grouper*	
Ir	*seamrog*	"	*shamrock*	(*sham + rock*)
Pers	*šir-o-šakkar* ("milk-and-sugar")	"	*seersucker*	(*seer + sucker*)
Cree	*oček*	"	*woodchuck*	(*wood + chuck*).

Another situation is one in which two words, due to phonetic evolution, are becoming identical. As a result of AD, one of them disappears or is replaced by a new item which is either based on the same root or entirely different. It is striking, for example, that French has kept none of the homonymic pairs produced by the diachronic loss of the voiced/unvoiced contrast in intervocalic position ((2)a below); the same is true of homonymic pairs created by the loss of final *-em* or *-um* in nouns and adjectives: one of the Latin words has either disappeared, its meaning being expressed by a new root ((2)b), or been replaced by a diminutive ((2)c) (Gougenheim 1972:301):

(2) a. *sūtōrem* "shoemaker" and *sūdōrem* "sweat" both yielded *sueur*, but today, this word corresponds only to *sūdōrem*; for "shoemaker", French has *cordonnier*. *grātum* "concord" and *gradum* "grade" both yielded *gré*, but today, this word corresponds only to *grātum*; for "grade", French has *degré*.

   b. *mūrum* "wall" yielded *mur*, but *mūrem* "rat" disappeared, and its meaning is expressed today by *rat*.

   c. *aurum* "gold", *collum* "neck" and *sōlum* "alone" yielded respectively, *or*, *cou* and *seul*, but *aurem*, *collem* and *sōlem* were replaced by *auriculam*, *collinam* and *sōliculum*, which yielded, respectively, *oreille* "ear", *colline* "hill" and *soleil* "sun".

This does not mean, of course, that the conflicts due to the existence of homonymic pairs have all been resolved. It is well-known that French, just like any other language, is far from lacking in homonyms. But note, first, that, more often than not, homonyms are distinguished in their written form, which suggests that AD is active primarily when there is nothing, not even an external pressure like writing, to prevent the fusion between two words. More importantly, examples like (1) and (2) show that, in applying either HA (which cannot always be reduced to what Förstemann 1852 has called 'folk etymology') or AD, LBs are moved by the need to ensure ease of comprehension whenever possible.

This need is at least as strong as the tendency to produce "natural" forms and structures, a tendency held to be the key to morphological evolution by the proponents of Natural Morphology (cf., for instance, Dressler 1987). In the course of morphogenesis, LBs seem to be constantly striving for clarity. As a consequence, they are often led to violate "naturalness" if it comes into conflict with AD. This seems to call into question the concept of naturalness itself. Many examples from noun and verb morphology in various languages could be cited here. To take just one, in spoken Lithuanian, the 1PL.PAST.INDIC *ėjome* "we went", is usually shortened, hence *ėjom*. Linguists using the Natural Morphology framework would claim that, thanks to this shortening, the plural is made simpler than the dual *ėjova* "we both went", which has three syllables, and is therefore formally more marked than the plural, just as it is semantically; however, in the conditional, this shortening, which seems to satisfy the requirements of naturalness so nicely, never occurs; if it did, the 1PL and the 2 SG.COND would be homonymous (Stolz 1988:482). Thus it appears that LBs here favor ease of communication over naturalness.

This same need for ease of communication can also explain countless cases of redundancy in the spoken styles of various languages. Thus, in a popular Hungarian folksong, which reflects the way people really speak, we find this example of morphosyntactic redundancy:

(3)   *Hát én immár kit válasszak, virágom, virágom?*
        Te engemet, s én tégedet, virágom, virágom
        (then I from-now-on whom should-I-choose flower-my
        flower-my
        you me-ACC and I you-ACC flower-my flower-my)
        "And me, whom should I now choose, flower, my flower?
        You (will choose) me and I (will choose) you, flower, my
        flower";

engem "me", PAT of *én* "I" and *téged* "you", PAT of *te* "you (agent)" do not need to be suffixed by *-(e)t*, the accusative marker, since they are already PAT forms (originally possessives). Nevertheless, in this spoken style, as opposed to standard Hungarian, they frequently get such a suffix.

Thus, LBs often reinforce grammatical marks, just as they often strive to avoid homonymy when it reappears in the course of evolution (AD) and to naturalize loanwords by reinterpreting them in locally transparent terms (HA). It is now time to examine what this implies with regard to the consciousness of LBs.

1.3 Degrees of consciousness

Most linguists take it for granted that the process of Lb is unconscious. This term refers not to the hidden motivations that may account for dreams, intellectual and emotional images, memories, omissions, desires, slips of the tongue, etc. (Freudian acceptation), but to the acts LBs perform without even realizing it (common acceptation). There are explicit claims that Lb is unconscious; one of the most famous and classical ones is Boas (1911: 67, 70-71):

We find objects classified according to sex, or as animate and inanimate, or according to form. We find actions determined according to time and place, etc. The behavior of primitive man makes it perfectly clear that all these concepts, although they are in constant use, have never risen into consciousness, and that consequently their origin must be sought, not in rational, but in entirely unconscious, we may perhaps say instinctive, processes of the mind [...]. The linguistic classifications never rise into consciousness, while in other ethnological phenomena, although the same unconscious origin prevails, these often rise into consciousness, and thus give rise to secondary reasoning and to reinterpretations [...]. The great advantage that linguistics offers [...] is the fact that, on the whole, the categories which are formed always remain unconscious, and that for this reason the processes which lead to their formation can be followed without the misleading and disturbing factors of secondary explanations.

This claim calls for some qualification. First, synchronically, there are varying degrees of consciousness, provided we do not lose sight of the important distinction between language as a system (*langue*) and speech as an activity (*parole*). While at one end of speech activity, that corresponding to grammar, there are mechanical processes such as the application of syntactic rules and, in many languages, constraints on word formation, as well as the ability to apply these rules to the contexts in which they are required, at the other end, the selection of lexical means from among the possibilities afforded by the stock of words of a given language is a highly creative activity, which implies a conscious knowledge of the relationships among words in the vocabulary. The most skillful form of this activity serves to determine style. Besides, even "linguistic classifications" are sometimes conscious (cf. 1.3.3).

Second, diachronically, a distinction should be made between change and creation, as well as between change and innovation. LBs have communicative and expressive needs, and language, being a system designed to fulfil these needs, is used as an organism which ensures the transmission of messages. Therefore LBs are not aware of most changes in syntax and the structure of the lexicon.

But what is true of grammar and of networks of semiotic relationships is less true of the process by which words (including neologisms) are created, and the individual use of expressive means (1.3.1). As far as sounds are concerned, it is far from true that their realization is unconscious (1.3.2). With regard to cases of innovation in morphosyntax, the initial steps are probably less unconscious than the subsequent ones, especially when there is an increasing process of freezing; at any rate, there are, here too, various degrees of consciousness (1.3.3).

1.3.1 Degrees of consciousness in lexicogenesis

Here we will study different cases of word-building, from the least to the most conscious. Seven points will successively be examined:
a. From *parole* to *langue*
b. Meaning-induced diachronic operations and the creative work of subjective reinterpretation
c. Hypocoristics
d. The shaping of the lexicon
e. Ideophone-making
f. Word-coining by individual users
g. Neological activity in literate societies.

a. *From **parole** to **langue***
I will begin with the least conscious cases of lexical building, whereby formulations appearing in LBs' speech (*parole* in Saussurean terms) become regular elements in the linguistic system (*langue*). This codification of spontaneous speech events has not, so far, been sufficiently studied, if only because mainstream linguistics, in the wake of Generative Grammar, has long underestimated many aspects of language related to concrete interpersonal communication as being relevant to performance rather than to competence.

One of the most interesting of these aspects is what Benveniste (1958) has called *delocutive verbs*. A *delocutive verb* is a linguistic sign that comes from a speech locution, not from another sign, hence its proposed name. Although materially derived from a base which is a specific word, it is really related to this base by a "say" relationship. Thus, in English, *to damn*, when it does not mean "to condemn as guilty", but "to swear at by saying 'damn' " (Webster's 1976:357), cannot be interpreted by simply referring it to its base *damn!*: the definition given by the dictionary clearly shows that it presupposes a speech occurrence; in other words, *to damn* = "to say *damn!*". The same applies to other verbs such as *to hail*, *to encore*, or American English *to O.K.*, as well as to French *pester*, *sacrer*, respectively meaning "to say *peste!* ("damn!")" and "to say *sacré...*" ("to swear"), Old French *mercier* = "to say *merci!* ("mercy!", and later "thank you!")", or Latin *negare* "to say *nec*" ("to deny"), *autumare* "to say *autem*" ("to argue") and *quiritare* "to shout *Quirites!* ("o Roman citizens!")" (Benveniste 1958).

It is proposed here to add the notion of *delocutive nouns* to that of *delocutive verbs. Damn* is a noun when it refers to the act of saying *damn!*. Thus, a delocutive noun, instead of being derived, as delocutive verbs are, by such processes as the use of English *to*, the suffixation of French *-er*, etc., is the locution itself, accompanied, as the case may be, by morphemes which indicate its nominal status, or *nominants* in Hagège's (1982) terminology. For example, in some languages, there are nouns which function as fillers, when speakers scan their memory for a personal name or a place name: in Ngandi, *jara*, translated by *watchamacallit* in Heath (1985), takes noun-class prefixes, regular case suffixes, and a *bi-* prefix referring, when necessary, to place names. Moreover, it serves as a base for derived verbs meaning "to do, or to become, *watchamacallit*". There is no kind of stigma attached to using such words, as is the case with English fillers like *um*. Quite to the contrary, *jara*, with its set of inflectional and derivational forms, belongs to perfectly normal Ngandi speech and has high text frequency.

Many surnames are delocutive nouns, such as French *Cheramy* (*cher* + *ami*), *Depardieu* (an oath meaning "God-damn!"), etc. The same is true of ethnic nicknames: French *bigot*, a derogatory nickname of the Normans (from English *by God!*), Middle French *dasticoteurs*, applied to the Germans (from German *dass dich Gott* "that God...thee"), Walloon *canifichtône* designating the Flemings and the Dutch (from Dutch *kan niet verstaan* "cannot understand"), Portuguese *camone*, a jocular name given to the English (from English *come on!*) (cf. Chambon 1986). Likewise, it is well-known that many geographical and ethnic names are derived from short messages addressed by, or to, foreigners whose knowledge of the addressee's language is inadequate. Among delocutive nouns that are lexemes, i.e., belong to the common vocabulary of a language, some are even derived from morphemes, especially from personal pronouns, such as Arabic *ʔanâniyya* "selfishness", from *ʔanâ* "I", and all the nouns derived from verbs which, in various languages with different levels of politeness, refer to the use of a certain personal pronoun as opposed to another. Thus French *tutoiement* is derived from the verb *tutoyer*. The verbs themselves are derived from these pronouns, related to them by a "say" relationship: French *tutoyer/voussoyer* "to say *tu*/to say *vous*", German *duzen/siezen* "to say *du*/to say *Sie*", Hungarian *tegezodik*/*magazodik* "he says *te*/he says *maga*". In all these cases, the important role played by language users in the process of communication is clearly reflected in the language system itself: they introduce a phrase which bears the marks of live interpersonal speech.

This case of Lb should not be confused with the common phenomenon by which an item entering the system originates in idiolectal speech activity. In the case examined here, we do not have a paradigmatic derivation yielding a new word from a root already present in the paradigm, but a word entering the paradigm from a certain context in which this word is uttered; its meaning is not simply "an x" or "to x", but "x as something which is uttered" and "to utter x", respectively.

In another interesting case, certain phenomena which are characteristic of spontaneous speech may result in innovations as regards the language system itself. There are, at least, two ways of interrupting the speech chain. One is to use what Hagège (1990b:199 ff.) has proposed to call *word sequence shatterers*, represented by such uses as those of **perhaps**, **of course** or **do you hear** in (4), (5) and (6) below, respectively:

(4)   *I will do it, unless,* **perhaps,** *you want to do it yourself*
(5)   *without,* **of course,** *intervening*
(6)   *he was afraid,* **do you hear,** *afraid.*

It goes without saying that word sequence shatterers are not a separate part of speech, but a specific and creative use of various word types, whose common effect is to allow speakers a brief respite from time by shaping it into manageable intervals.

Another way of interrupting the speech chain is left dislocation. Russian linguists use the term *lektorskij imenitel'nyj*, "lecturer's (proleptic) nominative" for the fronting of a nominal topic, followed by a coreferential personal index, whereby a speaker can put a distance between himself and what he is saying. In everyday speech there are many cases of such redundancies, which are of course condemned by purists, e.g.,

(7)   *Puškin on napisal stixotvorenie Ančar*
        (Pushkin he wrote poem A.)
        "Pushkin wrote the poem Ančar".

In examples like (7), there is no pause between the noun and its pronominal copy. In constructions requiring the dative of the personal index, the proleptic noun often remains in the nominative, an example of *casus pendens*, whereby speakers circumvent the declension of the noun and treat it as a topic (cf. 3.3):

(8) *Miša emu vsë ravno*
     (Misha(NOMIN) him(DAT) all equal)
     "Misha does not care";

on in (7) and *emu* in (8) indicate the gender and pragmatic function of the fronted noun. They are thus responsible for an ongoing innovation in the syntactic system, since contemporary spoken Russian, following an analytical tendency which it shares with agglutinative languages, is progressively acquiring pronominal gender markers (Comtet 1989). In other words, by producing in their speech "incorrect" but easily comprehensible sentences, LBs build new grammars. They thus reshape their language, in an effort to attenuate the effects of *the main obstacle to communication, i.e., the unavoidable quasi-simultaneity between discourse planning and speech transmission.*

b. *Meaning-induced diachronic operations and the creative work of subjective reinterpretation*
     At a level of consciousness which is still low, it is interesting to examine certain diachronic changes through which LBs leave traces of their aptitude to reinterpret, often in more subjective terms, a certain linguistic structure.
     The relationship between tense/aspect and the lexical meaning of verbs provides a good illustration of the operation whereby LBs elaborate a certain representation of things and "look for" the linguistic tools most appropriate to its expression. A revealing case is the identification, in certain languages, of the aorist tense with the perfective aspect, and, similarly, of the imperfect tense with the imperfective aspect. One of the factors leading LBs to such a treatment is that in the languages in question, these associations between a certain tense and a corresponding aspect are reflected in the normal use of many verbs, due to their meanings: those which refer to events that either are dynamic or have occurred only once or a few times without duration are more compatible with the perfective than those with a stative or durative meaning.

In Slovenian, this has resulted in a restructuring of the aspect system: the aorist and the imperfect have disappeared as tenses, and the semantic opposition they represented has been reinterpreted as one of aspect. The meanings of the verbs have probably been the decisive factor, but at least two adjacent conditions have helped to hasten the evolution. First, we know that in all Slavic languages, the primacy of aspect had already been furthered by the elimination of the future stem. This is in fact a partially fortuitous formal phenomenon, which did not correspond to a need of the speakers. It constitutes additional proof of the importance of a pressure which is very often opposed to (more or less) free semantic choice: *the pressure of form as an end in itself in the history of human languages* (cf. 2.1.3 below). As a result of the decay of the future stem, a periphrastic future was formed, with an auxiliary "to be" plus either the imperfective or the perfective; hence in Slovenian

(9)   *jaz bom pil*   (imperfective)
        "I will be drinking"

(10)   *jaz bom izpil*   (perfective)
        "I will drink up", "I will finish drinking (something)".

This is the situation in a South Slavic language. In Old Slavonic, the perfective present came to express the future, which is still the case today in Russian, where the perfective verb is incompatible with a periphrastic future form, and consequently the imperfective future is expressed by a periphrastic construction, which cannot be used with a perfective stem; (11) and (12) below have the same meanings as (9) and (10), respectively:

(11)   *ja budu pit'*[1] (imperfective)

and, instead of **ja budu vypit'*,

(12)   *ja vyp'ju*   (perfective).

Thus, depending on the language and even within the same linguistic family, LBs do not necessarily carry out the same operations. For the most part, however, they strive for well-balanced systems, even if these are doomed to decay within a relatively short period of time.

This *natural property of the human mind by which LBs tend to build, or to rebuild, well-balanced and economic systems* may explain the way LBs reacted to the second condition that hastened the evolution of the Slovenian aspectual system: the fact that this language lost its imperfect before its aorist, so that the system threatened to become asymmetrical, unless the elimination of one tense were followed by the elimination of the other. This is in fact exactly what happened, hence a significant economy with regard to the number of tenses, and a reinforcement of the pervasiveness of aspect. The consequences of the early decay of both the future stem and, at another historical stage, the imperfect tense, were more radical in Slovenian than in other Slavic languages. Slovenian distinguishes today between *delal sem* (imperfective) "I was working" and *izdelal sem* (perfective) "I have worked" or "I have worked (something) out". In Serbo-Croatian, as opposed to Slovenian, the imperfect and the aorist did not disappear, but there are two interesting qualifications: first, their use is limited to the spoken style and they are no longer found in the literary language; second, the situation in written Serbo-Croatian is the same as that which prevailed in Old Slovenian and which led there to the replacement of a tense opposition by an aspect opposition: the aorist is used exclusively with perfective verbs; hence in Serbo-Croatian we have

(13)   *(on) popi*   (perfective)
        "he drank up",

as opposed to

(14)   *(on) pijaše*   (imperfective)
        "he was drinking";

but there is neither *(on) pi* nor *(on) popijaše*.

This restructuring of a verbal system where a tense opposition is replaced by an aspect opposition is a typical illustration of the morphogenetic work done by LBs. (It should be added, however, that this evolution has no universal necessity. In Bulgarian, the aorist and the imperfect, far from having disappeared, are important parts of a very refined verbal system: in that system, such combinations as imperfective aorist and perfective imperfect are quite common. Thus the aorist/imperfect and perfective/imperfective oppositions do not function at the same level.)

Besides the relationship between tense and aspect, that between aspect and mood, also lying at the boundary between grammar and lexicon, is another interesting illustration. In many languages, there are polysemous words whose various meanings lie at such a distance from one another, that at first sight they seem totally unrelated. To take just one example, Cantonese *mai* may have one of (at least) three meanings: as a verb, "to bury"; as a verbal suffix, "end, completion of a process"; as an adverb, "also, even". If the relationship between the first two meanings may be understood, the only way of relating the second and the third meanings is to posit an operation whereby a set is divided into two parts, one of them being viewed as that which is left or must be recovered in order to reconstitute the set (cf. Tse 1986).

Not only do many aspects of speech activity imply precise semantic operations, but diachronically the subjectivity of LBs is also perceptible in certain general tendencies of the evolution of semantic systems. It has been shown, for example (Traugott 1989), that meanings linked to the external situation tend to become increasingly related to the speaker's subjective attitude; this applies in particular to three types of units: modal auxiliaries with both deontic and epistemic meanings, such as *must*, assertive speech act verbs such as *insist that*, and modal sentence markers, e.g., *probably, evidently, apparently*.

Finally, traces of LBs' subjectivity are also perceptible in the case of certain unstable forms. Such forms, precisely because their status is not stable within the subsystems of aspect and mood in a given language, remain at the disposal of speakers, who may thus commit themselves much more than with stabilized forms. In Moroccan Arabic, for instance, we find two perfects, one similar to the classical suffixed past, the other one formed on the present participle and invested with a much more subjective meaning (cf. 5.4.3 section a), as in (15) *vs.* (16) below:

(15)   *had-al-ḥotel, ʔanâ nʕast fi-h*
        (this-the-hotel I sleep~1SG.PAST in-it)
        "this hotel, I spent a night there"

(16)   *had-al-ḥotel, ʔanâ nâʕəs fi-h*
        (*nâʕəs* = present participle)
        "this hotel, I know it, I have spent a night there already!".

Aspect and mood are present in both (15) and (16), but not in the same way: the suffixal past form is more aspectual but not devoid of modal implications, and the participial form is more modal but with aspectual features.

Thus, the operational activity of LBs calls into question the legitimacy of clear-cut categories. Linguists need categories in order to study language, but LBs' activity is cross-categorial. It is largely meaning-induced (despite the pressure of forms), and it implies subtle operations whose study can reveal the creative work of human subjectivity.

c. *Hypocoristics*

Diminutive and derogatory, as well as apotropaic (exorcizing) expressions deserve special attention here; it often happens that the linguistic material which corresponds to a given intentional meaning is itself the subject of particular awareness. Yiddish, for example, is famous for a kind of verbal superstition, which results in numerous modifications of words whose real form is intentionally avoided. Early 20th century Alsatian Yiddish, and Bavarian Yiddish, designate the Virgin as *Schnerie* and *Schmarie*, respectively, instead of *Marie* (Lévy 1915). This substitution of *shn-* or *shm-* for *m-*, already known in 14th century German (in which *shn-* and *shm-* are ordinary (not in themselves funny) consonant clusters), is typically an intentional deformation, as is proven even today by the ironical replacement of *m-* by *shm-* in Yiddish and in Yiddish-influenced Israeli Hebrew when the word beginning with *m-* refers to someone the speaker wishes to disparage. Lithuanian Yiddish has gone even further, applying this alteration to any initial, and using the normal and the altered words contiguously, as in *dikduk-shmikduk* (*dikduk* "grammar" = a loanword from Hebrew) "grammar, this futile activity". In contemporary Yiddish, the substitution of any initial consonant of a foreign word by *shm-* or the prothesis of *shm-* before an initial vowel, as in *oedipus-shmoedipus* (speaking of a fashionable complex), always implies a belittling intention. The same funny use of *shm-* has also spread to certain variants of spoken American English.

d. *The shaping of the lexicon*

Even though it is difficult to set up rigorous lines of development in a domain characterized by fortuitous and unpredictable moves, the study of the shaping of the lexicon demonstrates the truth of a general principle: the history of words reflects the history of human ideas and representations of the world. This principle is borne out to a large extent by important works which study the vocabulary of institutions, economy, kinship, political power, social relationships, law and religion (cf., for example, Benveniste 1969b). Often, there is a restructuring of the lexicon when foreign objects and notions are imported into a culture and designated by words which, prior to acculturation, were applied to familiar entities. For example, in Tenejapa Tzeltal (Witkowski & Brown 1983:571-572), when sheep were introduced, they were equated with deer, which before the Spanish conquest were called *čih*, so that, in early post-conquest usage, sheep were labeled *tunim čih* "cotton deer", in which *tunim* "cotton" is the overt mark. But today the term for sheep is *čih*, while deer are called *te?tikil čih* "wild sheep". Thus, there is a marking-reversal, which is the linguistic manifestation of the fact that for these people sheep have gained, while deer have lost, in cultural importance. It also happens that LBs select a special characteristic in order to designate a formerly familiar animal, when its previous name has been assigned to a newly introduced animal whose cultural importance has become predominant. Thus, in contemporary Huastec, instead of *bičim* "deer"/∅ in pre-colonial times, we have *bičim* "horse"/*ic?āmal* "deer" (lit. "horned").

Comparable phenomena are found in other cultural areas. In Fijian a bow was *dakai*; when guns were introduced, they were called *dakai ni vâ lagi*, lit. "bow from overseas". An axe was *matau*; so, metal axes were labeled *matau ni vâ lagi* "axe from overseas". Eventually, as the native object became less usual, its name became the marked one. Today, gun is *dakai* and bow is *dakai ni Viti*, lit. "gun from Fiji", or *dakai tîtî* "gun of mangrove root" (Geraghty 1989:380-381). In all these cases, LBs shape the lexicon according to social and cultural evolution.

e. *Ideophone-making*

Another aspect of the lexicon whose study is in order here are ideophones. This label is applied to words whose structure presents some characteristics comparable to those found in onomatopoeia. Ideophone-making, though, does not necessarily imply an effort to dodge the law which establishes an arbitrary relationship between meanings and sounds. Rather, ideophone-making is a picturesque and vivid way of expressing perceptible (visual, auditory, tactile, etc.) properties of living beings and objects, mental characteristics, or various types of motions. From a syntactic point of view, ideophones are mostly adverbs, or, less commonly, adjectives or nouns.

Ideophones are not the same kind of phenomenon as the well-known phonaesthemes, or sequences of phonemes found in sets of words whose meanings are (often vaguely) related. In English, for example, the following words in -*ump* suggest bluntness and heaviness: *bump*, *chump*, *dump*, *thump*, etc. Phonaesthemes belong to the core vocabulary, and can often be traced back to a certain etymology, whereas ideophones have sounds and sound-clusters that are original with regard to the phonemic system of the language in which they appear. They are also more likely to be created by LBs gifted with individual talent.

This last point calls for further comment, however. Linguists doing fieldwork on African, South-East Asian and other "exotic" languages are struck by the seeming flexibility with which gifted old story-tellers intersperse their speech with various ideophones, many of which are not used, let alone known, by other villagers. Hence the temptation to conclude that ideophones may sometimes be invented by LBs according to their expressive needs. This is an unsupported conclusion, though. What is true is that the individual styles of speakers, if compared to one another, show a very broad range of variation in the use of ideophones. Those who most often resort to such expressive formations are conscious of the vividness thus gained by their style. But this does not mean that there is total creative freedom. Creativity exists, but only to a certain extent.

This applies in particular to one of the favorite means of ideophone-making: reduplication. In Moore, for instance, there are no theoretical limitations on the number of repetitions of *lūg* in *lūglūglūgí* "very high and stiff"; it seems to depend on subjective choice only: *lūglūglūglūgí* is used, and the recursive process can go even further. However, the choice of which syllable may be repeated is not free: it is only possible to repeat *lūg*, not *lūgí* (total reduplication), nor *lū* (another type of partial reduplication) (cf. Canu 1976:174). In Gbeya, all ideophones have isotonic syllables, with either high tones or low tones (Samarin 1965). Such is often the case in Mbum (Hagège 1970), and in Yoruba, where words like *gbàràgàdà* "wide open" are strictly coded (Welmers 1973:466), despite the apparent creativity. Korean ideophones express very subtle semantic nuances through precise sound associations (Diffloth 1972:442-443). The same is true of Japanese, which is known for the remarkable diversity of its ideophones. They are almost as numerous as the verbs to which they correspond, and they themselves often have predicative uses: *burabura* "to swing", *barabara*, "to be scattered", *parapara* "to splash", *taratara* "to be in a sweat", etc.

One could argue that these formal restrictions are also found in other original constructions, such as hypocoristics, examined in c. above, and that Yiddish *shm-*, for instance, is not just any consonant-cluster but is imposed by the linguistic system of Yiddish, just as sound-clusters are in ideophones. But if we consider meaning, and not only form, we see that *shm-* can be applied to any word, autochthonous or foreign, whereas ideophones, in languages where they exist in great numbers, constitute structured sets whose members occur only in certain contexts. It is true, however, that both hypocoristics and ideophones are subject to morphological constraints. The reason for these limitations on individual invention is not far to seek. These phenomena are everywhere part and parcel of the community-accepted lexicon, which is made of regular associations between sound and meaning. To a great extent, such associations are arbitrary, in the sense that they are fixed by social consensus.

Thus, ideophones are not completely free individual creations. Nevertheless, they have a property which is not found in ordinary phonology: a high degree of resistance to sound change. According to Diffloth (1979:57), this is "probably not an abstract and blind grammatical property of Expressives (=ideophones[CH]) as a word class. It only takes place when some active iconic pattern would have been weakened or destroyed by an impending sound change." Given that "Expressive phonology tends to have fewer systematic gaps than Prosaic phonology" (*ibid.*) and that, in Mon-Khmer languages for instance, ideophones do not use marginal phonetic material but only usual units and combinations, one can presume that ideophones are not the products of blind or random evolution, but rather reflect a relatively free organization of the phonic means. To that extent, they imply a kind of semi-conscious linguistic creation, although on a collective rather than individual level.

f. *Word-coining by individual users*

It is true that, as Boas writes in the excerpt quoted above (p. 14), speakers do not usually propose reinterpretations or secondary explanations of the processes by which linguistic categories are formed. If they did, they would themselves be acting as professional linguists, which in most cases they are not. However, as far as the lexicon is concerned, they may be perfectly conscious of their own word-coining activity. I will mention here a personal experience. In 1966, while I was doing fieldwork on Mbum, an African language spoken in North Cameroon (Adamawa-Eastern in Greenberg's (1963) classification), my elderly informant, having to designate in the course of conversation my tape-recorder, invented at once the compound *ŋáw-Bè* lit. "calabash-(for)speech". A new term must meet two requirements, if it is to be accepted by the community: first, it must conform to the word-formation habits of the language, second it must fill the gap that appears where a concept is in search of a form. The new term obviously met these two requirements, since it was a success, as was proved later by its wide diffusion within the village community. Everybody was perfectly aware of the newness of the term, and public rumor ascribed it to its inventor, recalling the circumstances of this invention, which I had myself witnessed.

The Mbums were then, and have remained, an exclusively oral society. This event suggests that it might be better to revise the claim according to which the absence of writing makes it less easy to remember newly-coined units. If an invented term serves a definite need and is well formed, its success will be guaranteed. LBs' awareness of its novelty gradually fades away, as I saw later when I went back to the village; this was further proof of its wide acceptance.

g. *Neological activity in literate societies*
Neological activity has long been, and is especially today, an important cultural phenomenon. It has much in common with the shaping of the lexicon and with word-coining by individual users, studied above, respectively, in sections d. and f.; but it requires special study, since we are concerned here with literate societies, in which LBs, and especially among them professional philologists and grammarians, explicitly leave their mark on the evolution of the lexicon by means of official decisions made at meetings of experts. Moreover, the government-supported creation of new lexical units in many cases (though not always) helps them to gain relatively wide acceptance; they thus cease being *terms* (technical designations) and become *words* (part and parcel of common vocabulary).

In many domains of modern life, word-coining is a worldwide enterprise, aimed at naming new objects, new techniques, new kinds of human relationships, etc. In Hagège (1983b:33), I have given the name *technolects* to sets of technical designations proper to a certain domain of human activity, and I have studied the various means by which members of technolects are formed: loanwords, calques, semantic extensions, descriptive compounds, truncated units, acronyms, etc. I have also shown how the affirmation by LBs of their cultural identity in neologisms is exemplified by many well-known cases, such as that of German *Fernsprecher* (farspeaker), which, in an attempt at "purification", replaces *Telephon*, a foreign word made of Greek elements and having an international status. Here, I will try to show the principles that underlie this concerted human action on the destiny of the lexicon, by examining some of the most remarkable known cases.

Many languages are notable for the care with which reformers have tried to adapt their vocabulary to new needs. Often, this effort begins very early. Hungarian intellectuals, for instance, have long cherished their language as a vehicle of self-affirmation, making it a point of duty both to enrich and to preserve it. The most important reform movement, which took place from the last quarter of the 18th to the middle of the 19th century, left in the Hungarian lexicon many words which had simply been coined by the reformers. A frequent device was the combination of two existing units into a portmanteau word: *higany* "mercury" is made from *híg* "watery" + *anyag* "material", here truncated, but itself a coinage from *anya* "mother"; *rovar* "insect" is from *rovátkolt* "grooved" + *barom* "animal, cattle", both abbreviated. Another device was the suffixation of certain elements, some of which were already productive, like *-alom/-elem*, *-mány/-mény*, *-kodik/-kedik/-ködik* (variations are due to vowel harmony), while others were obsolete, like *-nok/-nök*, *-ór/-ér*, or hypothesized from word-endings (cf. Fodor 1983:71). An illustration of this last case is *-da/-de*, as in *iroda* "office", from *ír* "to write", *óvoda* "kindergarten", from *óv* "to protect", *bölcsőde* "nursery", from *bölcs* "wise". It is remarkable that *-da/-de* aroused much controversy, and by no means gained immediate acceptance. Before it was admitted into the language as a new suffix, there was lengthy discussion in which writers, professors, and even non-specialists participated. Thus, the history of the lexicon bears traces of the attitudes of LBs with regard to certain aspects of neologization.

LBs leave even more precise traces of their near-to-conscious glossogenetic activity when they are reviving a language whose oral form had long fallen into disuse. The spectacular history of Modern Hebrew is probably most revealing in this connection. Many people in Israel are interested in the process of word creation, and it is a widespread form of game there to invent new words in order to express new realities, while trying to remain faithful to the morphology of the classical language. A striking example is the revival of old syllable patterns filled with borrowed phonic (consonantal) material. Israeli Hebrew has many verbs formed on the traditional (Biblical and Mishnaic) scheme called *piʃel* in Hebrew grammar (because it has this form in the verb taken as a model, i.e., *paʃal* in the base structure): *diklem* "to declaim", *tilfen* "to telephone", *pister* "to pasteurize", *pitrel* "to patrol", *sibsed* "to subsidize", *ʔirgen* "to organize", etc. The material is borrowed from German (*deklamieren*), Russian (*organizovat'*), etc. Two facts are worth noting, both testifying to the concerted activity by which LBs leave their imprint. On the one hand, very few verbs with three consonants have been introduced: *bilef* "to bluff" or *citet* "to cite" are among the rare examples. This is because triconsonantal verbs are quite characteristic of Hebrew verbal morphology, so that any borrowed verb with three consonants will almost automatically be associated with an existing Hebrew root with three consonants. It is unlikely that listeners will find such a root for any loanword with this structure, whereas they will easily associate borrowed verbs having four consonants, like *tilfen*, with a foreign word, simply because this structure is rare, and their scheme, *piʃel*, is well-known as characteristic of foreign words. Subtle as this may appear, such implicit reasoning is quite natural for Israeli Hebrew speakers. It accounts for certain gaps that would otherwise remain unexplained (cf. Masson 1986:61).

More generally, the mark left by Israeli LBs on contemporary Hebrew reflects an explicit and voluntary affirmation of cultural identity. Loanwords have either been hebraicized or not as regards stress, final in the first case (as in certain types of nominal and verbal patterns in classical Hebrew), penultimate in the second case (as in Yiddish and other European languages). Hebrew is the prestige language, even more so than Aramaic or English, let alone Yiddish, which is the (not yet extinct) language formerly spoken in Eastern Europe (Galicia, Ukraine, etc.), especially in villages (cf. Hagège 1992). It is true that Israeli Hebrew has accepted loanwords from these languages, as well as from Arabic, Polish, German, Russian, and others. But Hebrew was the main reference, since hebraicization was one of the main devices used in word-coining. The varying degrees of hebraicization of a loanword depend on the way the pioneers viewed it on a strictly defined scale of values.

The same feature appears in one of the most characteristic aspects of lexicogenesis: the making of puns. Israeli Hebrew has a large number of puns. Most of them reflect a nationalist view of lexical borrowing: the loanwords are readily accepted when, by a lucky chance, they happen to have both a semantic (even if not immediately obvious) and a phonic (albeit not perfect) analogy with an existing native unit. Examples are *ilit* "elite", from *ili* "lofty" + *-it*, a suffix of feminine adjectives; *abuv* "oboe", from Mishnaic Hebrew *abuv* "a kind of flute"; *pras* "prize", from Mishnaic Hebrew *pras* "salary", etc.

Hebrew, however, is not an isolated case in this connection. In other languages, too, artificial words have been made using native roots that happened to resemble a root in a language taken as a model: Turkish has *okul* "school", resembling both French *école* (or English *school*) and the Turkish verb *oku(mak)* "to read"; similarly, we have *soysal*, which calls to mind French *social*, but also Turkish *soy* "race"; Arabic has *ʃâzil* "isolator", which resembles the first syllables of the French and English words *isolateur* and *isolator*, but is in fact the present participle (noun of agent) of the verb *ʃazala* "to set aside"; just like the reformers of Modern Arabic, the Hungarian reformers, mentioned above for the love of their language, did not often resort to this type of punning, but they too coined some words by this method, e.g., *elem* "element", recalling French and English, but also the Hungarian preverb *elő-* "in front, in the first place".

The desire to follow a prestigious model can also apply to more abstract parts of the lexicon, such as word order in numerals. A famous case is the reform launched in 1950-1951 by the Norwegian government to replace, in numbers from 21 to 99, the Danish units-before-tens counting system, as in *fem-og-tredve*, by the Swedish (and English) tens-before-units system, as in *trettifem* "thirty-five" (Hagège 1983:23). The Swedish and English models were more highly valued than the Danish one, which recalled a long-lasting political dependence. Although the reform was not a total success, since both systems are in widespread use today in Norway (Jahr 1989:104), it clearly shows the attempt to leave an ideological mark on the language, as does more generally the promotion of Nynorsk, a semi-artificial medium established in 1885 as an official standard, on a par with Bokmål (Dano-Norwegian, formerly called Riksmål).

Finally, writers deserve a special mention here, for their participation in collective neological activity, even though their aim in fact is to cultivate their individual style. In this connection, an interesting, both literary and didactic, device consists of using native equivalents in order to explain terms borrowed from a prestige language. This is the way French words were made familiar to Middle English speakers in the 13th century. In *Ancrene Riwle* (*ca.* 1225), there are explanations such as *cherité, thet is luve* or *lecherie, thet is golnesse* (Jespersen 1955:100). This is strikingly similar to the situation in certain societies which have no written norm, or only some elements of one: in this case the diffusion of such a norm is helped by a kind of translating activity. Thus, according to Mühlhäusler (1989:139-147), Tok Pisin newspapers explain in Pidgin the English words introduced into the lexicon, hence a proliferation of passages in which the author interrupts himself in the middle of a sentence in order to give a Tok Pisin equivalent of an English word he has just used, and then goes on with what he is talking about, e.g., *ol* **pils** *o* **maresin**... "the pill, i.e., medicin...", **reprendum** *o* **vot bilong ol pipel yet**..."a referendum, i.e., a vote of the people themselves..."

1.3.2 The LBs' signature in phonology

Phonology is often held to be the domain of automatism, and the Neogrammarians believed in the blind application of rules which admit no exceptions. In fact, phonology offers many examples of the affirmation by LBs of their cultural identity. Such examples, along with theoretical interpretations, can be found in Hagège & Haudricourt (1978). Here, I would like to show how LBs can act upon diachronic processes and leave concrete marks of their cultural conceptions. It will thus appear that in certain cases we can both stress the manifestations of the consciousness of LBs and characterize various aspects of LBs' signature, left on the genetic history of their language.

An ongoing diachronic change in a given phonemic system can be deliberately halted if it does not meet the requirements of social evaluation. There are various examples of this, among which I will select only two, both taken from Scandinavian languages (data from Jahr 1989). When comparing Modern to Old Icelandic, it appears that the vowel system has been reduced by the loss of distinctive features. The last step of this long and regular historical development is the merging of /I/ and /Y/ with /e/ and /ö/ respectively, resulting in the homophony of words like *viður* "wood" and *veður* "weather", or *flugur* "flies" (PL) and *flögur* "slabs, flakes" (PL). However, a comparison between two statistical surveys conducted in 1945 and 1984 shows a spectacular decrease of this merging, from 38,5% to 2,6% of the informants. Between these two dates, an intensive campaign had been directed against the merging. This merging originated among fishermen in the 19th century, and has a low social value, as shown by the name given to the pronunciation which does not distinguish between /I/ and /e/ nor between /Y/ and /ö/: *flámæli* "slack or lazy speech", as opposed to *réttmæli* "correct speech". Thus, LBs in Iceland have reversed the normal evolution of their vowel system by stopping its last step through a campaign of eradication.

In Oslo Norwegian, dental /l/ has come to be realized as alveolar or retroflex, except after the vowels /a/ and /ɔ/. This uneconomical situation is only due to the fact that the urban/rural socio-professional parameter plays an important role in Norwegian: an alveolar or retroflex pronunciation of a lateral consonant after back vowels sounds very rural to the inhabitants of Oslo, who systematically avoid it.

On the other hand, the Danish pronunciation of /p/, /t/, and /k/ as *lenes* consonants, which was characteristic of upper-class Oslo Norwegian, and historically explainable as one of the results of 400 years of Danish rule down to 1814, has changed, after long resistance by this Danish-influenced class of Norwegian society, to an unvoiced, i.e., norwegianized, pronunciation, as a result of spelling reforms and school teaching.

Thus, the deliberate interruption of a natural ongoing change bears witness to the importance attached by LBs to their symbolic representation of how sounds should be pronounced in order to reflect their own cultural identity. This sociolectal index (cf. Hagège 1981b, 1983b) is a conspicuous signature left by LBs on the destiny of their languages.

1.3.3 Intentional morphosyntactic building

Having observed the importance of conscious word-coining (cf. especially 1.3.1 sections f. and g.) and the LBs' signature in phonology (cf. 1.3.2), we should expect a different picture as regards phenomena outside the lexicon. However, things are not that simple. The following five sections will try to show that

a.   In the derivation of personal pronouns from nouns (a particular case of a more general process which will be studied in chapter 7), there is a certain amount of choice as regards what specific nouns will be used;

b. There are cases of morphological analysis of complex words into their elements;

c. In certain rare situations, LBs have a kind of metalinguistic consciousness of grammatical structures;

d. There are striking cases of voluntary intervention of LBs on syntax;

e. Some products of poetic activity reveal a knowledge of certain grammatical characteristics.

a. *Deriving personal pronouns from nouns*

In some languages, such as those spoken in strictly hierarchized societies of East and South-East Asia, personal pronouns can often be traced back to master-servant, lord-subject, etc., relationships. Thus, Vietnamese *tôi*, usually translated as "I", is far from being as neutral as the English *I*. It coexists, in the Vietnamese system of personal pronouns, with *tao*, which implies a familiar relationship, whereas *tôi* is more formal. *tôi* originally meant "servant" or "subject of a king" (Thompson 1965:248). It is interesting to see, therefore, that at the first stage of this evolution, LBs selected for use as a personal pronoun a noun denoting a certain kind of social relationship between speakers, thus reflecting the original organization then prevailing.

Even if LBs are no longer quite conscious of this process today, they have, at least, a partial knowledge of the history, since *tôi* is clearly marked, and this is an indication of its special status.

There are analogous facts in other languages of the same area. Japanese *boku* originally meant "servant", but it is used today for familiar (not for formal) "I". Formal "I" is *watakushi*, which also means "private" as opposed to "public". Another word, *kimi*, originally meant "emperor", "lord" or "master", and is used today for familiar "you", normally between men, like *boku*.

Despite these differences between Vietnamese and Japanese, it appears that in both cases, LBs solved the problem of expressing the identity and status of partners in speech by using words which reflected their culture and social organization.

b. *Morphological analysis of Complex Words (CWs)*

In the activity of speech, one sometimes observes a certain amount of analysis of CWs, i.e., derivatives and compounds, into their constituent elements. Speakers of Spanish know that, in *langue* as a system, *clara-*

mente and *oscuramente* are independent words, just like *clara* and *oscura*. However, they use quite normally in their speech such expressions as *clara o oscuramente* "clearly or obscurely". Their linguistic behavior here shows that Spanish permits an etymological decomposition of adverbs in -*mente*, formed on the feminine of adjectives and seeming to simply retain the Latin structure, in which we have the ablative of a feminine noun.

Comparable phenomena appear in other languages, of course. To mention just one, in German, a suffix which is not normally separable can, nevertheless, be treated as common to two stems. Thus Stolz (1989:54) characterizes certain properties as being *tradier- aber nur schwerlich entlehnbar*, literally "transmit- but only with difficulty borrow-able". Such a formulation is typical of formal German, and the fact that T. Stolz is a linguist and, as such, professionally conscious of the possibility of analyzing a CW into its elements, probably has little to do with it. As far as the other example is concerned, it does not prove that Spanish speakers, even though they analyze a CW, do so quite consciously. But the fact remains that when speakers of languages such as Spanish and German use these kinds of formulations, they retrieve the very process by which CWs were formed.

c. *Metalinguistic consciousness*

Imposing a norm may reveal metalinguistic consciousness. Speakers of Nahuatl in the central Mexican States of Puebla and Tlaxcala have been found (Hill 1987:146) to be stigmatized by young men for using a Spanish-influenced possessive construction, with *de* between possessor and possessed, especially in cases of so-called alienable possession, e.g.,

(17)   *in tepāmitl den teōpantzīntli*
        (*den* = fusion of Sp. *de* and Nah. *(i)n*)
        (the wall of-the church)
        "the wall of the church".

Given that "good Mexicano" (= pure Nahuatl) is highly valued by men as one of the main markers of ethnic identity and is promoted as such into a solidarity code (in Brown & Gilman's (1960) sense), we have here a case of self-conscious purism. This attitude, when applied to morphology, has led to systematic avoidance, and immediate identification by men listening to women, of linguistic structures rejected as "castellano", i.e., as violating consciously established prestige norms. It is only fair to add, however, that women's speech shows broader use of noun incorporation, a typical Nahuatl (and, more generally, Uto-Aztecan) means of forming verbal compounds (cf. 6.2.2), as well as lesser use of calques on Spanish relative clause construction. Since it is men who, through male exercise of power, establish prestige norms, and given that women, as far as these two points are concerned, speak much "better Mexicano", it is clear that the conscious analysis of possessive constructions by men does not prevent them from being unconscious when it comes to other morphosyntactic phenomena. But at least with regard to possessive constructions, we may say that they have a metalinguistic consciousness.

d. *Voluntary interventions on syntax*

Although the term *morphosyntax*, widely used here, has the advantage of stressing the constant tie between syntax and morphology, certain facts can be presented as belonging to syntax proper, defined as that part of grammar which deals with the relationships between units and between phrases. In the history of modern languages, there is at least one very striking case of a decision taken by LBs on a syntactic problem: between 1952 and 1964, there was a strong and long-lasting controversy in Israel, arising from the explicit opposition of D. Ben Gurion (one of the founders, and first Prime Minister, of the State) to the use of the preposition *?et* in front of definite objects. Many letters were written by Ben Gurion to various periodicals, and many articles appeared in famous newspapers, such as *Ha-Tsofeh* "The Observer", *ſal Ha-Mišmar* "On Guard", *Davar* "Word"[2]. Ben Gurion claimed that *?et* was useful only to disambiguate the agent and the patient in cases where they might be mistaken for each other; such cases, he added, were very rare, and did not occur when it was obvious who was doing what; in most other cases, he concluded, using too many *?et* made the style clumsy, wasted paper, printing ink, money and time, and should therefore be abandoned. From the earlier to the later books of the Bible, Ben Gurion said, the number of occurrences of *?et* regularly decreased; furthermore, it often happened that two biblical passages, one with and the other without *?et*, were semantically identical, and who, Ben Gurion claimed, knows the language better than God, who created the world in Hebrew?

To this, the grammarian and journalist I. Avineri, one of Ben Gurion's main opponents, objected that the Prime Minister's counting was wrong.

Avineri gave statistics which tended to show the all-pervading presence of *?et* in the Bible. It was well-known, he recalled, that in Biblical and Mishnaic Hebrew, *?et* was the normal marker for definite objects. Avineri also rejected Ben Gurion's reference to the reservations of Rabbi Aqiba (a famous rabbi of the 1st-2nd centuries A.D.) and of Maimonides: Avineri said that the latter had written in a style strongly influenced by Arabic, which does not mark the patient with a preposition, but with a case-ending. Furthermore, Avineri stressed that *?et*, sometimes optional when the patient is expressed by a possessive noun-phrase, is obligatory when it is expressed by a noun-phrase with the definite article.

In the end, the conservative point of view prevailed, and Ben Gurion was forced to give up his project. The most striking fact, here, is that various arguments were put forward by writers, journalists, readers, often ordinary people who were far from being professional linguists, in favor of *?et* as a necessary tool to distinguish the subject from the object. In fact, most people, including Avineri, failed to note that *?et* does not only indicate that the patient of a transitive verb is definite: *?et* also serves to topicalize the patient (sometimes fronted in the Bible). This link between definiteness and topicality was already characteristic of the biblical uses of *?et* and we will see later (2.2.2) its importance in morphogenesis. That this was not noticed by people who were not linguists was to be expected, and does not detract from the high degree of consciousness shown by LBs in a domain that is generally thought to be quite mechanical: the explicit indication of a syntactic relationship between the predicate and the definite patient. LBs, here, literally made their syntax, by deciding that an element belonging to the classical stages of their language had an important syntactic role to play, and should therefore not be discarded.

Besides syntax proper, the voluntary interventions of LBs on the destiny of their language can also apply to aspects which are felt as characteristic of a certain conception of culture and society. It has often been reported that many languages in the Amerindian and Pacific areas were deeply affected by European conquest or colonization. In the Pacific area, under the pressure of cultural westernization, a very rapid change is taking place. But what is striking here is that, in many cases, the part of grammar threatened with decay is not random: it is the part which is the most marked, or notoriously man-made, often meant to reflect cultural autonomy and to express affirmation of group-identity (on this concept, cf. Hagège & Haudricourt 1978:138-158). This applies, in particular, to noun classifiers and to markers of honorific address. It is interesting to note that in certain societies, both were explicitly taught, perhaps even created, to be transmitted by elder teachers in ceremonial houses, which were considered as sanctuaries of lofty style and esoteric knowledge (cf. Voorhoeve 1977, for the Asmat; and Mühlhäusler 1989, for a general survey). The situation seems the reverse of that of *?et* in Israeli Hebrew, since units are being lost here and revived there, but the awareness of LBs as regards syntactic or morphological phenomena is quite remarkable since it can go as far as voluntary creation. Stressing this is not prescriptivism, but only an observation of the facts.

e. *Poetry and knowledge of grammar*

Poetry is a human activity often neglected by linguists, although it has much to teach us, since it illustrates an aptitude basic to language: creativity. Poetic works testify to a certain degree of grammatical consciousness on the part of poets. This applies to oral as well as written poetry. Both make use of a very characteristic device, called parallelism. *Parallelismus membrorum* is pervasive in the archaic Canaanite tradition reflected by the style of the Bible, as well as in Russian folksongs such as the *byliny* (heroic epics), and in the oral poetry of Finno-Ugric, Turkic, and Mongolian peoples.

As noted by Jakobson (1968:600), these devices

> give us a direct insight into the speakers' own conception of the grammatical equivalences. The analysis of various kinds of poetic license in the domain of parallelism, like the examination of rhyming conventions, may provide us with important clues for interpreting the make-up of a given language and the rank order of its constituents (e.g., the current equation between the Finnish allative and illative or between the preterite and present against the background of unpairable cases of verbal categories).

In this respect, one of the most striking examples in the history of grammar is the beginning of grammatical thought in China on the basis of the distinction between full and empty words, a distinction inspired by the need to establish precise lists of parallel words, i.e., words to be used at the same place in each verse of a distich. The list of full words contained names of tangible objects as well as verbs referring to actions. The list of empty words contained nouns and verbs referring to thoughts and feelings, but it also contained adverbs, prepositions and conjunctions (Hagège 1975:

23-24). Thus, the first awareness of a system of grammatical categories in Chinese was directly related to poetic activity.

1.4 Conclusion

It appears from the above that there are various degrees of consciousness in Lb. They all contribute to highlight specific features of speakers-listeners as LBs. All languages are pre-existent to the individuals of each new generation, whose personalities they will contribute to shape, while at the same time meeting their communicative and aesthetic needs. On the other hand, over their life, LBs constantly modify their language through daily use, and thus reshape it from generation to generation. These two propelling forces, communicative needs and search for new forms, are dialectically related: since human needs are constantly changing, they require new forms, which, in turn, modify the way languages function and meet human needs. This will be taken over in more detail in 2.3.

The first need, the need to say something to someone, implies an intention. LBs begin with a conscious choice when adopting a certain language as the channel through which this intention will find an expression. There still is a relatively free choice at the following stage, which consists of selecting a certain content or prelinguistic scheme (much more spontaneously and implicitly, of course, than this presentation in necessarily successive stages might lead one to believe). From there on, the freedom LBs enjoy begins to undergo certain restrictions. At the third stage, however, there is a curious phenomenon: we have both selection from among the lexical and grammatical material which defines every language, and necessary submission to the constraints implied by this very material.

This is the reason why LBs are characterized both by psychological and social features: psychological, because their activity corresponds to an intention; social, because the linguistic forms which express a given content are the result of the work done by generations of LBs. Consciousness is an individual phenomenon, even though it may concern a whole population, whereas Lb is a collective one. The partial consciousness of an operation based on an individual choice can combine with the unconscious application of rules reflecting a collective shaping. However, it is possible to go one step further. The task of selection, accomplished by LBs, from among lexical and grammatical elements is a voluntary activity, even though submission to the code cannot be so. Therefore, the question is: what is the relationship between what is conscious and what is voluntary? The two notions seem to overlap in some of the cases studied in this chapter. In other cases, recognizing that there are various degrees of consciousness, and often almost total unconsciousness, is not to deny the role of will, as has been done since the second half of the nineteenth century, especially by the Neogrammarians and their followers. M. Bréal rightly called this attitude into question when he wrote (1921 [1897]:314) that dismissing human will as an essential and objective factor in the genesis of languages amounted to ignoring the difference between intelligence as a natural property of the human species and reflection as a conscious faculty. Human intelligence, according to Bréal, is always present, if partly hidden, in the renewal of the shape of a language, and in such phenomena as polysemy and shortening of locutions; it avails itself of every opportunity to provide the mind with the new tools it needs.

It is probably true that human beings started speaking before analyzing exactly what they were doing when speaking. But this does not mean that the anti-constructivist hypothesis is well-founded. Such a hypothesis appears in some works which, in the wake of Wittgenstein's view (1967: §§ 7 and 23 among others) of "word games" as spontaneous "forms of life", state that human institutions do not stem from a consciously established program, but from natural evolution. Thus, Hayek (1978:15) writes that "man has [...] never invented his most beneficial institutions, from language to moral and law". In his opinion, therefore, the fundamental tools of culture result from spontaneous growth, not from an initial project. As far as language is concerned, it is true that there cannot be a concerted plan for the whole set of structures that define a given language. However, precisely because language is an institution, and, as such, related to the most characteristic forms of human culture, such as religions, myths, customs and behaviors, bodies of laws, etc., Lb is not quite so uncontrolled as one might believe. Language stands halfway between natural objects or processes, such as rivers, volcanic eruptions, etc., and voluntary creations of human activity, such as literature and art. This is because it is both imposed and constructed, both a set of constraints and a field of freedom.

Now the ability to select from among coded possibilities is itself related to another defining property: the aptitude for limiting energy costs without, at the same time, limiting efficiency; in other words, getting the best result at the lowest cost. Thus, there is an important economy of effort by the human brain. What makes this possible is the subtle distribution between customary and creative behavior. It is well-known that the human brain and the mechanisms of artificial intelligence have much in common, all the more since the latter are meant to simulate the performance of the former; thus, in the absence of sufficient scientific understanding, today, of underlying neurological mechanisms, the study of artificial intelligence can give a clue to how the brain functions. In certain (but of course not all) cases of automatic translation, a good machine can achieve results comparable to those of a human translator. We can therefore hypothesize that, under certain favorable conditions, the human brain and the computer use a particular faculty they both possess, i.e., time sharing. This term is not used here in the ordinary sense of "a system permitting the simultaneous employment of a computer or computer complex by many users at remote locations for solving their individual problems in real time" (Webster's 1976:1490). Rather, I use it in the general sense of an aptitude for accomplishing two operations at once. One of them is routine: it consists of a set of coded instructions which the machine automatically complies with at a low cost. As for the other, being more creative, it requires additional force; it will therefore use the energy left over by the other, more economical, operation.

It is easy to see that such a distribution of work ties in with the existence of lexical, as opposed to grammatical, elements in all languages. There is much more routine, and much less effort, in the choice of a grammatical element than in the choice of a lexical one (cf. Lüdtke 1986:40). Therefore, in the selection of an adequate lexeme LBs will invest the energy left over from the work of applying the grammar code. Such linguistic time sharing, since it allocates the rates of energy expenditure, is the main factor facilitating the construction of sentences in everyday linguistic exchange. The existence of two simultaneous operations is reflected in the lesser degree of metalinguistic self-consciousness required for grammatical elements, compared with that required for lexical elements. This difference itself is clearly proved by a very simple experiment: while laymen can easily give equivalents for lexemes and formulations they are consciously using, or propose descriptions of their meanings, it is generally difficult, and sometimes impossible, for them to indicate the exact role or value of a grammatical form, especially a short verbal or nominal affix, or a connective, when asked to do so. This time sharing between lexicon and grammar is also observable in language acquisition. While children, at the age of 4-5 (depending on the language and the social environment), master most grammatical structures of their language, they still have a long way to go before they can handle a lexicon comparable in size with that of adults. Therefore, they will invest more energy and time in selecting the adequate lexeme among their still scanty vocabulary than in applying the rules of grammar.

Thus, we are justified in concluding that the problem of consciousness in Lb is best tackled by establishing various degrees of this phenomenon, and investigating the reasons for such a variety. This is what the present chapter has tried to do.

CHAPTER 2

Adaptation of linguistic systems
to meet LBs' needs

In chapter 1, we have seen that in the lexicon, in the phonology and in the morphosyntax, there are various degrees of consciousness and voluntary intervention of LBs. It now remains to be shown that important parts of language reveal certain operations which, though not so conscious as those studied in chapter 1, also point to the permanent presence of LBs and the role they play in language making. This role is defined by a constant effort to adapt linguistic systems to meet LBs' needs.

In order to show this, I will begin with a study of Lb as problem-solving and as requiring a distribution of tasks between various linguistic components, thus highlighting the place of material form in language (2.1). I will then study an interesting activity by which LBs unconsciously introduce structural changes to meet certain new needs in expression: this activity is called reanalysis (2.2). Finally, I will show that the study of language morphogenesis reveals a dialectical relationship between two contradictory needs (2.3).

2.1   Problem-solving, the distribution of tasks and the role of form in languages

Like every human activity, Lb is not exclusively goal-directed: besides meeting the need for communication, it also fulfils an aspiration for intellectual and aesthetic self-accomplishment, which defines human societies no less than communication. However, the pressure of the latter is very strong. Languages are constantly on the move under the action of LBs, forced as they are to adapt their means of communication to social and cultural changes and to cope with new situations and requirements: in the lexicon (cf. 1.3.1 above), there is an ever-increasing number of things to be talked about, while others disappear as time passes; in the system of sounds (1.3.2) as well as in the grammar (1.3.3), there are complex propelling forces, between which no perfect balance is ever reached. Given these conditions, a large part of LBs' activity can be conceived of as problem-solving. Moreover, since languages are mechanisms which express meaning by material forms, two other aspects also call for examination here: the way tasks are distributed among the components of language, and the place of form as the material base which bears meaning. The study will therefore contain three parts: Lb as problem-solving (2.1.1); the distribution of linguistic tasks (2.1.2); the place of material form in language (2.1.3).

2.1.1 Lb as problem-solving

The features which characterize a language, as it is shaped by its users over a long history, are meant to meet various and complex needs. These are both external, i.e., related to the social context in which this language is used, and internal to the language in question, inasmuch as it functions as a system of communication. But it may happen that these very features in turn give rise to specific requirements. In other words, it turns out that LBs must meet the requirements they have themselves indirectly created. Examples of this situation abound, and on all levels. In order to show the usefulness of the notion of problem-solving as a characteristic aspect of Lb, let us examine a problem belonging to a particular component, syntax, in a particular language.

Classical Nahuatl has a striking property (Launey 1988:91-94, 1382-1383, 1434-1435): almost all parts of speech function as predicates. The only word-types that cannot be used predicatively are prepredicative clitics (about thirty morphemes) and the deictics *in* "this" and *on* "that". As a result, the use of any kind of word, other than these two, in a non-predicative function, raises a problem: not only verbs, but also nouns, locative phrases, etc., are inherently predicative. Therefore, a non-predicative function can only result from a derivation process. In order to get this result and thereby resolve the problem created by this particular feature of Nahuatl, LBs need an operator by which a non-predicative function can be assigned to inherently predicative words. They need an operator, that is, which can convert predicates into subjects or complements. The main operator meeting this need, evidently the word with the highest textual frequency in Classical Nahuatl, is *in*, the very same deictic mentioned above as characterized by the fact that it is excluded from the predicative function. In fact, *in* converts the following word not into a non-predicate but into a secondary, as opposed to main, predicate. The presence of *in* therefore guarantees that the word which follows it does not function as the main predicate. Thus compare (18) and (19):

(18) a. *ni-cochi*
          (I-sleep)
          "I am sleeping"
      b. *ni-cualli*
          (I-good)
          "I am good"
      c. *ti-tlaxcalteca*
          (we-T)
          "we are Tlaxcaltec [a nation]"
      d. *(ca)-0-tlācatl*
          ((OPTION.COP)-3-man)
          "he is a man"
      e. *(ca)-0-cualli*
          ((OPTION.COP)-3-good)
          "he is good"
      f. *(ca)-0-cualli tlācatl*
          ((OPTION.COP)-3-good man)
          "he is a good man"

(19)   *ni-kʷ-itta in-tlācatl*
          (I-him-see PRED.RED-man)
          "I see the man".

In (18)a, b and c, it appears that the predicate can be represented not only by the verb (a), but also by the noun (c) and by the noun of quality (b, where *cualli* is translated by an English adjective; but in Nahuatl, "adjectives" are, in fact, nouns[1]). In these three sentences, a clear mark of the predicative function is the presence of a prefixed personal index. In the third person, and when reference is made to an object or notion outside of the *ego-tu* dialogue, the personal index is zero; a *ca* copula may optionally be prefixed: as a result, the noun in (18)d, the noun of quality in (18)e, and their combination in (18)f all constitute full sentences coinciding with the predicate. In (19), on the other hand, we see that a noun, if it is to function as an argument, i.e., subject or complement in a sentence which has a verbal main predicate, needs an operator which derives a secondarily predicative term from this noun. It is not surprising that the main operator used for this purpose, itself, comes from a deictic, a word-type pointing to a term as a participant in the state of affairs expressed by the main predicate, which is here *ni-k*ʷ*-itta*, a transitive verb with an inserted patient-marker *k*ʷ, in coreference relationship with *tlācatl*. Specialists of Nahuatl often translate *in* by the article, in languages that possess this word-type. In fact, *in* is properly a *predicativity reducer*: it prevents the following term from functioning as the main predicate, making it the secondary predicate within a subordinate structure. The exact translation of (19) is "I see him, the [one who is a] man". (When having to express an indefinite entity (as in English *a man*), Nahuatl, depending on the meaning, resorts either to the numeral *cē* "one", or to the *incorporation* (cf. 6.2.2) of the noun.)

The use of inherently predicative words as modifiers in other languages that possess them raises similar problems. The so-called "adjectives" of Chinese, Japanese, or Melanesian languages like Iaai, for example, are a case in point. In these languages, LBs have resolved the problem by using an inherently predicative word within a subordinate structure, corresponding to an English relative clause. The situation is not the same as in Nahuatl, where the "adjective", being in fact a noun, may modify another noun by simple juxtaposition (cf.(18)f). But these examples, like that of Nahuatl, show that it is an important part of LBs' work to find solutions to the problems of expression raised by the structure of each individual language.

2.1.2 The distribution of linguistic tasks

In what follows, I will examine the distribution of linguistic tasks and try to show how the LBs organize this distribution, both within one and the same language whose various components are assigned different functions, and in a crosslinguistic perspective. In introducing the study, I would like to stress the importance of
– the diversity of processes which express a given meaning,
– the relationship between the components of languages, for what these two points teach us about the morphogenetic work of LBs.

With regard to the first point, we note that LBs, in an uninterrupted effort, try to exploit the possibilities made available to them by the evolution of their language, thus contributing to delineating well-defined types characterized by recurrent features. But LBs do not always depart from the conservative attitude of users who inherit a certain language shaped by the preceding generations. As a result, all languages possess devices thanks to which, in many semantic fields, a given meaning can be expressed by more than one structure, depending on the circumstances and the relationships between the speakers-listeners, as well as another, less often mentioned but no less important, factor, namely, the degree of knowledge, present in each speaker, of the resources of the language being used. This is a basic property of human languages, one that defines them as much as the fact that they all have a sound system and a syntax. I will call it the Stylistic Variation Property (SVP). The PP, studied below as the principle which defines, including within one and the same language, the difference between the preferred structure and the other ones, is, when considering language-internal paraphrases, one of the manifestations of the SVP.

With regard, now, to the crosslinguistic aspect of things, we may consider that, as illustrated below by two examples (Kalam and Telefol), for most processes defining a language type, there is at least one language which turns out to be atypical. The existence of atypical languages is a basic characteristic of Lb. This suggests defining LBs as both free and constrained: free as builders of efficient strategies, constrained to the extent that they must also abide by pre-existing rules. Thus, the solutions proposed by languages to the problem of expressing a certain content shed light on man's nature as a language maker.

As far as the relationship between the components of languages is concerned, certain principles may be proposed to introduce the following study. For one thing, the distribution of tasks between two components does not mean that an economy is realized in the long run; lightening the task of morphology amounts to loading syntax with a specific burden, and vice versa; we have seen for example (end of 2.1.1 above) that in languages whose "adjectives" are in fact stative verbs, LBs, when needing to use them not as main predicates, but in attributive function, have only one means: they must resort to a relative clause, i.e., a complex syntactic solution; but in languages possessing adjectives as an original category, there is an additional word-type, distinct from both verbs and nouns, and often submitted to constraints such as those of (gender, number, sometimes even case) agreement. For another thing, we will see that the two perspectives studied above and below, namely Lb as problem-solving and the distribution of linguistic tasks, are tightly linked: with regard to the VS (cf. section b. below) as well as to the expression of circumstances, LBs use either a synthetic-morphological or an analytic-syntactic solution; circumstances, for example, are expressed either by derivational morphology (cf. below Cokwe suffixes, Russian and Atsugewi satellites, Comox lexical suffixes), or by adverbial complements, and each of these solutions corresponds to a particular distribution of tasks. But things get even more interesting if we note that both the syntactic and the morphological solutions are also, to a certain extent, lexical: the syntactic one because the elements governed by a relator are lexical units, and the morphological one because even though this strategy associates affixes to roots, the complex words resulting from such associations are mostly lexical entries, let alone that the affixes themselves are sometimes, despite affixation as a formal device, lexical units, like the Comox elements which have been aptly named "lexical suffixes" (see comment on example (31)). A last point must be stressed: we will see, through the example of Hungarian satellites, Comox lexical suffixes and Spanish aspectual verbs, that in various domains, including aspect, the contradiction between syntactic primacy and semantic centrality is a factor that may contribute to trigger a grammaticalization (auxiliarization) process.

I will now focus on two aspects of the distribution of linguistic tasks in two sections, which I call[2]

a. The Paraphrastic Principle from a crosslinguistic point of view
b. The Verbal Strategy.

a. *The Paraphrastic Principle (PP) from a crosslinguistic point of view*
    Within one language, two or several different syntactic structures can correspond to the same, or roughly the same, semantic content. This is an important and universal property of human languages, which I will call the *Paraphrastic Principle (PP)*. The PP has often been studied, and it underlies much of the inspiration of early Generative Grammar. I would like to call attention, here, to another aspect of the PP, i.e., its crosslinguistic relevance. The comparison between various languages on specific points well-known to translators and specialists of contrastive linguistics reveals, if done in a theoretical linguistic perspective, an interesting kind of distribution of tasks. Consider the Spanish sentences (20)-(21) below (Talmy 1985:70-71):

(20)   *la botella cruzó el canal flotando*
          (the bottle crossed the canal floating)
          "the bottle floated across the canal"

(21)   *metí el barril a la bodega rodándolo*
         (I-put(PAST) the keg into the storeroom rolling-it)
         "I rolled the keg into the storeroom".

In these examples, it appears that there is an opposition between two strategies: the "Germanic" strategy, represented by English, and the "Romance" strategy, represented by Spanish or by French, in which the structure is the same as in Spanish, i.e., corresponding to (20) and (21) respectively,

(20')   *la bouteille a traversé le canal en flottant*

(21')   *j'ai mis le tonneau dans la cave en le roulant.*

We see that, given one identical content, i.e., an aim-directed motion and a manner, both applied to an object, the conflation of motion (due ((21) and (21')) or not ((20) and (20')) to an animate agent) with what Talmy calls "path" ("the course followed or site occupied by the Figure object with respect to the Ground object" (Talmy 1985:61)) is expressed in Spanish or French by the syntactic center, namely the verbal predicate, whereas manner is expressed by a peripheric element, the gerund complement. In contradistinction to this, the English sentences express manner by the verb, and motion by a resultative directional complement.

Resultative directional complements are just one case of a more general notion, that of adverbial complement (a function, not a word-class, despite this confusing label), whose crosslinguistic study sheds some light on an interesting distinction between paraphrases with the same meaning from one language to another. Among other possible solutions, the problem of expressing adverbial complements is mainly resolved either by making them grammatical satellites (Talmy 1985:102 ff.) of the verbal predicate, or, following another division of labor, by resorting to syntactic means outside the verb. Consider (22), from Atsugewi (Talmy, 1985:74):

(22)   */s-ʔ-w-cu-stʔaqʔ-cis-a/* → *scʔustʔáqʔcha*
         (I-SUBJ.M-3PAT.FACT-INSTR-for~runny~icky~material,
         like~gut, to~move-DIR("into fire")-DISC.M)
         "I prodded the guts into the fire with a stick".

The instrumental prefix *cu-*, meaning "from a linear object, moving axially, acting on the patient", and the directional suffix *-cis* "into fire" refer to the circumstances of the event, so that the literal translation of (22) is "I caused it that runny icky material move into fire by acting on it with a linear object moving axially". The two adverbial complements in this translation, like those used above, "into the fire" and "with a stick", represent syntactic solutions to a problem which can also be resolved by using morphological means: this is what is done, in Atsugewi, through the use of these two instrumental and directional satellites attached to the verb root.

Satellites often express the basic meaning, especially when they refer to the motion itself and its aim, the verbal root indicating a secondary circumstance. Thus, in Hungarian *fáradjon be!* "please come in!", the satellite *be*, focused by its final position (the infinitive is *befáradni*), means "into", whereas *fáradjon* (*-jon*: 3SG.IMP = polite "you"), literally "tire yourself!", just indicates manner. *in* in the English gloss is also a satellite, but it expresses the basic meaning, like *be* in Hungarian. What we have here is an interesting phenomenon, often occurring in languages using this kind of satellite, namely a *contradiction between syntactic primacy and semantic centrality*. The literal French translation of English *please come in!*, i.e., *entrez, s' il vous plaît!*, removes this contradiction by conflating motion and aim into a single verb, but the literal French translation of Hungarian *fáradjon be!*, i.e., *donnez-vous la peine d'entrer!*, does not remove the contradiction, since this translation has a finite verb (syntactically dominant) to express the secondary circumstance, and a governed infinitive to render the basic meaning. As expected, the languages using satellites are also those which, in sentences where motion and manner are both expressed, use a verb for manner, the task of describing the motion and its (reached) aim being assigned either to a satellite, like the prefix *át-* in the Hungarian sentence (23), or to a resultative directional complement, like *across the river* in (24), the English translation of (23) (cf. also (20)-(21)):

(23)   *át-úszta a folyó-t*
         (across-swam the river-ACC)

(24)   *he swam across the river.*

More often than not, languages in which satellites are widely used also possess a wider set of morphological means for the expression of certain contents which, if examined through Indo-European languages like French, or even English, might seem basically "lexical". Thus, to refer to the act of insulting, Hungarian uses a circumfix, *le...z*, within which the word indicating the insult is inserted, e.g., *le-hülyé-z* "to dub s.o., insultingly, an idiot", *le-fasisztá-z* "to dub s.o., insultingly, a fascist", etc.

The length of the English glosses which are necessary to translate certain associations of verbal roots with satellites in various languages sheds light on the typological differences resulting from the choice of a grammatical, instead of a lexical, strategy: there is no direct English equivalent to the many types of combinations of verbal roots with affixed satellites, which are a well-known feature of Slavic languages and should be considered a grammatical as much as a lexical phenomenon, since the satellites here are morphemes belonging to specific paradigms, e.g., Russian *ot-stuk-iva-t'* "to blow several times, insisting on each blow", *iz-o-lgat'-sja* "to become an arrant liar by dint of lying", *v-čitat'-sja* "to read carefully, striving to understand" (the hyphens in the transliteration are meant to indicate that the set satellite + reflexive suffix *-sja* or satellite + imperfective suffix *-iva* may be treated as a single discontinuous affix). The comparison of English with languages from other parts of the world also illustrates the PP as applied to the distribution between satellites in one language and lexical strategies in another: Cokwe has an intensive-depreciative-reversive suffix *-unuk* whose combination with *kas* "to bind", for example, yields *kas-unuk* "to loosen something small which was fastened" (Van Den Eynde 1960: 4-7); certain polysynthetic languages not only provide illustrations of satellite-genesis (see below for Comox), but also assign to some of their satellites highly specific meanings which, in most languages of the world, are expressed by free lexemes; in some rare cases, it is a noun which is the root, and the suffixed satellite which gives the whole word its verbal status, as in Kwakw'ala *ləx̣'-wətəla* basket to carry along in the hand, hence "to go along carrying a basket", or *gəgewas-g* deer(REDUP)-to eat, hence "to eat deer" (Anderson 1985:29). This example, furthermore, shows that *there is no inherent nounhood or verbhood of any given notion*, and that LBs can organize in highly various ways the grammatical grid through which they express the world. More generally, there is much to learn, with regard to the distribution of tasks between grammar and lexicon, from a crosslinguistic study of the PP.

b. *The Verbal Strategy (VS)*

A particular aspect of this distribution deserves a separate study. I call *Verbal Strategy* the choice, made by LBs in certain languages, of successions of verbs or of VPs containing various sorts of affixes, as opposed to the use, in other languages, of the structure verb + adverbial complement, where this complement depends syntactically on the verb, but is morphologically autonomous, which makes it quite distinct from a satellite. For speakers of English, structures like

(25)   *John said to Mary...*

or

(26)   *I am angry at you,*

in which the person spoken to and the person who causes anger, respectively, are both represented by relator-phrases, appear quite normal. Consider, though, their equivalents in Trique, given below as (27) and (28) respectively:

(27) $ga^3ta^{34}h$ *juan gu^3ni^3 maria*
         (said J   heard M)

(28) a^3 $?ma^3$ ru^3wa^2h ni^3 $?i^{21}$ re^5 $?$
         (angry I see-I you) (Longacre 1985:263; numbers = tone levels and glides (1 highest, 5 lowest)).

Here, instead of a verb and a relator-phrase functioning as indirect object, which is the structure in (25) and (26), we have two juxtaposed clauses, recognizable as clauses by the very fact that each of them has its own predicate: a finite verb. (27) and (28) are illustrations of the VS, which produces polycentric sentences, as opposed to monocentric sentences.

Besides polycentric sentences with successions of finite verbs, the VS can also be represented by VPs, in which various affixes correspond to the adverbial complements of the non-verbal strategy (NVS). The polycentric VS is an analytic device, whereas the VP-centered VS is a synthetic device. An interesting crosslinguistic division of labor can be observed here: just as languages using the VS and languages using the NVS are not the same ones, the analytic and the synthetic types of VS do not normally coexist in the same language. This can be illustrated within a single language stock, for example in Papuan: while Hua, Enga, and Kewa have the synthetic type of VS, which yields structures with the form Adjunct Nominal + Verb, Alamblak, Barai and Yimas have verb serializing, i.e., the syntactic or analytic solution, and they either lack synthetic constructions entirely, or possess very few of them. Seen in this perspective, the crosslinguistic distribution of tasks, precisely because it shows what unconscious choices LBs make when having to resolve a given problem of expression, has typological consequences: even within the same language stock, here Papuan, a language which would possess both adjunct constructions and verb series would contradict the assumption that these two devices have the same function and that consequently, they should not, according to the principle of crosslinguistic distribution of tasks, coexist in the same language; if they do, the language in which they appear concurrently must necessarily be considered as atypical. It so happens that such a language exists: Kalam has both adjunct constructions ((29)) and verb series ((30)):

(29)   – combinations of *ŋ* "to perceive" with adjunct nominals *wdn* "eye", *tmwd* "ear", *wsn* "sleep", *gos tep* lit. "thought good", yield, respectively, *wdn ŋ* "to see" (eye perceive), *tmwd ŋ* "to hear" (ear perceive), *wsn ŋ* "to dream" (sleep perceive), *gos tep ŋ* "to like" (thought good perceive)
        – combinations of *d* "to hold" with adjunct NP *waŋ sy* lit. "penis illegal" or adjunct NP *mgn sy* lit. "vagina illegal" yield, respectively, *waŋ sy d* "to commit adultery (of woman)" or *mgn sy d* "to commit adultery (of man)"
        – combinations of *ag* "to sound" with adjunct nominals and NPs such as *kmap* "song" and *mnm jwj* lit. "speech basis" yield *kmap ag* "to sing" and *mnm jwj ag* "to explain", respectively.

(30)   – *am mon pk d ap ay*
        (go wood break get come put)
        "to fetch firewood"

– *am alŋaw kab tk d ap ad ñb*
(go pandanus nut cut get come cook consume)
"to gather pandanus nuts" (Pawley 1985:96-97).

This atypical character of Kalam might be due to areal diffusion, since Kalam occupies the border between Highlands and Sepik languages, in which adjunct constructions and serialization, respectively, are prominent features (cf. Foley 1986:127-128). Be that as it may, the very fact that Kalam is unique among Papuan languages lends support to the idea that there is in most cases a crosslinguistic distribution of tasks.

When the strategy chosen by LBs is the synthetic type of VS, the center of the complex verb resulting from this choice is not necessarily a generic verb belonging to a limited list, as illustrated by Kalam in (29). There are languages in which the situation is just the opposite: the center may be any verb, and it is the affix combined with it which belongs to a limited set of elements. In certain polysynthetic languages, this affix often refers to a circumstance, whose expression is thus tightly linked to the verb by the VS. Consider (31) from Comox (Hagège 1981c:64):

(31)   *joθ-šən-t-ə-s*
         (push-foot-3PAT-LV-3AG)
         "he pushes him with his foot".

Comox *šən* belongs to a set of forms which constitutes one of the most characteristic features of Salishan languages. These forms have successively been called "substantival","nominal","etymological" and finally "lexical suffixes" by specialists of Salishan languages (Hagège 1981c:58). Seen in the perspective of the distribution of tasks among the various components of a language, this label reflects the contradiction between the semantic centrality of the word referring to a concrete object generally assigned to the lexicon (a body part in (31)) and, resulting from the choice of the VS, its treatment as a bound element belonging to the *morphology*. Salishan lexical suffixes are not reduced forms of nouns, as would be the case if they resulted from the process called *incorporation* (cf. 6.2.2). They are *not* incorporated nominals; striking as it may appear, most of them are original forms, totally different from the nouns with which they are synonymous: in Comox, for example, "human being" and "hand" are *tómeš* and *čéyeš* respectively when free nouns, but *-áye* and *-ʔóje* when lexical suffixes. We must conclude, then, that in several vocabulary fields such as those of body parts, food, tools, intellectual life, LBs, for one and the same semantic content, have unconsciously distributed the task of expressing this content between the lexicon and the grammar; consequently, they have developed two kinds of forms: one belonging to a non-limited collection of free units, the other a member of a limited set of morphemes; interestingly enough, the latter is reserved for uses whose equivalents in languages without lexical suffixes are NPs functioning as objects or (like in the English translation of (31)) adverbial complements, i.e., having a specific grammatical status.

We have studied so far, based on Papuan and Salishan examples, the various realizations of the synthetic type of VS, and we have seen that there is much to learn from this study of the division of labor between the grammar and the lexicon. But there is also much to learn from comparing the two types of VS themselves, namely the synthetic and the analytic types. This appears clearly in the field of aspect. Spanish and Portuguese possess relatively rich sets of aspectual verbs and auxiliaries. These yield structures whose characteristic features can be defined, as in (32), by opposing them to the Slavic structure with aspectual preverb + verb:

(32)   Spanish   Russian   gloss
          rompió a reir   *zasmejalsja*   "he burst into laughter".

To express the ingressive, which is one of the meanings of the Russian aspectual preverb *za-* (mostly yielding a perfective verb), Spanish here uses an aspectual finite verb followed by a dependent verb in the infinitive. The first of these two elements can also be an auxiliary instead of a full lexical verb, and the second one can be another type of non finite dependent verbal element, namely a gerund; these cases are realized in (33), where the aspect, this time, is progressive:

(33)   *María está escribiendo una carta*
          "Mary is writing a letter".

Depending on the element which occupies the first position and on whether the second element is an infinitive or a gerund, e.g.,

(34)   a.   *acabó comiendo*   b.   *acaba de comer*
              "s/he ended up eating"   "s/he has just eaten",

these Spanish aspectual structures may express a variety of aspects, such as reiterative (*volvió a* + infinitive = "s/he V-ed again") and continuative (*continua a* + infinitive = "s/he keeps on V-ing"), in addition to ingressive (example (32)), progressive ((33)), terminative ((34a)), and immediate past ((34b)). But the important common point between these structures is that in all of them, the first element, the aspectual one, whether a full lexical verb or an auxiliary, is the main verb from the syntactic viewpoint, while the second element, which is the semantic center, is syntactically dependent: it is not even a finite verb, but only a nominal form of the verb. The situation is almost the reverse in Russian: the syntactically main verb is not the aspectual element, but the very verb which receives aspect, and the latter is expressed by a peripheric element, a preverb. Therefore, on a crosslinguistic scale of aspect marker morphogenesis, Russian has gone one step further than Spanish, which itself has gone one step further than English, as is shown by the English translations of the Russian and Spanish examples: although English has aspectual auxiliaries, it also uses aspectual full verbs as well as adverbs; although Spanish allows adverbs as markers of aspect, its main and, in some cases, only system of aspect-marking is the structure illustrated in (32)-(34); and although Russian does not exclude this structure, since it is possible to use, for example, *prodolžat'* + infinitive = "to continue to", Russian has categorized the expression of aspect, making it the central paradigm of its verbal system.

Thus, there are cases in which the two types of VS, the synthetic and the analytic types, represent two different paths followed by the genesis of aspect markers: Spanish has begun to specialize verbs as aspect markers, but it still uses to that effect, besides true auxiliaries, full lexical verbs which inflect like any other verb, and are the syntactic centers of the structure; hence a discrepancy between syntax and semantics, as opposed to Russian, where the syntactic center is also the main semantic element; the adverbs of English represent the lowest step of the scale, and the same can be said of the aspectual adverbs of German, given that they have not been regrouped into a class with specific formal properties. While the VS is a basic strategy in the morphogenetic history of many languages, and plays its part in grammaticalization (cf. chapter 7 below), the same cannot be said of the adverbial strategy[3].

Despite this deficiency of adverbs in the morphogenetic history of languages like German, adverbs as verb modifiers often have an important function when the VPs produced by the VS are not powerful enough as far as the expression of tense and mood is concerned. This appears both in the comparison between two languages through the exercise of translation and, language-internally, in languages that do not have verbal affixes but "compensate for" this by the importance of certain adverbs in the sentence. To begin with the latter, an obvious sign of the crosslinguistic distribution of tasks is the following: the verb in inflectional (e.g., Indo-European) languages often contains mood markers, whereas many languages whose verb is invariable, especially monosyllabic languages of West Africa or South-East Asia, have a number of forms submitted to several, and sometimes very strict, rules that determine their position and combination possibilities, as a result of LBs' problem-solving activity in languages without verbal morphology. An interesting example is Chinese zài, whose general semantic content is reiteration (Renaud & Luo 1987).

With regard to the function of adverbs, in a contrastive perspective, as tools for the expression of tenses which are underspecified in the VP, consider (35), from Hungarian:

(35)   elveszt-ett-em a könyv-ek-et, amely-ek-et ve-tt-em
         (lose-PAST-OBJCTV.1SG ART book-PL-ACC REL-PL-ACC
         buy-PAST-OBJCTV.1SG.)

Hungarian has only one past tense in the indicative (as well as in the conditional). (35), literally "I lost the books which I bought", can mean either that the books were lost immediately after they were bought, or some time (or very long) later. If the latter is the intended meaning, or if a translator starts from "I lost the books which I had bought" as an English sentence for which an exact Hungarian equivalent is required, then an adverb will be inserted before the verb, in order to give information on the anteriority of the second clause: előzőleg "previously", útközben "on the way". Similarly, the durative meaning of the French imperfect, e.g., in:

(36)   depuis qu'il était parti, nous riions
         "since he had left, we had kept on laughing"

is rendered, according to Kelemen (1988:85) by the adjunction of an adverb, *egyfolytában* "continuously", hence

(37)   *mióta elmen-t, egyfolytában nevet-t-ünk*
          (since leave-PAST continuously laugh-PAST-SBJCTV.1PL).

This is because the verbal system of Hungarian, which opposes the objective conjugation (definite patient) and the subjective one (indefinite patient or no patient), does not express the opposition between a punctual and a continuous event, the latter being rendered in (36) by the French imperfect. The choice of an adverbial strategy in (37) and in the revised version of (35) implies a less advanced stage, since Hungarian, given its verbal system, must resort to the lexicon in order to express aspectual contrasts. What makes these examples interesting is that they show how the personal choice of the translator in such a situation results in the use of a lexical means, thus stressing again that crosslinguistically, the grammar and the lexicon are complementary to each other: where a given language lacks the grammatical means to express an aspectual contrast (affixed morphemes distinguished by their aspectual meanings), the solution, often prompted by the need to translate from another language in which this paradigmatic opposition does exist, is lexical, and therefore less mechanical and more open to individual initiative. If used not only by an isolated translator, but rather on a large scale by an increasing number of LBs as a result of long-lasting cultural contact, this solution may lead to the creation of a new aspectual category.

The question should be raised, then, whether the opposite situation is possible or not. In other words, are there cases in which the VS produces VPs which are so pregnant with indications of time, aspect, and mood, that the modifying adverbs are underspecified in that respect, and must rely on the VP for a part of their meaning? Such a situation is, in fact, not exceptional at all. As far as tense is concerned, for instance, in Hindi, the adverb *kəl* "the day just 24 hours from today" does not specify whether the time referred to is past or future, leaving the task of saying it to the VP. Thus there is no Hindi word for "yesterday"; nor is there one for "to-morrow": *kəl* means both, depending on the tense of the verb. The same is true of Huron *(h)ē?(t)*. Likewise, Malagasy *vao* means "recently", "shortly", or "a few minutes ago", depending on whether the prefix on the verb indicates past, future or present. As for French *tout à l'heure* and Japanese *tadaima*, they both mean "a few minutes ago" if the verb is in the past, and "within a few minutes" if it is in the future.

The last manifestation of the VS which must be mentioned here has to do not with the adverbial, or other, complements which modify the verb within the same clause, but with those which themselves take the form of a clause. In languages possessing *diaphorics* (cf. 3.2.1), the task of conjoining clauses is done by the non-final verb, which bears an indication of *isophoricity/anisophoricity* with the following verb, as well as simultaneousness/non-simultaneousness, consecution if required, etc. The kind of crosslinguistic division of labor related to the choice of VS appears with particular clarity here, since in many languages which do not use *diaphorics*, the task of conjoining clauses is done by conjunctions. Therefore, it is not surprising to find that in Wojokeso, a language in which medial verbs receive *isophoric* or *anisophoric* suffixes, as well as morphemes indicating simultaneousness *vs.* succession in the non-future, there is only one conjunction. Given this correlation, just as Kalam appears atypical since it associates two features which are, crosslinguistically, in complementary distribution within its stock (cf. (29)-(30) above), another language of this stock, Telefol, also appears atypical: it has both the verb morphology typical of Papuan languages (with *diaphorics*), of which Wojokeso is a clear illustration, and another feature doing the same task, i.e., a rich inventory of free conjunctions (Longacre 1985:286 n.11).

Thus, the study of the distribution of linguistic tasks sheds light on the fact that, both synchronically and diachronically, the components of language are very flexibly related to one another. The permanent morphogenetic work of LBs, adapting as they do each language to its users' needs, is in fact the real force which shapes these relationships and triggers linguistic evolution.

2.1.3 The place of material form in language

The preceding discussion has shown that, contrary to what the relegation of forms to "surface" has long led linguists to believe, language types are determined to a large extent by the type of solution chosen in each case, in order to resolve the problem of having to express a certain meaning by certain forms. It has, therefore, shown the importance of typology in the study of *the relationship between form and meaning, a relationship which is the most fundamental characteristic of human languages.* Far from being only the crosslinguistic examination of various issues in descriptive grammar, *language typology is a basic contribution to theoretical linguistics, since it sheds light on the place of material form in language.* The importance of form is established, among other things, by two types of phenomena which I will comment on successively now. The first one has to do with formal constraints as reflected by what I have called (Hagège 1990b:142-143) the Heavy Close Law (HCL). Many known languages have binomials, expressive (including ideophonic) or ordinary, whose order is irreversible – the second term being mostly, by virtue of an *iambic affinity* typical of speech, "heavier" than the first: it has more syllables, longer (or more) back consonants or vowels, or it has phonemes in the lower frequencies of the acoustic spectrum: *flip-flop, by guess and by gosh,* etc. (cf. Cooper & Ross 1975). The HCL may happen to come into conflict with the ego-centered deixis, an important aspect, if not the only relevant one (cf. the discussion in 3.2), of the *anthropophoric system.* In terms of ego-centered deixis, things which, in space or time, are close to ego, e.g., "here" and "soon" as opposed to "there" and "late" respectively, are ordered, with regard to both intrinsic value and word-sequence, *before* those which are less close; similarly, "more" has priority over "less" on the scale of values as defined by ego. French *de-ci de-là, tôt ou tard, plus ou moins* are examples of this deixis-triggered word order in binomials. But there are cases in which obedience to the HCL results in binomials that violate the ego-centered deixis. Thus we find Russian *tam i sjam* ("there and here"), Spanish *tarde o temprano* ("late or soon"), and Urdu (under the influence of Persian) *kəm o béš* ("less and more"). All three are applications of the HCL such as defined above. We can therefore conclude that a purely formal constraint has priority, here, over ego deixis. In other words, the *iambic affinity* of speech, which reflects an articulatory and acoustic tendency of LBs, is stronger than the word-order affinities, which reflect LBs' representation of the hierarchy of beings.

Structural homologies are the other type of phenomena that demonstrate the importance of form in language. The notion of *structural homology* refers to the homology established by certain revealing languages between two formal structures whose respective meanings, in most other languages, are not expressed by homologous structures. The very fact that they can, if in few languages, be treated alike points to the syntactic and semantic homology between them. Yaka is a striking example (Van Den Eynde & Kyota 1984). In this language, the unmodified form of the noun and the absolutive mode of the verb are both unmarked; nouns when followed by modifiers and verbs when followed by a nominal complement are marked by the tone lowering of all the vowels in the root; nouns when modifying a preceding noun or pronoun and verbs when they are in a relative clause modifying a noun or pronoun are also marked by a tonal morpheme, this time a high tone on the first mora of the root. Thus, the *structural homologies* observed in Yaka are a clear manifestation of the link between the functions of the noun and those of the verb. They reveal that despite the crosslinguistic difference between nouns and verbs, there is a tight relationship between them, since in at least one language, they are marked in the same way for each of the three functions which both of them can have.

The importance of form in language could seem to be sufficiently demonstrated by the foregoing. But some authors, going one step further, have argued that there is, in many cases, a direct dependency of content on form. Thus, Nichols, studying (1986b) the opposition between two marking strategies, head-marking an dependent-marking, examines its realization in two domains, the expression of possession on the one hand (cf. examples (82) and (84) in 2.3.3) and split intransitivity on the other. As far as the former is concerned, she observes that the alienability contrasts are most frequent in languages using head-marked possession, either exclusively (Diegueño, Greenlandic Eskimo, Lakhota, Nanai), or as one of the types in a split system (Eastern Pomo, Maidu, Hittite, Ge'ez). As for split intransitivity, she notes that where the distinction between active participants (inflected like the agent in transitive constructions) and stative participants (inflected like the patient) is head-marked (personal indices on the intransitive verb), as in Dakota or Mangarai, the form-content relation is reflexive, i.e., verbs are strictly classified as having either active or stative inflection; one of these two classes contains verbs that all refer to body processes, like "to cough", "to shout", etc., and it is lexical choice which appears to trigger inflection type. In dependent-marking languages, on the other hand, like Eastern Pomo or Batsbi, in which ergative *vs.* nominative is marked on the subject, she notes that there is a systematic choice between volitionality and non-volitionality, i.e., the form-content relation is not reflexive but straightforward. Since she has shown, based on her data, that the existence of head- *vs.* dependent-marking strategies is the factor which controls the possibility of making certain semantic distinctions in these two domains, she concludes that the availability of a content distinction depends here on specific formal properties.

In fact, this model, if applied to a wider set of languages, raises some problems. Semitic languages (not represented in Nichols's data), though they are head-marking, do not contain a clear alienability contrast, and conversely, among African languages (not represented either), those of the Mande stock, for example, do have this contrast but are not strictly head-marking. One could rather think that inalienably possessed objects, in NPs of possession, inherently (but not automatically, since there are exceptions) call for a modifier indicating the possessor; hence the correlation that LBs' activity has established, at least in the initial stages of the process of language-making, between alienability/inalienability contrasts and head-marking. If this is true, head-marking would be a meaning-induced phenomenon, i.e., just the reverse of Nichols's claim. But, despite these objections and counter-examples, it is true that there is a correlation between certain formal or structural properties of languages and certain semantic phenomena. Thus we note that some languages whose grammar offers a choice between two declension cases, each one expressing a particular semantic content (e.g., non-referential nominative *vs.* referential accusative in Turkic and Tungusic families, permanent (dative) *vs.* temporary (allative) transfer of possession in Chechen-Ingush and Lezgian), are dependent-marking: LBs leave themselves wider possibilities for semantic distinctions expressed by specific forms when they mark the function of the complements not within the VP, which is already loaded with many indications, but on these complements, which, being outside the VP, are easier to mark.

Thus, there is no doubt that material form has a central place in the process of Lb. A less often observed influence is the one they have on the makers of linguistic theories themselves. As noted by Nichols (1986a:115), "Chomsky's analysis of case and government can be read as making the following implicit assumptions: a. Dependency and government are the same thing. b. Every dependent must bear the marker of its syntactic relation. c. Heads govern dependents, and assign formal marking to them." This confirms what she had noted earlier, i.e., that "the effect of Chomsky's system is to build into the fundamentals of core grammar the dependent-marking nature of English (and generally IE) morphosyntax." The correlation suggested here between certain features of English and some of the methods used in Transformational Grammar is also apparent if we consider that English, with its grammar relying mostly on word order and prosody to mark syntactic relationships, its almost total lack of syntactically-driven morphology, and its plethora of meaning-invariant syntactic processes, provided rich material for a theory of transformations. By contrast, inflectional languages like those of the Slavic family, in which syntactic relationships based on meaning are predominant, have inspired dependency models such as Tesnière's (1959) structural syntax or Mel'čuk's dependency syntax (Mel'čuk 1988:311).

We have here another, external, manifestation of the importance of material form in human languages. The material form of words is not only the result of the work done by generations of LBs striving to adapt morphosyntax to their needs. By a symmetrical move, it also influences the thinking of LBs, including the most conscious ones, i.e., grammarians and linguists[4]. It even happens, sometimes, that the latter do not take advantage of the clues provided by certain features of their language, because they are attached to the concrete shape of units. Thus, Roman grammarians, who thoroughly studied the morphology of Latin, did not develop a syntactic model (Baratin 1989), probably because, even though inflected Latin words, as meaningful syntactic units, contained the indication of all their relationships with the rest of the sentence – thus requiring syntactic study - they were viewed as members of regular declension and conjugation paradigms and, last but not least given the importance of didactic considerations, they were taught as such by the Grammatici.

2.2 Reanalysis

I will first propose a definition (2.2.1) and then an illustration concerning "be" and "have" structures (2.2.2).

2.2.1 Definition

Reanalysis has been variously defined in modern linguistic work. Langacker (1977:58) considers it to be "a change in the structure of an expression or class of expressions that does not involve any immediate or intrinsic modification of its surface manifestations", and distinguishes two broad types of reanalysis, "resegmentation" (itself subdivided into boundary loss, boundary creation, and boundary shift), and "syntactic-semantic reformulation" (symmetrically subdivided into semantic loss, semantic addition, and semantic shift). As for Timberlake, to mention only these two authors among many, he distinguishes (1977:141) reanalysis, defined as "the formulation of a novel set of underlying relationships and rules", from actualization, defined as "the gradual mapping out of the consequences of the reanalysis".

In the perspective of the present research, these definitions cannot be retained, since the main criterion here is the amount of change in the real substance of linguistic utterances, rather than the resegmentation or reformulation of just the underlying structures. The latter are artifacts created by linguists, perhaps useful for representing relationships, but of limited use in the study of morphogenesis. Reanalysis will therefore be defined as the operation by which LBs cease to analyze a given structure as they did previously, and introduce a new distribution of, and new relations between, the syntactic units that constitute this structure. These innovations are always manifested by changes in the formal substance. Thus, in Teso, we can observe three successive stages in the transition from subordinate to main clause: in (38), although the old verb *bu* "to come" has been desemanticized to a past tense marker, it keeps its personal inflection, and continues to govern the verb of the subordinate clause, *ner*, as evidenced by the use of the subjunctive personal prefix *ke-*, regardless of the fact that the subordinate verb is now, in semantic terms at least, the main verb:

(38)   *a-bu ke-ner*
          (I-come I(SBJC)-say)
          "I said".

The following stage is represented by *eroko* "not yet", which still governs the subjunctive, but is not itself inflected for person:

(39)   *eroko ke-buno*
          (not~yet he(SBJC)-come)
          "he has not yet come".

The last stage is represented by *mam*, formerly a negative copula "not to be", and today a simple negative marker: *mam* is not inflected for person; moreover, the transition from subordinate to main clause has been completed, as is evidenced by the use of the indicative personal prefix *e-* in front of the following verb (Heine & Reh 1984:104-105):

(40) *mam petero e-koto ekiŋok*
      (NEG Peter he(INDIC)-want dog)
      "Peter does not want a dog".

Thus, while at the stages illustrated by (38) and (39) the semantically main verb is still syntactically subordinate, in (40) it has been reanalyzed as a main verb, and the former main verb has been reanalyzed as a verbal marker.

2.2.2 Reanalysis of a "be" structure as a "have" structure

The transition from a "be" to a "have" structure is observed in a number of languages. It deserves a special study, as it shows with particular clarity the morphogenetic activity and signature of LBs.

A well-known situation is that of languages in which the transitive perfect and the possessive phrase are structurally homologous; in Old Persian, there is an obvious parallelism between (41) and (42) (Benveniste 1966:180):

(41) *manā pussa astiy*
      (I-GEN.DAT son is)
      "I have a son"

(42) *manā krtam astiy*
      (I-GEN.DAT done is)
      "(here is what) I have done".

Just as in Old Persian the agent of the perfective event is in the genitive-dative, in Classical Armenian it is in the genitive, and thus treated, likewise, as the possessor of the action, since this language shows the same parallelism as in Old Persian between the possessive and perfective structures, illustrated below in (43) and (44) respectively:

(43) *nora ē handerj*
      (he-GEN is cloth)
      "he has clothes"

(44)   *nora ē gorceal*
         (he-GEN is done)
         "he has done".

We can see that in these old Indo-European languages, the perfect is a stative form, since the agent is treated as a possessor. However, Classical Armenian has gone one step further. When the transitive perfect, represented in (44) by the verb-phrase that contains the participle with an *-al* suffix, has an object, corresponding to a patient in semantic terms, this object is marked as accusative, by a *z-* prefix, as in (45):

(45)   *z-ayn nšan arareal ēr nora*
         (ACC-this miracle accomplished was he-GEN)
         "he had accomplished this miracle".

In examples (41)-(44), we had a possessive structure with a verb "to be", as well in possessive expressions proper ((41) and (43)), where the possessor is a genitive-dative experiencer and not a nominative subject, as in perfective sentences, where the subject is the patient of the transitive action, corresponding to the possessed in possessive structures. The new fact in (45) is that the patient is marked as an accusative in *z-ayn nšan*: this is one of the defining features of a "have" structure, even though it is only in a loose sense that some linguists would call *nora* a subject, since it does not agree with the verb (cf. 3.3) and remains genitive. Thus, (45), like (127) below, is a hybrid structure, in which LBs leave both a trace of the former analysis (here the genitive *nora*) and a sign of the new analysis (the accusative marker *z-*).

Comparable facts may be found in Semitic languages. Among the speakers of substandard Israeli Hebrew, for instance, there is a frequent use of *?et*, the definite object marker (cf. 1.3.3 section d.), before the NP representing the possessed object:

(46)   *lo haya l-i ?et ha-kesef ha-darûš*
         (NEG was(MASC) to-me *?et* the-money the-necessary)
         "I did not have the necessary money" (Rosén 1965:83).

Here *ha-kesef ha-darûš*, lit. "the money the necessary", would be considered to be the subject of *haya* "was", since both are masculine singular, were it not for the presence of *?et*: *?et* is the object marker. As for *l-i*, it is a dative NP, just as in Classical Hebrew: without *?et*, (46) becomes a common Classical Hebrew sentence; the same dative NP *l-i* "to-me" is found in Mandean, Talmudic Babylonian and New Syriac, as seen in such forms as Mangesh Aramaic *griš-li* (drawn-to~me) "I drew"; cf. also, in the same dialect, *qtila-lux* (killed(FEM)-to~you) "you killed her" (Cohen 1984:513). These structures have been hastily dubbed "ergative" for the sole and insufficient reason that "das Objekt war bereits in der Flexions-basis enthalten" (Jacobi 1973:153 n.1). At that rate, ergativity should be considered a general feature of Chamito-Semitic languages whose perfect has a possessive structure, including the most ancient one, Old Egyptian, in which we have *śdm n-f* (heard to-him) "he has heard", and this without further justification.

The structure illustrated by (46) is not unattested in Biblical Hebrew, but it is much less frequent there than in colloquial Israeli Hebrew, and where it appears, the *?et* it contains is a topic marker rather than a definite object marker. The transition from the latter to the former is a relatively spontane-ous, and understandable, process: a participant already identified can easily be mentioned as undergoer of an event (cf. Persian *-râ*). But since in collo-quial Israeli Hebrew *?et* is not only used as a topicalizer but has acquired the specific syntactic role of a patient marker, *?et ha-kesef ha-darûš* in (46) cannot easily, despite gender and number agreement with the verb, be treated as a subject. *l-i* would then appear as the subject, were it not dative (cf. 3.3 on "dative subjects"). At any rate, we may consider *lo haya l-i*, lit-erally "not was to-me", as a frozen VP, corresponding, in fact, to "I did not have". This is typically a case of reanalysis, since in (46), as in (45), we have both a trace of the former analysis (*haya l-i*) and a sign showing that a new grammatical interpretation has taken place: the use of *?et*. In other words, the "be" structure has shifted to a "have" structure.

As noted in 3.3, verb agreement control can apply to gender, number, or person, and preferably to all three when we want to be sure that a given NP has subject status. In (46) *l-i* might appear as a "subject", but there is no agreement of any kind: in Israeli Hebrew, if a woman is speaking, the feminine, unmarked in the pronoun for "I", is necessarily marked by the personal index *-t* affixed to the VP; but in (46), the resulting feminine form *hayta* "she was" is ruled out: thus, there is no gender agreement here. There is no number agreement either; if we replace *l-i* "to me" by *la-nu* "to us", the verb remains singular: the plural form *hayu* "they were" is also ruled out. Finally, there is no personal agreement: *hayiyti* "I was" is equally ruled out in (46). However, in another Semitic language, Maltese, which, unlike Israeli Hebrew, does not have an accusative marker (the only serious criterion to consider (46) as a case of reanalysis), there is person agreement in the "have" structure resulting from the reanalysis of a "be" structure: as opposed to Classical Arabic

(47)   *zayd-un sa-ta-kûnu la-hu ḫubzat-un*
          (Z.-NOMIN FUT-3SG.FEM-be to-him loaf(FEM)-NOMIN)
          "Zayd will have a loaf",

in which the verb "to be" agrees in gender with its feminine subject *ḫub-zat-un*, hence the SG.FEM personal index *-ta-*, in Maltese we have

(48)   *Pawlu sa-j-kol-l-u ḫobža*
          (P. FUT-3SG.MASC-be-to-him loaf(FEM))
          "Paul will have a loaf" (Comrie 1981:215),

in which *kon* "to be" (which becomes *kol* by assimilation of its final *-n* to the following *l*, which is the dative marker corresponding to the *la* of Classical Arabic) agrees with *Pawlu*, i.e., the sentence-initial subject and topic, the affinity between these two notions being stressed by this position, much more frequent in Maltese than in Classical Arabic. If we add that when the verb is negated, the two members *mâ* and *š* of the discontinuous negation, a characteristic of the Western dialects of Arabic (cf. 5.2.2) also found in Algerian and Tunisian, are immediately pre- and postposed, respectively, to the VP, we must conclude that (48) illustrates a further stage when compared with (46): although Maltese, like Israeli Hebrew, continues to use, literally, a verb "to be", the shift from a "be" to a "have" structure is more advanced, since the VP has not only become a frozen whole which can receive negation as such and in which the "be" and dative meanings have disappeared, but also agrees in gender, number and person with the subject NP. It is even possible to overhear an object pronoun, e.g., feminine, added to dialectal *ʃand-î* "(to-me=)I have" and inserted with it in a *mâ...š* negation: *mâ-ʃand-î-hâ-š* "I don't have her" (in Syrian Arabic, according to Hewitt, personal communication).

The next stage is represented in other (in fact much older) languages, by the transition from Classical to Late Latin, and from there to the Romance languages, for example in the well-studied evolution from *id mihi factum est* (this to-me done is) "I have done this" to *id habeo factum* (this I-have done), reproducing in the system of the auxiliary VP the transition from *est mihi liber* (is to-me book) "I have a book" to *habeo librum*. This evolution had already started, for verbs denoting the result of an intellectual activity or an appropriation, long before Classical Latin, in the language of the Early Republic, and it was well advanced in the 3rd and 2nd centuries B.C. in the Latin of Plautus, Terentius, and Cato (Rosén 1980:311 fn.3). Even within Indo-European, however, other branches have not reached the Latin-Romance stage: they have not extended the use of a verb "to have" to all contexts, including VPs with an auxiliary. Nevertheless, reanalysis has often occurred.

Slavic languages, for instance, have reacted in various ways to the early decay of the theme of the future. A conservative language like Slovenian introduced, and still uses today, an auxiliary "to be" in association with a perfect participle ending in *-l* and functioning like an adjective, as in example (9) above (cf. 1.3.1 section b.); this is quite an ordinary association, which was not exposed to reanalysis. Other languages did not react that way. Russian LBs, for instance, had recourse to a "be" possessive structure, expressing futurity as an obligation. In this structure, therefore, the possessor of the future event, i.e., its agent or patient, was originally expressed in the dative. Thus we had, for example, with *platiti* "to pay", *vam platiti budet* (to-you pay will-be) "you will have to pay", i.e., "you will pay". When this structure with a dative subject was reanalyzed by replacing the dative *vam* with a nominative *vy*, yielding *vy budet platiti*, a new problem was created, since there was a discrepancy between this nominative subject and the impersonal form *budet* "it will be", a trace of the stage in which "you will pay" was expressed by a structure whose literal English equivalent would be "it will be to you to pay". The problem was resolved by making the verb agree with the nominative subject pronoun, hence the present stage: *vy budete platit'*, in which *budete*, the 2PL.FUT of the verb "to be", is frozen as an auxiliary; it cannot be interpreted synchronically, since it is followed, not by a verbal adjective as in Slovenian, but by an infinitive, a structure requiring a dative experiencer. Thus, Russian has gone even farther than Georgian (example (127) in 3.3) and Israeli Hebrew (example (46)): there is number and person agreement, and, furthermore, the "dative subject" has shifted to a nominative subject, even though the verb "to be" is retained.

A comparable kind of evolution is found in Breton, a language without noun inflection (although there is consonant mutation), but in which, as a result of the topicalization (and fronting) of the possessor, the original "be" structure is reinterpreted as a "have" structure, e.g., in *me m'eus plijadur* (me to-me is pleasure) "I am pleased", literally "I have pleasure" (same structure in the present perfect, where *m'eus* functions as an auxiliary). In 19th century Manchu, the possessor simply loses the dative marking and it is reanalyzed as subject (Adam 1873:69). It even happens that the word interpreted as a verb "to have" in the new structure is not even an old verb "to be", but a noun-phrase of possession. In Malay, *punya* "to have" is a reduced form of *empu-punya* "its owner". Hopper notes (1986:132) that "the original syntax was (and often still is) of the form *rumah ini saya punya* 'this house I [am] its owner', requiring the possessed object to be a definite topic." Nowadays, *punya* is, for every speaker, a verb "to have": *saya punya rumah* "I have a house".

One might consider that verb agreement and accusative marking are not sufficient, and that the ultimate stage of the transition from a "be" to a "have" structure is reached only when a new verbal form meaning "to have" has been substituted for the verb "to be" in sentences expressing possession and in the auxiliary-based VPs, as in Latin and, more decisively, in the Romance languages. What is interesting, however, for the present study, is the clash, illustrated by Israeli Hebrew (ex. (46)), Maltese (ex.(48)) or Russian, between the vestigial form of a verb "to be" and the new organization of the sentence according to a "have" structure. This clash shows that LBs strive, at all levels of consciousness, including the lowest one, to satisfy various, not always convergent, expressive necessities.

2.3 The dialectical relationship between two contradictory needs

The change from a "be" to a "have" structure just studied in 2.2 above is a creative process, which renews an old pattern, but at the same time gives rise to some constraints such as subject-verb agreement, etc. More generally, there is a dialectical relationship between contradictory needs. I will examine this relationship below in three parts dealing successively with morphology and lexicon (2.3.1), syntax (2.3.2), and agreement (2.3.3), a phenomenon which, although already mentioned above in various places, deserves special consideration in the perspective of the present study.

2.3.1 *Morphology and lexicon*

By an interesting paradox, typical of their nature, LBs need at one stage to create constraints, which establish full-fledged new structures, and, at another stage, to free themselves from the stranglehold of these very constraints, which have finally resulted in frozen forms.

Two pairs of opposite tendencies are responsible for a significant part of the evolution of human languages, throughout their entire histories. These are, on the one hand, the opposition between ease of production and ease of perception (corresponding in part to Langacker's (1977:103-105) "signal simplicity" and "perceptual optimality"), and, on the other hand, the opposition between material integrity and the search for expressiveness. Ease of production implies reducing the number, length, and difficulty of the units and groups to be produced, both from the phonetic and the grammatical points of view, hence various phenomena such as the elimination of unstressed vowels, fusion of adjacent words into a single whole, cliticization of originally independent elements, sound assimilation, vowel or tone merger, reduction of consonant clusters, condensation of phrases into compounds, etc. This continuous reduction process eventually becomes an obstacle to ease of perception, because the various changes it brings about progressively blur morpheme boundaries, obscure clause relations, etc. On the other hand, the search for expressiveness leads to the renewal of worn out expressions; but the new forms in turn, precisely because they become the established norm, are progressively frozen, thus losing their motivation: the signal of this change, which makes them more and more opaque, is the reduction or elimination of various elements, i.e., the loss of material integrity. At a later stage, the frozen forms get expressive remotivation and the cycle (cf. chapter 5) starts again.

These two pairs of tendencies are interrelated. Ease of perception by the listener, whose task is rendered less difficult, is often a result of the search for a periphrastic formulation, which replaces a frozen structure and substitutes the expressive transparency of an analytic strategy for the opacity of a synthetic whole. As for ease of production, it often jeopardizes material integrity, since it brings about, as noted above, several kinds of reduction. Moreover, the search for expressiveness, through the addition of new elements, may impair the ease of perception, which is itself reinforced by the respect of material integrity. As long as the latter is not in turn destroyed by factors cyclically triggering linguistic change, it preserves languages from the violations of the "one form-one meaning" principle (Hagège 1990c). All these correlations between various tendencies are schematized in (49):

(49)   ease of production ⟶ ease of perception

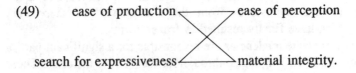

search for expressiveness ⟶ material integrity.

To take just one example among many, relators (cf.7.2.1), in a number of languages, have often been renewed, but exposed again, at a later stage, to a demotivation process. In particular, speakers of languages in which relators may govern nouns or NPs with a fairly broad meaning – these associations giving birth to new relators, both longer and more complex – are often in search of novel nouns, held to have the capacity to refresh old and stale function words. But these new structures, becoming more and more frequent as time passes, are progressively more and more frozen, so that they are finally condemned to demotivation. This process is sometimes very fast, as is observable today in complex relators such as French *au niveau de* or German (Lehmann 1987a:202) *im Zuge* + GEN (instead of *bei* + DAT), as in *im Zuge der Regierungsumbildung* "in the government change" and *im Vorfeld* + GEN (instead of *vor* + DAT), as in *im Vorfeld des Kongresses* "before the Congress".

In other cases, the evolution is much slower, and contradictory forces act simultaneously, without one of them overcoming the other. Human languages are replete with forms which are both expressive and, because uneconomical, less and less easy to handle. Lithuanian can illustrate this state of tension between tendencies. While the old Indo-European case system has been simplified or lost in a number of modern languages, in some dialects of Lithuanian, three new cases have been added to the seven inherited ones. In the 16th and 17th centuries, they still were part and parcel of the morphology of the common language itself, without being restricted to dialectal use. Brought about by the influence of the agglutinating languages long used in the neighboring Finnic-speaking territories (Stolz 1987a:26-30), the presence of these three additional cases makes dialectal Lithuanian, already known for its conservatism, one of the most complex languages in the world as regards nominal inflection. The new cases, the illative, the allative, and the adessive, are formed by adding the suffixes *-na*, *-p(i)*, and *-p(i)-k* to the accusative, the genitive and the locative, respectively, according to a method called *hypostasis*, also applied in such languages as Ossetic, and which consists in agglutinating a suffix to an inflected stem. Two, at least, of the new cases, the illative and the adessive, have practically the same meaning as the old cases, from which they furthermore are derived. There is therefore an obvious contradiction between two needs: expressive diversification and paradigmatic economy, the latter being one of the main factors underlying ease of production.

The freezing of forms originally motivated by the search for expressiveness is illustrated by an important phenomenon of natural languages, idiomatic expressions. English *to kick the bucket* and its French equivalent *casser sa pipe* are analyzable into elements some of which are inflected in the usual way: it is impossible to say, for instance, **he kick-the-bucketed* or **vous casser-sa-piperez*. However, it is easy to see that these idioms remain quite opaque in terms of semantic analysis: they do not mean that one gives kicks to a bucket or that one breaks one's pipe, but that one dies. Similarly, in Yoruba, *kpā-rí* (cut-head) means "to terminate", not "to cut the head" (Hagège 1981a:77). Idiomatic expressions should be thoroughly studied in as many languages as possible (for English, cf. Makkai 1972). They cannot be treated in the classical generative framework, since no deep structure can retrieve their meaning (cf. Chafe 1968). Therefore, LBs learn them by heart, and if this, despite the tremendous number of idioms in any language, does not bring about an intolerable burden on individual memory, it is because idioms constitute a part of the culture of native speakers. This is shown by the well-known fact that a non-native speaker has some trouble in understanding, let alone producing, such expressions, for lack of the cultural model on which many of them are based, whereas native speakers, possessing this model, can understand a number of idioms they have never heard, and in some cases create new ones to satisfy their need for expressiveness.

LBs can even remotivate a frozen idiomatic expression, for instance by inserting between its terms other terms adapted to the desired meaning. It is possible to remotivate in this way, for example, some of the immutable and irreversible quadrisyllabic idioms of Chinese known as *chéngyǔ*: thus, in Hao Ran 1972 (I, p.498), the following exhortation is attributed to Mao Zedong:

(50)   *wǒmen yīngdāng gāo hǎn chén rè dǎ tiě chén duóqǔ le quán guó*
shènglì de rècháo dǎ shèhuìzhǔyì de tiě
(we must aloud shout take-advantage-of hot strike iron take-advantage-of gain-by-war PAST whole country victory CONN enthusias-
tic-stride strike socialism CONN iron)
"we must shout: 'let us strike while the iron is hot; let us take
advantage of the warm enthusiasm arising from the national victory
in order to strike the iron of socialism.' ".

Here the author splits the frozen idiom *chén rè dǎ tiě* by inserting, between
the two V + Object Noun associations of which it is made, a dependent
structure, which, in prenominal position as required in Chinese, determines
the object noun. Thus, *rè* "heat; hot" and *tiě* "iron" both receive a
determiner, respectively *duóqǔ le quán guó shènglì* "gain by fighting a
national victory" and *shèhuìzhǔyì* "socialism". The author, therefore,
without destroying the parallelism of these two V + N associations, which
is characteristic of many expressions built on syllable-grouping in this
monosyllabic language, renews the idiomatic expression in a creative
manner, by both preserving and jeopardizing its material integrity, since
new elements are inserted, that break it up into four parts.

2.3.2 The syntax-semantics clash

The morphological and lexical aspects of the conflict between opposite
tendencies schematized in (49) has just been illustrated by examples taken
from the domain of relators (such as French or German prepositions, or
Lithuanian case morphemes) and idioms. Another important aspect of this
conflict is the syntax-semantics clash. If viewed in a purely synchronic perspective, syntax may appear as a field with its own context-free mechanisms; in certain cases, the processes that control linguistic productions
seem to be directly governed not by communicative functions, but by syntactic categories operating to some extent independently of these functions
(Bock & Kroch 1989). But it is also common knowledge among linguists
that much of syntax is a frozen state of semantics. This characteristic feature of linguistic evolution should be studied in the light of the LBs' glossogenetic activity. LBs need rules in order to build utterances as speakers
and to decode them as listeners. Thus, in the course of linguistic evolution,
the semantic motivation of many a structure gets lost and gives way to the

automatism of regular constraints, which define grammar. However, LBs, following a symmetrical tendency, also strive periodically to remotivate frozen syntactic structures. They often leave concrete traces of this effort; at times, syntactic constraints overcome semantic motivations, at other times, the reverse happens. I will examine below, successively, these two phases of a dialectical evolution.

In many inflectional languages, the genitive originally had a concrete partitive meaning, as we can see in Latin: *farinae* first means "some (a part of the) flour"; but this vague indication can be made more precise by combining it with a word pointing to an exact quantity, as in *farinae libram addito* (Cato, *Agr.*, 75) "add a pound of flour", or in Homeric Greek *oînoio kúpella* (wine(GEN.SG) cups(ACC.PL)) (*Il.* 4, 346) "cups of wine"; it appears here that the genitive has started losing its original partitive meaning and is progressively becoming a mere indicator of a dependency relationship between two nouns (cf. Serbat 1988:59-61). This includes fairly abstract uses, such as the conversion of noun government by the verb into a dependency between a modifier noun and a deverbal substantive functioning as a head noun. Thus a case-ending which at an earlier stage had a concrete meaning has become a syntactic tool. A similar situation is that of Japanese *o*: originally an interjection denoting exclamation, lamentation or wish, it lost its emotional overtones and became a mere object marker (cf. Shibatani 1990:340-347).

Just as LBs need to create abstract syntactic instruments, they sometimes submit clause structures to the requirements of similarity to a complete sentence. In certain languages, there is a marked tendency towards structural parallelism between subordinate clauses and independent sentences. Japanese is such a language: it is possible to say, for example,

(51)   *mon kara deru Sugiko ni atta*
         (door from leave S. to meet-PAST)
         "(he) met Sugiko who was going out of the door"

or

(52)   *kowareta kuruma o naosimasita*
         (was-damaged car OBJ.M repair-POL-PAST)
         "(he) repaired the damaged car",

but if we want to stress the circumstances in which the agent met Sugiko
or to insist on what has happened to the car, the usual Japanese structures
are, respectively,

(51')   *Sugiko ga mon kara deru no ni atta* (*ga* = SUBJ.M)

and

(52')   *kuruma ga kowareta no o naosimasita,*

literally, "(he) met with the fact that Sugiko was going out of the door"
and "(he) repaired the fact that the car was damaged", since *no* = "the fact
that" serves as nominalizer of a whole clause, which can thereby, as in
(51') and (52'), be governed by a postposition. In fact, what is met in (51')
is not the fact that Sugiko is going out of the door, but Sugiko herself, and
what is repaired in (52') is not the fact that the car is damaged, but the car
itself. This discrepancy between syntactic and semantic dependencies can
appear strange for a Westerner, but it is quite normal in Japanese, a
language where syntactically complete clauses are favored (cf. Mel'čuk
1988:123-124; Hagège 1991).

The importance of syntactic requirements often goes much further,
resulting in partial or total demotivation. The loss of the original meaning
of a lexeme which has become a grammatical instrument is illustrated by
the case of auxiliaries used together with the verb from which they are
historically derived, even when there is a contradiction between the
meanings of the verb and of the auxiliary (cf. 7.4.2 section a.).

In contradistinction to the cases examined so far, it often happens that
meaning plays a decisive role in the core syntax of a language. Thus, it has
been shown (Dixon 1979, Plank ed. 1979, Hagège 1982:40, 117-118,
among others) that in split-ergative systems, the choice between ergative
and non-ergative strategies depends on such factors as person, aspect,
degree of animacy, degree of control, type of clause, lexical meaning of the
verb. Another illustration is provided by the phenomenon which I call
diaphoricity (cf. 3.2.1). Telefol, like a number of other Papuan languages,
has two distinct morphemes indicating, when there is clause-chaining (one
of the most typical syntactic features in that area), whether the subject of
the dependent verb is (*isophoric* marker) or not (*anisophoric* marker) the
same as that of the following verb. The *isophoric* marker is *nal* and the

anisophoric is *ól*. They both appear in (53):

(53)　　*tál-nal-a-ta sook ang-ko-ól-u kaán-sé*
　　　(come-ISOPH-3SG.MASC.AG-then rope wrap-finish-
　　　ANISOPH-3SG.FEM.AG die-3SG.MASC.FAR~PAST)
　　　"he came an committed suicide and died" (Foley 1986:191).

The subject, *sook*, of the second clause, *sook ang-ko-ól-u*, is an inanimate belonging to the class of feminines, as is shown by the class suffix *-u*. Therefore, this clause is marked, by the *anisophoric* marker *ól*, as having a subject different from that of the following clause, *kaán-sé*, whose subject, *-sé*, is masculine and human. Since the subject *-a-* of the first clause, also masculine and human, is different from the subject, *sook*, of this second clause, the first clause should also be marked by an *anisophoric* morpheme. Instead of that, it gets *nal*, the *isophoric* marker. The reason for this discrepancy is not far to seek: the inanimate actors, here as in many languages, are fairly low in topicality. Therefore, if a clause containing an inanimate actor acting on a human undergoer appears between two clauses whose common participant is human, as in (53), not only will the verb of the medial clause receive an *anisophoric* marker, but, in addition, the verb of the first clause will be marked by an *isophoric* morpheme, because its subject is coreferential with the human undergoer of the medial verb. This human undergoer is not expressed in (53), where the subject is *sook* "rope", represented in the VP by *-u*. Thus, the syntactic rules organizing *diaphoricity* are overruled by semantic factors, since coreference is controlled by meaning (viewpoint 2 in the three viewpoints theory: cf. 3.1), and consequently the element treated as coreferential with the subject of the first clause is not the subject of the second (viewpoint 1), but (viewpoint 2) the undergoer (unexpressed in this second clause).

The primacy of semantic factors can go even further. In Eastern Pomo, the *isophoric* and *anisophoric* suffixes are normally used, as in Papuan languages having this type of distinction, to mark, respectively, coreference and non-coreference between the verbs of two successive clauses. However, in spontaneous speech, i.e., in texts other than those elicited under the pressure of translation from English sentences with formally identical pronouns, Pomo speakers use the *anisophoric* suffix *-qan* when a patient-taking verb occurs in one clause and an agent-taking verb occurs in the other, even though there is no change in person. Thus consider (54) and (55):

(54)   *há: xá:qákki-qan, wi q̓a:lál tá:la*
        (I(AG) took~a~bath-ANISOPH I(UND) got sick)
        "I took a bath and got sick"

(55)   *wi q̓a:lálma-qan, há: kʰúyhi qóyuhù*
        (I(UND) got~sick-ANISOPH I(AG) NEG come)
        "I got sick, that's why I didn't come" (McLendon 1978:8
                                                   and fn. 13).

In both (54) and (55), the subject of each of the two clauses is 1SG. Therefore, *isophoric* suffixes should appear. But the subject is expressed by pronouns belonging to two distinct paradigms, agent and then undergoer in (54), undergoer and then agent in (55). The undergoer paradigm is used with stative verbs, and the agent paradigm with active verbs. Thus, the factor controlling the choice between the *isophoric* and the *anisophoric* suffixes is not the identity or non-identity of syntactic person, but the semantic class of the verb.

There are even more striking cases, in which syntactic rules seem to be squarely violated. It appears, in fact, that a semantic shift is responsible for a seemingly odd structure. Russian, for example, has an *autophoric* pronoun, whose accusative-genitive (animates) is *sebja*, instrumental *soboj*, etc. It is used like any *autophoric*, when reference is made to the subject of the clause. However, we find in the spoken language examples like (56) and (57):

(56)   *večno tebja ždjoš*
        (always you(ACC-GEN.SG) wait-2SG)
        "you keep people waiting all the time"

(57)   *s toboj ne sgovoriš′ sja*
        (with you(INSTR.SG) NEG agree-2SG)
        "there is no way to come to an agreement with you"
                                                   (Zolotova 1989).

If literally translated, (56) and (57) should mean, respectively, "you are always waiting for you" and "you don't agree with you". "yourself" would be more correct, but it is ruled out here, precisely because there is no *autophoric* in the Russian sentences. This is by no means a violation of the rule imposing the use of the *autophoric*, for a very simple reason: the two "you" in (56) are not coreferential, and neither are those in (57); only *tebja* in (56) and *toboj* in (57) refer to the listener and mean "you". The 2SG personal indices in the inflected verbal forms *ždjoš* and *sgovoriš'sja* are only formally 2SG. Due to a semantic shift, the second person singular, in some of its uses in Russian conversational style, has come to refer to a universal person, roughly corresponding to French *on* or English *one*. English *you* is also used in this meaning.

Conversational style often brings more light than literary usage, because it reflects experiments, some of which may eventually become the norm. Of course, meaning-induced violations of coreference constraints have not everywhere reached this extreme point, but certain revealing languages provide interesting illustrations of the trends which characterize LBs' morphogenetic work. In conversational Lhassa Tibetan (Tournadre 1992), we come across interrogative sentences in which the subject pronoun is first person and the personal index in the VP is second person:

(58)   *khyedrang-tsho phebs-payin-pas ?*
        (you-PL go-PAST+1SG-INTERR)
        "did you go (there)?".

This striking absence of coreference between the pronoun and the affixed index is not due to a semantic shift as in spoken Russian, but to an anticipation of the answer: the Tibetan speaker uses in the VP the personal index corresponding to the listener replying as ego, and, in this way, the elements of the answer are already provided in the question, making the conversation much more vivid and cooperative. Obviously, such a structure cannot be interpreted in a theoretical framework which makes no room for the concrete interaction of dialogue by which LBs build linguistic systems together.

2.3.3 Agreement, or the LBs as both skilled and clumsy workmen

In many languages, LBs have invented specific means by which certain important syntactic and semantic features can be stressed and thus made easier to produce as well as to interpret. Agreement is one of the main such devices. But the skill it implies does not go without some clumsiness, given the cost, in terms of linguistic material, required by its application. I will not present here a general study of agreement. I will only summarize some previous observations, and add some new ones, so as to emphasize certain properties of agreement which are of interest in the perspective of the present study.

Agreement may be defined as the expression of a relationship between two or more constituents, of which the main one belongs to a certain category (generally gender, number, person, or case) possibly marked on it, but more often on the other(s). The former is the agreement-triggering and the latter the agreeing term(s). A link is thus established between them, with the proviso that the agreeing term or terms do not determine the meaning of the agreement-triggering term; if it does, the process should be called concord rather than agreement (Lehmann 1982a:249-250, where concord is illustrated by the classical example of classificatory verbs in Athapaskan languages). This definition already shows what is implied by two terms agreeing with each other in a given linguistic utterance: LBs have built structures which appear as a discontinuous projection of a single unit on one or more points, thus giving a clue for the identification of those elements in the utterance that are linked by a certain kind of relationship.

I have proposed (Hagège 1982:75-89) to call *nominants* the morphemes (such as gender and number markers, demonstratives, articles, possessives, etc.) which are characterized both as having access to the sentence only when the noun itself appears (except in some of their anaphoric uses) and as helping, by their appearance, to define the very noun-ness of the noun. Similarly, I call *verbants* (*ibid.*) the morphemes which play the same role for the verb. Certain languages, like those of the Bantu stock, are known for presenting quite alliterative structures, resulting from agreement between *nominants* and *verbants* rhyming with one another; (59), from Kukuya (Paulian 1975:197), may serve as an example:

(59)   *kì-kò kíí mè kì kì-bvé kì kíí-bààkì*
        (7CLSF-loincloth CONN(7CLSF) me this(7CLSF) 7CLSF-
        beautiful this(7CLSF) 7CLSF+PAST-to~be~torn(NARR))
        "this beautiful loincloth of mine has been torn".

In languages where the CLSF on the noun is masked by fusion or has disappeared, the agreeing *nominant* alone indicates the class of its head noun, thus clearly marking the link between *nominant* and noun. This is illustrated by (60), from Godié (Demuth *et al.* 1986:460-461):

(60)   *nyú wɔt-u*
(water cold-CLSF)
"cold water".

Here *nyú* results from coalescence of the stem *ní* "water" with the CLSF *u*, used for liquids; but this CLSF appears overtly on the following word, which, in this context, functions like a *nominant*.

Noun class agreement, a general phenomenon under which gender and number agreement can be subsumed, is a widespread characteristic of human languages. It has often been described (for a recent work, cf. Craig ed. 1986). I will only note that the noun to which reference is made need not appear in the sentence, not even in the linguistic context: it may suffice for it to be indicated by the situation. Its use is even ruled out, more often than not, with 1 or 2 PER, in languages whose verb must express person; sentences like English *I man will come* or *you girl do not work enough* are therefore ill-formed, the 1 and 2 person indices being already totally specified by themselves and hence not needing any new specification by a noun (for some exceptions, cf. Hagège 1982:99-100). Consequently, in that case, there is no noun in the vicinity with which the personal indices could agree: they refer, in fact, to the very person who is speaking or spoken to, and, in languages whose verb is also inflected for gender and number, they indicate the sex, as in Slovenian *vîdiva* "we (MASC.DUAL) see" and *vîdive* "we (FEM.DUAL) see", or Arabic *katabti* "you (FEM.SG) wrote".

In most other cases, of course, the agreement-triggering element must appear. This element is mostly a noun. However, cases of verb-triggered agreement also exist. I would prefer to call this phenomenon *attraction*. In Lardil, for example (Hale 1966), the future marker, when it appears on the verb, also appears on direct objects, adverbs, directional and other complements. Moreover, Gabelentz (1891) mentions some Germanic dialects in which, at least in the beginning of the 19th century, there was an attraction of a conjunction by the verb; in fact, the attracting element here is not the verb itself but the personal index suffixed to the verb of the clause introduced by the conjunction, as in *dassen wir kommen* "that we come", *obt ihr geht* "whether you go". In any case, this device, like the one illustrated by Lardil, testifies to the importance of structural cohesion as an aim towards which LBs, through gender and number agreement as well as through attraction, are periodically striving.

As a result of this tendency to *structural cohesion*, agreement sometimes becomes a pervasive phenomenon. In Avar, for instance, the class of the subject noun, not marked on this noun itself, is marked on all the other constituents of the sentence – not only the *nominants* and the VP as in Bantu, but also the complements whatever their nature, e.g.,

(61)   *a-w hit' ína-w či w-áqaraw rosnó-w-e w-úss-ana roq' ó-w-e*
          (this-CLSF little-CLSF man   CLSF-boarding two~oar~boat-
          CLSF-in CLSF-return-past house-CLSF-in)
          "this little man, having boarded a two-oar boat, went back to
          his house" (Charachidzé 1981:32).

In Brazilian Arawakan, the scope of class or gender agreement is even broader: it includes, in addition to those mentioned for Avar, such verbal morphemes as subordination, interrogative and aspect suffixes in Dení, and intransitive subordinating and thematic suffixes in Paumarí (Derbyshire 1986:531-532).

If, in those languages where agreement plays an important role, gender and number agreement must be assigned the function of strengthening the solidarity between the constituents of the sentence, things are different with regard to the other two types, person and case agreement. In many languages, person agreement reflects the importance of human participants. Sometimes, there are affixed verbal morphemes which express, in addition to the agent, both the patient and the beneficiary: this is the case in Kiowa, where the prefix *mǫn-*, for example, contains the three fused elements "you two" + "them" + "for them" (Merrifield 1959:168). But in other languages, the ditransitive verb of attribution generally agrees with only one of the participants: the agreeing index selects the beneficiary, i.e., the person to whom something is given, or said, etc., rather than the patient, i.e., the thing given. In Hayu, one of the so-called 'pronominalized' languages of the Tibeto-Birman family, 50% of the ditransitive verbs agree with the beneficiary, selected as object, since they take indices from the applicative paradigm (Michailovsky 1988:139-144). It is interesting to note that in a language whose ditransitive verb contains, in the active voice, indices referring to the agent, the patient, and the beneficiary, only the beneficiary, not the patient, can have subject status when the sentence is passivized: this language is Classical Nahuatl (cf. (130)-(131) in 3.3).

The grammatical promotion of human participants as a trace of LBs' place in nature is also perceptible in languages whose verbs show person agreement referring to the possessor, including even metaphorical humanized artifacts. Romanian is a case in point, as well as languages of a fairly different type in other respects, namely those of the Algonquian stock. In Romanian, for example, we have:

(62)   *ei mi-au luat portofel-ul*
         (they me(DAT)-have taken wallet-the)
         "they have taken away my wallet"

(63)   *a-şi lua zbor-ul*
         (to-itself take flight-the)
         "to take off (plane)"

(64)   *a-şi trăi trai-ul*
         (to-oneself live life-the)
         "to live one's life".

Literally, these examples would mean "they have taken me the wallet", "to take oneself the flight", and "to live oneself the life", respectively. Other Romance languages also have this type of structure. But, in French for example, it is limited to human possessors, as in:

(65)   *il s'est cassé la jambe*
         (he himself AUX broken the leg)
         "he has broken his leg",

whereas in Romanian, possessor-triggered person agreement is all-pervading and includes (as in (63)) non human-possessors, treating them as human-centered, since possession is essentially a human characteristic.

The tendency towards *structural cohesion*, aimed at insuring *ease of production*, often results in *cohesion constraints*, i.e., in the necessity of following certain agreement rules. These agreement rules produce complex associations, whose *material integrity* must be respected by LBs. This in turn brings about some inertia, which may have consequences on *ease of production*. LBs try to strengthen the links between units, even at the cost of establishing severe constraints; and they need to preserve these constraints, even at the cost of increasing the complexity of utterances. A striking illustration of this conflict between contradictory needs (cf. (49) in 2.3.1

above) is provided by the other type of agreement, case agreement. It often produces a very strong cohesion of adnominal complements with the head noun. Thus, in Old Georgian, a noun functioning as an adnominal attribute is both in the genitive, marking its dependency upon its head, and in the case of the head, marking the agreement between them:

(66)   *saxel-ita mam-isa-jta*
          (name-INSTR father-GEN-INSTR)
          "by the name of the father" (Mel'čuk 1982:127)

In another Caucasian language, Chamalal, the genitive attribute also agrees with its head, but this agreement, certainly a rare feature (illustrated, likewise, by gender agreement in Awngi), applies to class (not marked on the head noun itself; *id.* in (61), from neighboring Avar), whereas in Hurrian (67) below, the genitive attribute agreed in *case* with its head, so that if the head was genitive, there were two genitives marked on the same noun:

(67)   *sen-ifu-we-ne-we asti-we nihari*
          (brother-my-GEN-SG-GEN wife-GEN dowry)
          "the dowry of my brother's wife".

Case agreement with the head is also attested when the adnominal attribute has the complex form of a relative clause, as is shown by Shoshone, Yaqui, Kaititj, Dyirbal, and Hurrian itself (Lehmann 1982a:208-209). Thus, in Dyirbal, we find such sentences as

(68)   *yibi yara-ŋgu njalŋga-ŋgu djilwa-ŋu-ru buṛa-n*
          (woman man-ERG child-ERG kick-REL-ERG see-REAL)
          "the man whom the child had kicked saw a woman" (Dixon 1969:38).

In this example, the relative clause *njalŋga-ŋgu djilwa-ŋu* depends on *yara-ŋgu* which is itself in the ergative, since it expresses the agent of *buṛa-n*; hence the case agreement with *ru*, between this noun *yara-ŋgu* and the relative clause, thus as tightly linked to the noun as though it were any non-complex *nominant*. It is well-known that in Classical Greek too, there was optional agreement of the relative pronoun itself with the head noun, as in

(69)   *émeine sùn toîs thesauroîs hoîs ho patèr katélipen*
       (remain(AO.3SG) with ART(DAT.MASC.PL) treasure(DAT.PL)
       REL(DAT.MASC.PL) ART(NOMIN.MASC.SG) father(NOMIN.SG)
       leave(AO.3SG))
       "he remained with the treasures that his father had left [to
       him]" (Xen., *Cyr.*, 3,1,33).

In some languages, the conflict between different needs, such as those
illustrated here by the example of case agreement, results in quite contradictory structures. This is shown by an interesting phenomenon of Arabic,
known, among Arab grammarians, as *naʃt sababî*, whereby a participial
attribute (*naʃt*) agrees with an agreement-triggering (*sababî*) noun external
to the NP constituted by this participial attribute and its head noun, but also
agrees with this head noun itself, the two kinds of agreement being of course
different. Consider (70)-(72) taken from Polotsky (1978: 161-165):

(70)   *yu-lâhizu bi-ʔanna ʔahad-a l-ʔafrâd-i faqada šayʔ-an min*
       muhimm-ât-i-hi l-masʔûl-i ʃan-hâ
       (he-notices on-that one(MASC)-ACC ART-individual(MASC.PL)-
       IND.C lost(MASC.SG) thing-ACC from equipment-FEM.PL-IND.C-
       3MASC.SG ART-responsible(MASC.SG)-IND.C for-them)
       "he notices that one of the men has lost some equipment of
       his for which he is responsible"

(71)   *tadahraǧ-at ʔilà l-kûh-i l-muqîm-at-i fî-hi l-ʃaǧûz-u*
       l-marîd-at-u
       (tumbled-she towards ART-hut(MASC.SG)-IND.C ART-settled-
       FEM.SG-IND.C in-3MASC.SG ART-old~woman(FEM.SG)-NOMIN
       ART-sick-FEM.SG-NOMIN)
       "she tumbled towards the hut in which the sick old woman
       lived"

(72)   *ya-ʔbà ʔan ta-ʃʃur-a bi-hi hattà l-ʔard-u d-dâriǧ-u ʃalay-hâ*
       (he-refuses that 3FEM.SG-feel-SBJC with-3MASC.SG even ART-
       earth(FEM.SG)-NOMIN ART-treading(MASC.SG)-NOMIN
       on-3FEM.SG
       "he does not wish that even the earth upon which he is treading
       should become aware of him".

The striking feature of these sentences is that the three participial attributes, namely *mas?ûl-i* (70), *muqîm-at-i* (71), and *dâriǧ-u* (72), all agree in case with the noun, which they follow, namely *muhimm-ât-i-hi*, *kûḫ-i* and *?arḍ-u*, respectively, of which two are in the indirect case (-*i* suffix) and one in the nominative (-*u* suffix); at the same time, these participial attributes agree, in gender and number, not with this noun, but with another, seemingly external, NP, to which they are not contiguous: they either follow it (example (70), with anaphoric agreement, in gender and number, between this NP, here represented by the accusative indefinite pronoun *?ahad-a*, and the participial attribute, here *mas?ûl-i*) or precede it (example (71), with cataphoric agreement, in gender and number, between the noun *ʃaǧûz-u* and the participle *muqîm-at-i*); in (72), the agreement-triggering NP is represented by the MASC.SG personal index *ya-* on the verb of the main clause, hence the MASC.SG participle *dâriǧ-u*.

At first sight, these three sentences seem odd from a semantic point of view: despite the contiguity and the case agreement between the participial attribute and its putative head, it is not the equipment which is responsible in (70), the hut which lives in (71) or the earth which treads in (72). Not only does it appear that case agreement does not reflect a real relationship here, but on closer examination we can explain the gender and number discrepancy between the noun and the participle, the former being FEM.PL, MASC.SG, and FEM.SG in (70), (71) and (72) respectively, while the latter is MASC.SG, FEM.SG and MASC.SG. The participle, being the adjectival conversion of a finite verb form in the third person, must agree, like a verb, with the noun or pronoun representing this person, as though this verb had actually been present with the noun as its subject. Thus, *gender* and *number* agreement is *syntactically and semantically* motivated, whereas *case* agreement is more mechanical. However, being triggered by contiguity, it contributes to *structural cohesion*. Although *naʃt sababî*, as illustrated in (70)-(72), is more frequent in administrative than in literary style, it has long been commented upon by the Arab grammarians as quite characteristic of Arabic syntax (cf. Al-Zaǧǧâǧî 1962). It sheds light on the conditions in which LBs build their syntax and on the conflict between contradictory needs, which is one of the elements of this enterprise. By studying this aspect of the syntax of Arabic, we see how the respect of case agreement, meant to strengthen syntagmatic unity, sometimes results in obscuring the functional relationship, stressed by gender and number agreement, between two or more elements in the sentence.

What, then, if gender or number agreement link together certain elements which have no syntactic relationship whatsoever? Such a phenomenon, strange as it may appear, does exist. The subject and the object, in particular, or the subject and the adverbial complement, being defined by the relationship linking each of them to the predicate, should not have "logical" reasons to agree. Consider, though, the following sentences, from the Italian dialect of Ripatransone (Lüdtke 1977: 174):

(73)   *lu frəkí ča fámu*
         (the boy has hunger)
         "the boy is hungry"

(74)   *le frəkíne ča fáme*
         "the girl is hungry"

(75)   *li frəkí ča fámi*
         "the boys are hungry"

(76)   *lə frəkína ča fáma*
         "the girls are hungry"

(77)   *lu frəkí ε ítu a r:óma*
         "the boy has gone to Rome"

(78)   *le frəkíne ε íte a r:óme*
         "the girl has gone to Rome".

In (73)-(76), the object agrees with the subject, this agreement being marked, depending on the final vowel of the subject noun and/or its article, by the vowel -**u** in the MASC.SG, -**e** in the FEM.SG, -**i** in the MASC.PL and -**a** in the FEM.PL. Even more curious, (77) and (78) show gender and number agreement between the subject and the adverbial (directional) complement: -**u** ... -**u** ... -**a** in the MASC.SG, -**e** ... -**e** ... -**e** in the FEM.SG. What can we learn from these examples?

One of the purposes of gender agreement is to give information about a constituent by projecting onto other constituents the marks of some of its properties. Examples (73)-(78) above show that there is no theoretical limitation on the type of constituent on which such marks may be projected.

In other words, the constituents which bear these marks need not be functionally related. It is true, however, that there is a functional relation in most cases, and that Ripatransone represents an exceptional situation. But like other revealing languages, it has the interesting property of showing that the limitations observed in most languages are not universal and therefore cannot be retained as defining features. The pervasiveness of gender agreement (recall also Bantu and Avar, illustrated in (59) and (61), respectively) testifies to its importance in those languages that possess it. Not only is gender (in the broad sense including number and implying noun classes, as indicated above) one of the main categories to which agreement applies, but agreement may, in many cases, have played a role in its very advent (cf. Hagège 1990a).

In another rare case, it is *person* agreement that links together two constituents which do not have direct syntactic relationships, for instance two nouns functioning as subject and object respectively. Consider (79) and (80), from Coahuilteco (Troike 1981:660, 669):

(79)   *cin anillo apa:-n na-k-a:x*
         (I ring DEM-1AGR 1SUBJ-2OBJ-give)
         "I give you the ring"

(80)   *na-k-um pin na-k-pa-ta:nko tuče:-m ma-ho:y san ino:*
         (1SUBJ-2OBJ-say thing 1SUBJ-2OBJ-SUB-command DEM-2AGR
         2SUBJ-do FUT 1AGR.AUX)
         "I advise you to do what I command".

The agreement affixes on the object show person agreement with the subject and may take one of three forms. Two of these are represented here: the predominant form is mostly a suffix on the demonstrative terminating an NP; for the first person, this suffix is *-n*, as in (79), where the subject *cin* "I" and the object *anillo* "ring" thus agree in person; for the second person, the suffix is *-m*, as in (80), where there is thus person agreement between the subject *ma-* "you" of the verb *ho:y* "do" and the object of this same verb, namely the noun *pin* "thing" and the whole clause which is in apposition to this noun, i.e., *na-k-pa-ta:nko* "what I command to you": the agreeing suffix, here, is attached, as in (79), to a demonstrative, which, like the clause itself, depends on *pin*, hence *tuče:-m*; but (80) also contains another less frequent type of agreement suffix, whose main use is to mark a clause as object; this form is a person-differentiated copular auxiliary, which is *ino:* for the first person: in (80), *ino:* agrees with the first person *na-* in *na-k-um*, this agreement yielding a structure whose literal English equivalent would be "I-say that-you-do-I".

Coahuilteco subject-object agreement may have something to do with the absence of case markers in the language. At any rate, it provides a morphological signal of the fact that subject and object, although not directly related, are dominated by the same propositional node. In this respect, it is reminiscent of another device which, on the level of the whole sentence, also meets the need LBs have to keep track of reference in discourse, namely *diaphoricity*, illustrated, for Papuan languages, by example (53) above. Thus, Coahuilteco subject-object agreement, despite its seeming oddity, is, in fact, related to the perceptual strategies resorted to by LBs in order to resolve a fundamental problem of linguistic communication.

It is important to note that there is a limitation to the often stressed redundancy which, in many languages, is the result of agreement as a factor of *structural cohesion*. This limitation is illustrated by NPs expressing possession (when not marked by word order only). Head-marking mostly implies person-agreement between the head (possessum) and the modifier (possessor), as in Palauan, e.g.,

(81)   *məlk-él a-ŋálək*
         (chicken-his SPEC-child)
         "the child's chicken" (Hagège 1986:83)

or, with the reverse sequence, in Abkhaz, e.g.,

(82)   *sarà sə-y'nə*
         (me my-house)
         "my house" (Nichols 1986a:60).

The Mayan languages represent a variant of the Palauan pattern, with personal index before possessum, as in Mam

(83)   *t-q'ab' a?*
         (its-hand water)
         "branch of a river" (England 1983:71).

On the other hand, dependent-marking may consist of a case morpheme (genitive or dative) affixed to the possessor, as in Chechen, e.g.,

(84)   *de:-n a:xca*
          (father-GEN money)
          "father's money" (Nichols, *ibid.*).

But there is no example, as far as I know, of dependent-marked possession with person agreement of the modifier with itself. This would yield a hyper-identifying structure of the type X (head) + Y (modifier)-y or the reverse order, where, the dependence being marked by juxtaposition only, the possessor, already expressed by Y, would in addition be identified again by a personal index.

Thus, *agreement has an identifying, hence mnemonic, function, but not at the cost of total redundancy.*

PART II

THE PLACE OF HUMANS

IN

LANGUAGE MORPHOGENESIS

Manifestations of human presence in language at the levels of both full and partial consciousness have been studied in the first part of the book. But even when consciousness is zero or close to zero, human presence in language still manifests itself strongly. This is what I am going to show in the second part of the book. This part will be divided into three chapters. The first chapter (chapter 3) will show that languages are anthropocentric systems, in which LBs leave the trace of their conception of the universe. The second chapter (chapter 4) will examine how the presence of LBs manifests itself through an important historical process, i.e., the genesis of pidgins and creoles. Finally, the third chapter (chapter 5) will show that language morphogenesis follows cycles triggered by the human search for expressiveness.

CHAPTER 3

Languages as anthropocentric systems

Various grammatical phenomena recognized in contemporary research as central to the study of morphosyntax show clear traces of LBs' activity and of the way in which they express through linguistic forms, although at a very low, or zero, level of consciousness, their conception of the relationship between the world and themselves. This will appear in the following three parts: the humanization of grammar (3.1); man's place in deixis (3.2); subjecthood and subjectivity (3.3).

3.1 The humanization of grammar

Many phenomena in natural languages reflect an effort to assign topic status, or subject function, to NPs which refer to humans, and first of all, to ego. Since the publication of Silverstein 1976, many studies have shown that, in split ergative systems, the transition from accusative to ergative, or the converse, is triggered by a lexical hierarchy controlling markedness relationships among NP types, with ego or the group ego + others ranking highest, NPs ranking lowest, and the other persons falling between these two extremes. For instance, in Bandjalang, we have, from top to bottom, first person plural, first singular, second singular, third plural, third singular feminine, third singular masculine, human nouns, other nouns (animates, etc.); and in Dhirari, inclusive dual as the upper boundary and lexical nouns as the lower one (Silverstein 1976:125-126).

In the light of the theory of glossogenesis underlying the present study, one can say, more explicitly, that human beings, as LBs, locate themselves at the highest level on the agentivity scale. This is a universal tendency: it does not characterize a particular language to the exclusion of others and therefore cannot serve as an argument in favor of the old conceptions, according to which there is a relationship between a given language and the psychology of its speakers. But although languages all share this conception, they have various ways of manifesting it. While certain languages resort to lexical means, others possess explicit grammatical means, such as agreement-marking or case-marking. This is the well-known situation of Dyirbal and Chinook, as well as Montagnais (Martin 1982) and Navaho (Foley & Van Valin 1977). It also occurs in languages less often mentioned, such as those of the Tibeto-Burman stock, like Hayu (Michailovsky 1976:14-15), or Tangut, in which there is direct agreement with the highest nominal, whatever the syntactic relationship (Comrie 1980); and in Tibetan, human volition is central to syntax, a characteristic that might reflect old religious conceptions, which are common to Buddhism[1] and to the three western monotheistic religions.

Other illustrations are to be found among Siberian and Papuan languages. In Chukchee, for instance (Comrie 1980), the only available agreement slot is for intransitive subjects or for direct objects; so when the nominal element which is highest in animacy happens to be a transitive subject, it is assigned the properties of an intransitive subject by the use of an "antipassive" suffix. Another case is that of Fore, where we find such sentences as

(85)   *yaga: wá a-egú-i-e*
           (pig man 3SG.PAT-hit-3SG.AG-DECL)
           "the man hits the pig".

In this sentence, despite the respective positions of *yaga:* and *wá*, the meaning cannot be that the pig hits the man, because on the animacy scale humans rank higher than animals. In order to get this meaning, it is necessary to mark *yaga:* with the ergative suffix *-wama*, yielding

(86)   *yaga:-wama wá a-egú-i-e.*

It is also possible to say, with the same meaning,

(87)   *wá yaga:-wama a-egú-i-e,*

which proves that word order is free in this case. However, in Iatmul, a language spoken in the same area, the agent must precede the patient. But whatever the contribution of word order to case-marking, in Fore *yaga:* must remain marked.

What is formally reflected here is an anthropocentric conception of world phenomena. Some phenomena are expected, others are not. When an unexpected phenomenon occurs, attention must be drawn to its unexpectedness, whereas expected phenomena do not need to be emphasized. Therefore, a marker will be added to the NP referring to the unexpected participant. Thus, *during the history of language morphogenesis, languages receive certain markers of the LBs' anthropocentric conception of the universe; these markers stress the degree of expectedness which, according to this conception, is characteristic of a given event.*

Similar observations may be made about the notion of control (cf. Thompson & Thompson 1971). The animacy scale refers in fact to an inherent property of NPs, while the control scale refers to the relationship between NP and predicate. Although the animacy scale may interact with other parameters, such as the degree of definiteness (e.g. in Persian: Lazard 1982), it overlaps in many cases with the control scale. We may consider that the overt features opposing controlled to uncontrolled states or actions are traces of the work by which syntax is constructed as a mirror image of the humanness scale. These features appear all over the world, in such diverse languages as those of Africa, New Guinea or North America. Moore typically uses the verb *tár(à)* "to have, possess" (speaking of physical or psychological events) either with an animate or an inanimate subject, according to the way the situation is viewed in purely human terms. While a sentence like

(88)   *à tárà ráōōdō*
         (he possess courage)
         "he is courageous"

is quite usual, informants deem it very strange to say

(89)   ? *ráōōd n tár à* (*ráōōd* and *tár* = context forms; *n* = TOP.M
         with nouns).

Conversely

(90)   *kòjūūd n tár tūndò*
         (thirst TOP.M possess us)

and

(91)   *sūkíir n tár à*
         (jealousy TOP.M possess him)

are the normal ways of saying what English expresses, respectively, by

(92)   *we are thirsty*

and

(93)   *he is jealous.*

It is not possible to switch the two NPs across the VP. Now, if one wants to speak of the lack of a favorable state, the noun referring to the animate being whose state is thus described must be made the subject:

(94)   *à ká tár láafí jē*
         (he NEG possess health NEG (NEG is discontinuous in Moore))

is the usual way of saying "he is not in good health", which is not normally expressed by

(95)   ? *làafí ká tár à jē.*

As these examples show, positively valued events and physical or mental states such as health, courage, etc., are expressed by postverbal NPs: since, in terms of value as established by human societies, it is normal for these events and states to be positive, the NPs will occupy an unmarked position; the human experiencer, on the other hand, is in the conspicuous subject, i.e. (in this language), preverbal, position, since he controls them. Negatively valued events or affects will be marked as abnormal, hence the elements which will occupy the conspicuous subject position will, this time, be those which express these events.

Like Moore, Usan (Foley 1986:123) expresses the human experiencer of a negatively valued event as a patient: in this case, another means, the opposition between paradigms of personal affixes, is added to word order:

(96)   *wo toar war-a*
         (he sickness 3SG.PAT~hit-3SG.AG)
         "he is sick".

Thus, in languages like Moore and Usan, syntax itself indicates whether or not something is positively valued, and therefore whether or not it is under control. Other languages show a different distribution of controllable and uncontrollable, or less controllable, events. This applies of course to transitive processes involving an agent and a patient, as illustrated in languages possessing two distinct paradigms of personal indices. In this case, we may speak of *strong* and *weak transitivity* (Hagège 1981c, 1982) and say that this dual system reflects the way LBs, in the course of Lb, have, less and less consciously, adapted their language to the expression of the various relationships they have with the world. Thus, in Comox (Hagège 1981c:71-72), the same verb can take one of two distinct transitivity markers, according to the degrees of agent volition and the degrees of patient affectedness: *tləpxʷ-ə-t* "to break (purposely)"/*tləpxʷ-ə-xʷ* "to break (by accident)", *qē-t* "to kill (intentionally)"/*qē-xʷ* "to kill (without premeditation)", *maʔ-t* "to take"/*maʔ-ə-xʷ* "to receive", *c'ē-t* "to listen"/*c'ē-xʷ* "to hear" (*-ə-* is a link vowel). Even physical affects may imply various degrees of control. For example, in Newari, we have either an ergative or a dative marker, according to the speaker's assessment of the degree of control exercised by the subject on such emotions as anger (Delancey 1985a:10):

(97)   *wɔ-ɔ̃ tɔ̃ɔ̃ wɔekɔɔ-lɔ*
         (he-ERG anger come(CAUS)-PERF)
         "he got angry" (with the implication that he could have controlled his anger if he had chosen)

(98)   *wɔ-etɔ tɔ̃ɔ̃ wɔ-lɔ*
         (he-DAT anger come-PERF)
         "he got angry" (with the implication that he was unable to control his emotions).

Comparable pairs may be found in Papuan languages, such as Kalam, in which the distinction between controlled and uncontrolled emotions (as well as events) is pervasive: in (99) below, the actor is an animate performer controlling the action, as indicated by the agreement between the nominative form of the first person pronoun and the suffixed form (first person index), as well as by the use of an auxiliary, while in (100), the animate participant exerts no control over the physical state, as indicated by the agreement between ϕ and the inanimate cause functioning as actor, as well as by the accusative case of the pronoun and a different word order (Foley 1986:121):

(99)   *yad swk a(g)-jp-yn*
         (I~NOMIN laughing do-PROGR-1SG)
         "I am laughing"

(100)   *swk yp ow-p-ϕ*
         (laughing I-ACC come-PERF-3SG)
         "I feel like laughing".

In contrast to these variations among languages as regards the criteria which define controllable and uncontrollable states or events, the universal tendency to place human beings at the highest level on the animacy scale often results in constraints on the use of prominence markers. Thus, in Barai (Foley 1986:124-125), it is always the animate (usually human) participant which receives prominence, no matter whether it represents an actor or a patient: in (102) below, the clitic -*ka* "really" cannot be attached to *ije*, although *ije* plays the same role as *fu* in (101):

(101)   *fu-ka na kan-ie*
         (he-really I hit-1SG.UND)
         "he really hit me"

(102)   *ije na-ka visi-nam-ie*
         (it I-really sick-TRANS-1SG.UND)
         "it really sickened me".

In the framework of the three viewpoints theory (Hagège 1980a and, in a renewed and expanded version, Hagège 1990b), linguistic utterances are studied according to three different and complementary perspectives: morphosyntactic (viewpoint 1), semantico-referential (viewpoint 2), and information-hierarchical (viewpoint 3). The phenomena studied above refer to viewpoint 1: they illustrate both the syntactic promotion of NPs representing human participants (or what comes closest to them on the animacy scale), and the distribution of states and events in terms of degrees of human control. Parallel with this morphosyntactic marking of LBs' assessment of their position in the hierarchy that they establish to give linguistic organization to the world surrounding them, LBs also tend to promote human participants according to another perspective, that of viewpoint 3. From this viewpoint, a topic is opposed both paradigmatically to other possible topics, and syntagmatically to the rest of the utterance. To take just one example among many, Chamorro has no less than five different constructions involving participants in the action expressed by the verb phrase: it has two types of nominalizations, an active transitive construction, a construction containing the ergative infix -um-, it also has in- and ma- passives and finally, an antipassive. The remarkable fact here is that in Chamorro, topic continuity is practically always maintained by the application of rules imposing, from among these constructions, that which makes it possible to promote to subject, as the most topic-worthy, the highest referent on the animacy scale. According to Cooreman (1987:212),

Chamorro speakers seem to be biased toward pronominal, animate, and singular referents as highest topics in the clause [...]. Chamorro speakers even seem to have grammaticalized these biases since even in cases where for instance the plural Agent is numerically more topical than the singular Object, the use of an active transitive construction is considered ungrammatical.

In this case, a passive construction must be used instead, as the author shows in chapter 4 of her book.

Thus there is a harmony relating viewpoints 1 and 3. (With regard to viewpoint 2, cf. 1.3.1 section b., where certain general tendencies in the evolution of semantic systems are shown to reflect LBs' subjectivity.) As a result, we observe a coincidence between the highest syntactic function, i.e., subject, and those elements which refer to animate beings; LBs are biased towards the latter as more topic-worthy.

To sum up the contents of this part of the chapter, we may say that the linguistic phenomena that bear witness to the humanization of grammar may be interpreted in both social and psychological terms: *communication is easier to establish when it is about subjects more familiar to both partners, as is the case with animate beings*; on the other hand, *humans have greater cognitive salience, as a topic, for humans themselves*.

3.2 Man's place in deixis

Two points will be studied here: the anthropophoric system (3.2.1) and the LBs' personal sphere (3.2.2).

3.2.1 The anthropophoric system

Humans as centers of deixis form the base of a morphological system whose manifestations are a universal characteristic of languages. It is proposed here to call this system *anthropophoric*. It is represented in the chart below:

(103)   The anthropophoric system:

chorophorics			⎧ - anaphorics
			⎪ - cataphorics,
			⎪ including dia-
			⎪ phorics, i.e.,
	exophorics	endophorics	⎨ isophorics/
			⎪ anisophorics
chronophorics			⎪ - autophorics
			⎩ - logophorics

The labels in (103), based on technical Greek terms, are meant to meet the need for terminological consistency. The suffix *-phorics* (etymologically = "carrying") means "elements that refer to", and the roots indicate the domain to which reference is made: *choro-* for space, *chrono-* for time, *exo-* for individuals, objects and notions of the external world, *endo-* for the linguistic material of the discourse itself [2], within which there can be reference to the speaker or to the grammatical subject of a sentence or a clause (*autophorics*), to a preceding (*anaphorics*) or following (*cataphorics*) word, phrase or sentence, or to the author of an explicit or implicit speech (*logophorics*).

Chorophorics, *chronophorics* and *exophorics* have been studied in detail in Hagège 1986 (101-104). Among *endophorics*, three classes deserve to be mentioned here. The first contains the *cataphorics*. As a particular sub-division I introduce here *isophorics* and *anisophorics*, grouped together under the label *diaphorics*. This adjunction is meant to make the chart more comprehensive, by taking into account a phenomenon hitherto known as switch-reference, a term introduced in Jacobsen 1967 (cf. Haiman & Munro 1983 for a general survey). The concept of *diaphoricity* makes it possible for switch-reference to become a constituent part of the *anthropophoric system*, which itself forms a consistent set of interrelated operations, among which is found the operation known to be characteristic of such languages as those of the Papuan or Yuman families. In the course of the history of these languages, LBs' unconscious operations have resulted in linking two clauses together: the verb of a following clause is linked to the verb of the preceding clause. The semantic relationship between them is of an adverbial type (temporal, final, consecutive, etc.); the linking element is a suffix indicating coreference (hence the label *isophorics* which I propose) or non-coreference (hence *anisophorics*) between their respective subjects (cf. examples (53)-(55) and comments); the suffix in question often adds to this indication, in a single fused form, other parameters such as the simultaneousness or non-simultaneousness of the two events.

Anaphorics have been abundantly studied. But two other classes of *endophorics* deserve special attention here, because the traces of LBs' shaping activity are particularly clear in the elements of which their members are made up. One of these classes contains what I call *autophorics*, rather than *reflexives*, since these personal or possessive markers establish identity of reference (*-phorics*) with self (*auto-*) as the experiencer or syntactic subject of the verb in the same sentence or in the higher clause. In many languages, we find, instead of a specialized and frozen marker, a still recognizable trace of the way self is semantically interpreted, i.e., an NP "head, or soul, or body + a mark of possession" to express "myself", "yourself", etc.: Fula *hoore-mum* (head-his (or her)) "himself (or herself)", Mbum *sóà à ké* (head of he (or she)) "himself (or herself)"; a lexical base with a similar meaning also appears in other languages: Shilluk *ri* and Logbara *rö*, both meaning "body" (Kohnen 1933, Crazzolara 1960), Moroccan Arabic *ras* "head", Amharic *əǧ* "hand", Basque *buru* "head", Georgian *tavi* "head, self" (Vogt 1971:40), Mokša Mordvinian *prä* "head" (Geniušienė 1987:303), Vietnamese *minh* "body" (*ibid.*), Malay *diri* "body, person".

The third class deserving special emphasis here contains what I proposed to call *logophorics* in Hagège 1974, a work whose main points have been taken up in a number of subsequent books and articles, including Clements 1975, Voorhoeve 1980, Hyman & Comrie 1981, Frajzyngier 1985, Sells

1987, Kuno 1987, Von Roncador 1988, Yoon 1989, Koster & Reuland 1991, mostly within a framework which has little to do with what I meant when I invented the term *logophorics*. I coined it in order to insert the morphogenetic activity by which self-reporting pronouns and adjectives are created by LBs within the general framework of the *anthropophoric system*. Most of the above-mentioned works, on the other hand, exploit the concept of *logophorics* by acclimatizing it in quite another issue, namely the role of anaphora within the Government and Binding theory and the ability this theory has to handle long-distance anaphora and related phenomena. A *logophoric* pronoun or adjective (personal or possessive) refers to the author of a discourse which is either explicit, the main verb being a "say" verb, or implicit, the main verb having in this case one of the meanings "to think", "to want", "to wish", "to order", etc. In (104) below, the LOG (= *logophoric*) *z̀* appearing as the subject of the complement clause refers to *à*, which is the subject of the declarative verb of the main clause; this Mundang example is taken from Hagège (1974:291):

(104)   *à rɛ̀ z̀ lwà fàn są̄*
        (he say-PAST LOG find thing beauty)
        "he said he had found something beautiful".

In Tuburi, a language related to Mundang, the *logophoric* can appear even in a relative clause, although such a clause determines a noun and not a declarative, or implicitly declarative, verb. In the Tuburi example below (Hagège 1974:299), the use of the LOG *sē* means that the speaker prefers to leave the responsibility for a certain thought to the individual represented by the subject pronoun, *á*, whereas this is not the case if the pronoun *á* is used instead of *sē* :

(105)   *á Dīk tí mą̄y mà:gā sē kó n sú: mònò*
        (he think to girl REL LOG see ANAPH.RESUMPT yesterday
        CORR)
        "he is thinking of the girl he saw yesterday".

Logophorics play an important role in discourse. In the languages where they have special forms and are not simply special uses of already existing elements, *logophorics* illustrate the way discourse can be embedded within the speaker's discourse itself: LBs can refer to themselves not only by first and second person pronouns in present instances of discourse, but also by *logophorics* in reported instances of discourse.

Thus, the existence of *logophorics* testifies to the importance of the LBs' discourse in the *anthropophoric system*, no matter whether this discourse is explicit or implicit. The fact that implicit discourse is as important as explicit discourse has a consequence in yet another domain besides *logophoricity*, namely the use of certain verbs which, although not explicitly related to an act of saying, can nevertheless appear in *inquit* position, i.e., as inserted or postposed quotation indices. Literary Hungarian is remarkable for having a fairly large number of such reporting verbs, which belong to semantic fields often located at some distance from that of discourse, since they are not only "verba non dicendi", but also in many cases outright *verba agendi*. They refer to body movements, like *ölelte meg* "he put an arm around her", facial mimetics, like *vigyorgott* "s/he grinned", nonverbal human sound-making, like *ásított* "s/he yawned", emotive attitudes, like *bosszankodott* "s/he became annoyed", social behavior, like *harcolt* "s/he struggled" (Fónagy 1986:264-266). Strikingly, these verbs and VPs (often including patients or adverbial complements) are treated as if they were, by their meaning, introducers of direct discourse, or referred to conversational strategies, like *terelte el a szót* "s/he shunted the conversation" or *fogalmazta át* "s/he changed the wording".

The interpretation of personal indices in direct discourse controlled by special verbs in certain languages seems to point to the central position of ego in the *anthropophoric system*. In the Hare dialect of Slave (Rice 1986), there are two verbs "to want", both introducing direct discourse, i.e., behaving as if they meant "to want, saying that". One of these verbs, *yeniwę*, does not require an object pronoun, and any first person in the preceding direct discourse (the language is SOV) will refer to the subject of this verb. This is why

(106)   *se-ts?ę ráwodí yerinewę ?*
          (1SG-to 3SG~FUT~help 2SG~want),

literally "do you want (saying:) 'he will help me!'?", means "do you want him to help you?". The other verb "to want", *-udeli*, requires a proleptic object pronoun, a pronoun which is coreferential with one of the pronouns in the direct discourse. If the subject pronoun of the direct discourse verb is third person and its oblique pronoun is first person, as is the object pronoun of the matrix verb, then these two first person markers will not be coreferential, since there are two possible first persons, namely the speaker, who accomplishes the speech act itself, and the person whose desire is reported, and who is represented here by the grammatical subject of the matrix verb; the speaker, being designated in the direct discourse as someone else, will therefore be referred to by a third person, hence

(107)   se-tsʔę́ ráwǫdi s-udeli-ø
         (1SG-to 3SG~FUT~help 1SG-want-3SG),

literally "he wants me (saying:) 'he will help me!' ", that is, "he$_i$ wants me to help him$_i$". Now if the object pronoun of the matrix verb is first person and the oblique pronoun of the direct discourse verb is third person, then the former will control the latter, hence

(108)   be-tsʔę́ ráwǫdí s-udeli-ø
         (3SG-to 2SG~FUT~help 1SG-want-3SG),

literally "he wants me (saying:) 'you will help him!' ", i.e., "he wants you to help me". Finally a second person object pronoun on the matrix verb does not control a third person in the complement clause, so that the latter will refer to some other third person:

(109)   be-tsʔę́ ráwǫdí n-udeli-ø
         (3SG-to 2SG~FUT~help 2SG-want-3SG),

literally "he wants you (saying:) 'you will help him or her!' ", i.e., for example, "he wants you to help her". The other two interpretations, "he wants you to help him" and "he wants you to help yourself" are ruled out, the first because -udeli is a verb requiring direct discourse and therefore the third person be in be-tsʔę́ cannot refer to the author of the reported speech, and the second because a third person cannot be used as the reflexive of a second person. Slave has a special pronoun ʔéle to express reflexivity.

It is true that the above facts represent an extreme case, such as can be found in revealing languages. But strange as they may appear, the complex rules underlying the interpretation of (106)-(109) are only an "exotic" illustration of a very common phenomenon: the primacy of ego as a speaker, no matter whether as the author of the main discourse or as the person whose discourse is being reported or quoted.

This central position of human speakers-listeners in the deixis system is also evidenced by the relationship between what I propose to call the *itive* (Latin *ire*, supine *itum*) and the *ventive* (Latin *venire*, supine *ventum*). These notions are originally expressed, as these Latin designations show, by a verb "to go" and a verb "to come", respectively. In the course of the history of many languages, these verbs yield various morphemes such as demonstratives, tense and aspect markers, relators, conjunctives, directionals, etc. What is interesting in the present connection is that the reference to ego may help to account for seemingly strange phenomena found in certain languages. Thus, Catalan, as opposed to Spanish and Portuguese, has lost its synthetic preterite. In the modern language, this tense is expressed by an auxiliary, *anar*, which directly precedes the infinitive. In its use as a lexeme, *anar* is the verb "to go". This seems rather odd, since most languages with an *itive* marker use it to express the future, not the past. But let us recall that the *itive*, as opposed to the *ventive*, describes motion through space or, metaphorically, time, without specifying or implying a final destination. With regard to the time before ego's discourse, then, the *itive* implies motion starting from ego, crossing a past event which has really occurred, and becoming thereafter more and more distant from ego. This explains such Catalan examples as (110) below, in which the *itive* indicates the past:

(110)   *ahir vaig esmorzar amb el meu germà*
          (yesterday IT~1SG lunch with the my cousin)
          "yesterday I took lunch with my cousin".

If, on the other hand, the *ventive* is used, it will correspond to the (mostly recent) past, since in this case, consideration of the final point, which coincides with the time of ego's discourse, makes part of the meaning; hence French *venir de*, Malagasy *avy*, Teso *bu* (cf. (38) above), Rarotongan *mai*, which, interestingly enough, may also refer to the first person pronoun itself (Buse 1963:163-164), thus highlighting the relationship between spatio-temporal deixis and personal deixis (Bourdin 1992), and confirming the central position of ego. Symmetrically, for any reference to a point located in the time after ego's speech, the *itive* means a move starting from ego, as in English, Luiseño, Palauan, Tamil, Worora, and most dialects of Arabic, while the *ventive* means a move starting from the unknown future and reaching ego, as in Cherokee, Finnish, Luo, Mbum, Norwegian, Rheto-Romance, Swedish, etc. In some languages, but by no means all, the *ventive* corresponds to a distant future (this is the case, for example, of Mambar *ba* and Moore *wa*; but in Zulu, the *itive* and the *ventive*, i.e., *ya* and *za*, indicate a distant and a near future, respectively), and the *itive* corresponds to a near future, as in Catalan *anar* + *a* + infinitive, a structure differing from the rare one illustrated in (110) by the sole presence of *a*, whose directional meaning indicates a prospective attitude, of course absent from (110). All the explanations given above are summed up in (111):

(111)

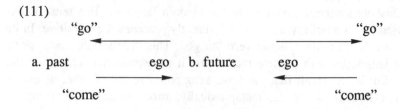

The chart in (111) is not an abstract and purely formal model. It is meant to reflect the flexibility and diversity of spatio-temporal deixis as a trace of LBs' morphogenetic work in the process of building the *anthropophoric* systems of real languages. It must be stressed that the move starting from ego does not necessarily go farther and farther from ego into the past or the future. Nor does the move oriented towards ego necessarily indicate that the event is close to ego in the past or in the future. But the arrows can be, and often are, interpreted that way. This explains the distant future meaning of the *ventive* in Mambar, Moore (cf. above) and many languages of West Africa. It also explains tense systems considered to be among the most complex in the world. Kiksht for instance, according to Hymes (1975), has two directional prestem prefixes *u-* and *t-*, expressing, respectively, direction from and direction towards the speaker, i.e., *itive* and *ventive* markers in my terms; with three (out of four) of the tense markers referring to the past, the *itive* means distant past (like in Catalan), and the *ventive* near past, while with the tense markers referring to the future, the *itive* means near future and the *ventive* distant future. A last point deserves to be stressed: with regard to ego as deixis center, the two seemingly opposite movements may be incompatible in logical terms, but they are not necessarily so in linguistic terms; an event starting from ego may well come back to ego, thus indicating that it is imminent. This explains why in Afrikaans (Van Schoor 1983:168) and in Margi (Hoffmann 1963:222), we find the *itive* and *ventive* markers associated in the same VP.

Besides their specialization as tense markers explained in (111) above, the *itive* and the *ventive* may yield various other types of morphemes, depending on the morphogenetic history of each individual language. Here I will single out the directionals, because their behavior sheds light on the status of ego as a deixis center. West Caucasian and Mayan languages are known for having a rich array of directionals: Mam, for instance (England 1983) has a dozen such elements, indicating direction of motion with respect to ego. In Korean, many compound verbs of motion are paired according to the same criterion: the second part of the compound is either *ka* or *o*, respectively "to go" and "to come" in their lexematic use, but functioning here as *itive* and *ventive* markers: *til-ɔ-ka-ta* (enter-LV-IT-CIT.SUFF(ASS)) "to enter" (a place away from speaker)/*til-ɔ-o-ta* "to come in" (when speaker is in), *nɛli-ɔ-ka-ta*/*nɛli-ɔ-o-ta* "to descend away from/towards the speaker". Ego-centered deixis is not necessarily interpreted in spatial (or temporal) terms only. A directional may refer not to ego's topographic location, but to ego's empathic choice (Kuno & Kaburaki 1977). In Tikar (Hagège 1969:32-33), the participant towards whom or away from whom there is a motion, indicated by *-î* and *-ɔ̂?* respectively, is not always the speaker, as in

(112)   *φ-î mæ̀*
          (give-ALL.DIR me)
          "give (it) to me"

and

(113)   *φ-ɔ̂? nú̧*
          (give-ABL.DIR him)
          "give (it) to him".

The participant can also be someone with whom ego empathizes, as in

(114)   *φ-ɔ̂? mæ̀ plè*
          (give-ABL.DIR me clothes)

or

(115)   φ-î nú plè
          (give-ALL.DIR him clothes).

In (114) ego adopts the addressee's point of view, according to which the latter, as a result of the act of giving, will be deprived of his clothes; in (115), ego explicitly shares the referee's desire or need for the clothes; the translations by "give me the clothes" and "give him the clothes", respectively, do not render these meanings. The projection of ego's representations and feelings onto someone else sometimes yields a potential meaning, as in

(116)   mà̀ íl-ɔ̀ʔ nú
          (I love-ABL.DIR her)
          "I might love her"

as opposed to

(117)   mà̀ ílí nú
          (I love her)
          "I love her".

In other languages, the *ventive* directional is used to indicate various ways by which ego participates in the event: in Quechua (Kirtchuk 1987:166), the directional -*ku* gives the verb a subject-oriented (but not necessarily beneficial!) meaning: *puṇu* "to sleep", *puṇu-ku* "to sleep at will"; *waṇu* "to die", *waṇu-či* (*či* = CAUS) "to kill", *waṇuči-ku* "to commit suicide". In Hausa (Bachir 1978:120), the suffixation of the *ventive* directional -*yóo* to the verb in

(118)   y-áa shá gíyà-l shì
          (he-PERF drink beer-of 3MASC.SG)
          "he has drunk his beer"

yields

(119)   y-áa shá-yóo gíyà-l shì.

(119) also means "he has drunk his beer", but the directional contains further information, not easy to translate into English: it indicates a motion towards the speaker, implying that the referee is getting close to the speak-

er at the moment when the sentence is uttered; the directional suggests, therefore, that the fact that the referee has drunk beer is perceptible to the speaker, through behavorial or olfactory or other signs.

Finally, in certain revealing languages, the centrality of ego is even more clearly stressed in the mood expressing ego's pressure on the surrounding world, namely the imperative: in Maidu (Shipley 1964:51), the imperative bears the obligatory indication of the speaker's presence (*-pi* suffix) or absence (*-padá* suffix); in Lakhota (Foley & Van Valin 1977:315), imperatives are formed by the addition of the clitic *-yo/-wo* for a male speaker, or *-ye/-we* for a female speaker, to the end of the verb.

The facts examined above point to the central position of ego in the *anthropophoric system*. This applies to the complex rules underlying the behavior of direct speech verbs with regard to personal reference in a language like Slave, as well as to the phenomena related to the functioning of the *itive* and the *ventive* in many languages, regardless of whether these markers are tense morphemes or directionals. This is the reason why for a long time I called the system schematized in (103) above the *egophoric system* (Hagège 1982, 1990b.) before I decided to call it *anthropophoric*. The reason for such a change is that at least one of the interrelated domains that constitute this coherent system, namely the *exophorics*, does not seem to be always, or necessarily, ego-centered. The term *exophorics* refers mainly to demonstratives and, where they exist, articles (on the morphogenetic relationship between the two, cf. 5.4.3 section b.). In languages like Chinese, Vietnamese and others in East and South-East Asia, deixis is based on an opposition between demonstratives implying reference not to ego alone but to the first and second persons taken together on an equal footing against all the rest: Chinese *zhèi/nèi* "this/that", Vietnamese *đây/đấ´y*, same meanings. Moreover, in many cases the demonstrative subsystem cannot be interpreted in purely personal terms: it is also geared to spatial parameters. The same is true of Japanese, where the famous *ko/so/a* trilogy is not always an *ego/tu/alii* system, as is the case, for instance, in *ko*-derived deictics, such as *kochira*, when used not in its ordinary meaning of "(on) this side", but with the meaning of "(polite) I" (in telephone conversations, letters, etc.). Often, spatial and social positions control the assignment of persons. Facts like these had already led me, in Hagège 1982:44, to speak of *lococentric structures* in order to characterize this type of situation in Chinese (and also Russian, Luyia, etc.). In this case, space controls person assignment as much as the reverse. In many

African, Amerindian and Austronesian languages, *exophoric* subsystems are organized according to landmarks such as houses, mountains, rivers, cardinal points and other criteria whose role can be considered as *ecolinguistic*. However, the primacy of human speakers, as established above, is not incompatible with this importance of spatial parameters. It is to avoid the implication that ego is always and necessarily the sole organizer of deixis that I have replaced the concept of *egophore* by the broader concept of *anthropophore*.

Among the other manifestations of the *anthropophoric system*, at least four are worth recalling briefly here (for more details, cf. Hagège 1982:116-119): *case anthropology, linguistic expression of social hierarchies, axiological scales,* and *cultural indexing*. By *case anthropology* (taking *case* in the broad meaning of the syntactic relationship, marked by special tools, between nominal complements and verbal predicate), I mean the formation of spatio-temporal pre- or postpositions by means of names of body parts or spatial landmarks, pointing to an appropriation and humanization, by LBs, of space through language. In languages of all the parts of the world, it is easy to find *relators* (cf.7.2.1) meaning "in front of", "behind", "in", "on", "under", identical with obsolete or still current nouns meaning "face", "back", "belly", "head", "foot", respectively (cf. 7.4.1 section a., table 224).

The *linguistic expression of social hierarchies* is a well-studied phenomenon (cf. Brown & Gilman 1960, Winter ed. 1984), by which, in many languages, not only personal pronouns of address, but also verbs and nouns, according to the unit chosen among available lists, reflect the way ego expresses the social, cultural, economical or political position of the participants in dialogue and of the persons or things referred to. Very often, especially in languages of South and East Asia, the historical sources of the (mostly polite) pronouns for "you" and "I" are nouns whose meanings are "master" or "prince" (cf. 1.3.3 section a. for Japanese) and "slave" (e.g., Burmese *cun-to*, Khmer *khnom*) or "servant", respectively (cf. *ibid.* for Japanese again). In certain languages, such as Kawi or Dyirbal, animate and inanimate beings are organized along *axiological scales*, i.e., scales defined by the relative values assigned to these beings within a given culture, and illustrating a particular relationship with the universe, also expressed in mythological representations. Finally, I have proposed to call *cultural indexing* the assignment of linguistic designations to objects, places or activities which play an important role in a given culture. For example, a correlation can be established between the many landmarks built by western societies and the relative scarcity of place adverbs in English, French, German, etc., compared with Kikuyu or Eskimo (cf. Denny 1978), where LBs have created a profusion of linguistic elements related to human visual, aural and tactile perception. Another case of *cultural indexing* is represented by place names which, in certain (e.g., African) languages, do not require the use of a spatial *relator*: it suffices, in this case, to say something meaning literally "I'll go bush" or "he walked mountain", because the ecological and professional relevance of some particular places is enough for these places to imply by themselves their space-like nature. The last illustration of *cultural indexing* which is worthy of mention here lies in systems of personal pronouns. In PortSandwitch, for example (Charpentier 1979:49-51), there is a distinction between inclusive and exclusive in the dual, trial and plural, not only for the first person, but even for the second and third persons: special forms make it possible to indicate whether the group of people to whom (second person trial and plural) or about whom (third person trial and plural) one is talking does or does not include the addressee proper. Although this is speculative, there might be a correlation between this high degree of precision and the need for accurate identification: LBs needed to know, in case of argument or war, who was who, who was for or against whom. A high degree of precision along another dimension is also to be found in certain languages: in Aranda and Lardil, for instance, "we two" and "you two" both have two distinct forms, depending on whether or not the relationship between the two individuals in question is defined in terms of agnation (descent by male line from a common male ancestor).

3.2.2 The LBs' personal sphere

The notion of *personal sphere* is not taken in the meaning it has in Bally (1926), the article which introduced it. It is applied here to the many aspects of grammar which bear the marks of human deixis, i.e., of the omnipresence of LBs in seemingly fossilized structures that are governed by strict rules. It will appear that such structures often point to mental operations reflecting the human representation of the relationships both between man and the world and among speakers in communication. The notion of *personal sphere* seems to be able to account for several puzzling facts in various languages.

A fairly frequent fact of this kind is the existence of morphemes whose functional and semantic versatility seems at first sight surprising. Yuman languages provide good illustrations here. In Diegueño for instance (Gorbet 1979), -*k* is an allative-adessive marker when suffixed to a noun and a hypothesis marker when suffixed to a verb, while -*m* is ablative-abessive when suffixed to a noun but indicates, when suffixed to a verb, that the following verb has a different subject. This -*m* suffix is thus an *anisophoric*, according to the terminology adopted here in order to include the phenomenon hitherto known as switch reference in the general scheme of the *anthropophoric system* ((103) above). In another Yuman language, Yavapai, -*k*, in addition to having these uses, is also suffixed to verbs meaning "to say", "to ask", "to think", "to want", "to feel", as well as to clauses expressing aims or intentions, and -*m* is also used as an accusative marker in Kiliwa and as a completivizer in several other Yuman languages (Jacobsen 1983). According to Kendall (1975:8-9), "-*k* might be designated a 'personal' or 'egocentric' construction marker and -*m* an 'impersonal' or 'allocentric' construction marker", because the -*k* structures "have in common a speaker-centered semantic force [...]. These constructions contrast with the ones describing events or states having existential reality outside of the speaker or at a distance from him. The latter are, predictably, marked with -*m*". Ego is taken as a target when -*k* is used, hence the allative-adessive meaning, and as submitted to the outside world, itself taken as a target, when -*m* is used, hence the ablative-abessive meaning. With regard to *diaphoricity* procedures, Kendall, in order to account for the use of the speaker-centered member of the pair in case of *isophoricity* but not in case of *anisophoricity*, hypothesizes that if the speaker "switches topics or subjects, he is metaphorically moving away from the point at which he was located. The notions of *location* and *moving away from* are certainly parts of the definitions of -*k* and -*m*, respectively". It is interesting to note that in other languages, as well, the same morpheme is used as an adessive marker with noun and an "ego-centered" mood marker with verbs; Quechua -*man*, illustrated in (120) (from Grondín 1971:190), is such a morpheme:

(120)   *fiesta-man jamu-yku-man*
         (feast-ALL come-we(EXCL)-POT)
         "we might come to the feast".

Another less direct manifestation of the *personal sphere* as the domain of representation of man's place in deixis can be observed in an important area of grammar, namely transitivity. Uralic languages provide interesting illustrations here. The Finnish partitive is used to refer to the patient after verbs implying the latter's non-affectedness or partial affectedness, like *rakastaa* "to love" in (121):

(121)   *rakasta-n sinua*
          (love-I you(PART))
          "I love you".

Thus, we find the grammar of Finnish explicitly reflects the fact that the person who is the object of an emotion like love is not necessarily affected by it[3]. Similarly, a given verb may have different meanings according to whether the following noun is in the accusative or in the partitive (this is not unrelated to the often stressed fact that, in Finnish, a transitive verb in the past has perfective meaning if the object noun is in the accusative, but progressive meaning if the object noun is in the partitive): thus *ampua* "to shoot" means that the patient has been shot dead if the accusative is used, but that the patient is only shot at when the partitive is used. In Hungarian, the rules prescribing the use of the subjective conjugation, whose relation with the objective conjugation is a much debated issue, can be lumped together under one principle: this conjugation is used when the object is partial or partially affected, as opposed to the objective conjugation, which implies control of the subject over the object, as marked by a definite article, a demonstrative, a possessed or proper noun, a third person pronoun, etc. This also explains why the object pronouns of the first and second persons cannot be used with a verb in the objective conjugation: if they could, it would mean that *ego* and *tu* are pulled out of their personal sphere and assigned to the sphere of dominated objects. Strikingly enough, although the latter is a quite ordinary situation in everyday life, human languages are so structured that LBs seem to have constantly striven to dodge the direct linguistic expression of such a situation, or to hedge it with various constraints, as appears in the often marked formulas that correspond to it (cf. 3.1 above). This is one more confirmation of a general tendency: *the more unexpected the situation, the more strongly marked its linguistic expression.* Thus, the Finnish and Hungarian forms that indicate a partial affectedness of the patient or a partial completeness of the action are a faithful reflection of LBs' *personal sphere*, i.e., of LBs' anthropocentric representation of the events of the world.

The same can be said of various kinds of formal affinities which reflect interesting semantic associations. Some of these affinities are found only in a restricted number of revealing languages, such as those which use the verb "to do" in the structure expressing negation: English, Korean (for one of the two formulas appearing in this case, i.e., the long one, $V + ci + an + ha(ta)$ ("to do"), considered to be the more literary), two Tungusic languages, Nanai and Ulcha, and seven Papuan languages: Ankave, Baruya, Kapau, Korafe, Orokaiwa, Simbari, Telefol (Boisson 1984). This affinity between the concepts of non-realization and negation may be compared with the affinity between negation and irrealis (Palauan, cf. Hagège 1986:-128-130, Walmadjari: Hudson 1978, Yuman languages: Munro 1977), and with the one between interrogation and irrealis (Haiman 1978). The link between all these is the operation by which LBs suspend an assertion, leaving formal traces of their doubts as to its validity. This oscillation between assertion and doubt can explain seemingly contradictory phenomena, like Nahuatl *tla*, used both as a mark of strong affirmation and as a dubitative morpheme: what is affirmed by the speaker may be contested if the speaker's and listener's *personal spheres* coincide, that is, if the speaker espouses the listener's viewpoint (de Pury-Toumi 1981). We can likewise explain the affinity found in Japanese (*no* in the language of women), Khmer (*tè*), Mangarai (*ji*), Tamazight (*is*) (Boisson 1984) between such different phenomena as interrogation and emphasis. The concept of *factivity* (Givón 1979:93 ff.), despite its usefulness, is too narrow to account for this range of phenomena. If certain morphosyntactic structures (viewpoint 1 in the three viewpoints theory: cf. end of 3.1 above), are so close to one another in such different languages, it is because they contain traces of information-hierarchical operations (viewpoint 3), by which LBs express meanings (viewpoint 2) reflecting their *personal sphere*.

The same considerations can explain in a unified way certain apparently random features in various languages. For example, how can Ainu, Chamorro, Georgian, Nahuatl, Russian possess homologous structures to express such diverse contents as passive, reflexive, reciprocal, but also plural, potential and honorific address? It has been proposed (Shibatani 1985) to treat this correlation of passive with various semantic zones in terms of *prototype*. Though this approach is interesting, it is not the only possible one. If we consider the operations by which concrete traces of LBs subjectivity are left in the web of grammar, such correlations are not surprising: the use of the passive in order to avoid mentioning an external agent as the direct cause of a given event is an operation semantically related to the polite suppression, by use of honorific address, of this agent's singularity (hence the plural); similarly, what is also suggested by the absence of an explicitly mentioned agent is spontaneity, and therefore propensity of occurrence (potential) of the action that the patient performs either reflexively, or in reciprocal relationship.

Finally, one of the activities most intimately connected with the verbal representation of the world by LBs in the very process of communication is explicitly present in the metalinguistic distancing by which certain languages use the verb "to say" as a formative in compounds: thus in Enga, of 1068 examples of specific verb + generic adjunct verb constructions, 334 have been found to take *lengé* "say" as generic adjunct; among these 334, a little less than half involve the core meaning of "sound", other common associations being with states, and, even, with motion. Moreover, of these 1068, another 247 contain *pingí* "to do" as an adjunct, and among these 247, almost half are not associated with activities (Foley 1986:120-121). A comparable situation exists in other Papuan languages, and also in Amharic (cf. 6.3.3). What is covert elsewhere is overtly expressed in these revealing languages, namely, that saying and doing are two basic human behaviors, likely to be treated, in linguistic terms, as constituent elements of situations that do not necessarily refer to speech or to an action. Although the Papuan formulas soon get frozen, this is another testimony of the omnipresence of human representations in the structure of languages.

3.3 Subjecthood and subjectivity

Besides the traces of LBs' personal sphere that appear in the various aspects of grammar studied above, there is, in the specific domain of syntactic functions, a tendency towards equating subjecthood with subjectivity. However, some methodological precautions must be taken here.

In order to identify syntactic functions, a number of linguists, in line with Keenan (1976:324), make use of two kinds of properties: behavorial and control properties, such as deletion, movements, control of cross-reference, etc., on the one hand, and on the other hand, coding properties, i e., position → case marking → verb agreement (meaning that "if an NP acquires the verb agreements characteristic of subjects, then it must also acquire the case marking and position; and if it acquires the case marking, then it must acquire the position."). The linguists who make use of this framework are sometimes faced with difficulties when dealing with what have been called "dative subjects" in the literature. In many languages with a case system, noun-phrases referring to the experiencer appear in the dative when the predicate expresses physical states (whether inherent or transient), mental dispositions, and various intellectual attributes such as judgment, belief, doubts, knowledge, diverse perceptions, affects like desire, hatred, etc., ability, obligation, and, fairly often, kinship and possession. "Dative subjects" are well represented in the languages of South Asia. Masica (1976:164) notes that "a high development of this feature is characteristic of India", since it is "present in all the major languages to a degree that seems to be unparalleled elsewhere". It is interesting to examine to what extent the notion of dative subject is justified here.

Taking examples from two languages of South Asia, one Indo-Aryan, Hindi, and one Dravidian, Kannada, let us study the overt formal (in Keenan's terms, "coding") properties possessed by NPs with one of the meanings noted above, when these NPs are subjects: sentence-initial position in stylistically unmarked utterances, verb agreement control for gender, number and person, nominative case-marking. This last property being ruled out by definition since the case is the dative, we note that, of the other two properties, only word order applies: in Hindi as well as in Kannada (Saxena 1981, 1985; Sridhar 1976), there is no verb agreement; the verb agrees with the unmarked term, the one referring not to the experiencer, but to the affecting entity or feeling, event, etc. Thus, in the Hindi sentence

(122)   *Rām-ko angrezī nəhį̃ āt-ī*
          (Ram-DAT English(FEM) NEG known(PARTCP)-FEM)
          "Ram cannot speak English",

the verb takes the feminine suffix *-ī*, hence *āt-ī*, because it agrees with feminine *angrezī*, not with masculine *Rām*, which refers to the experiencer. A literal English translation reflecting that would be: "to Ram English is unknown".

Since the coding properties yield negative results, let us examine the behavorial properties. In Hindi, they all designate the dative NP as "subject". In Kannada, the situation is less simple: while reflexivization and participial subject deletion yield positive results, two other important tests, namely Equi NP deletion and causativization, yield negative or, at best, ambiguous, results. Thus, in

(123)   *nān-u nan-age talenōvu baralu ishtapaduvudilla*
(I-NOMIN I-DAT headache come wish~not)
"I don't wish to get a headache",

the dative *nan-age* fails to delete under identity with the matrix subject *nān-u*. Faced with such conflicting evidence, Sridhar, who cites this example, writes bluntly at the end of his article (*ibid.*:590): "Frankly, I don't know!" All we can say is that it is less easy to speak of "dative subject" in Kannada than in Hindi.

Turning to languages from other parts of the world, we find similar situations. In Russian, for instance, datives referring to the experiencer function like indirect objects, not like subjects with regard to their overt formal properties, but they have behavioral properties of subjects: in

(124)   *vidja čto proisxodit, emu stydno za svoego brata*
(seeing what happens he~DAT shameful for REFL brother)
"seeing what happens, he feels ashamed for his brother"
(Shaumyan 1985),

the dative pronoun *emu* controls Equi in a participial construction, *vidja čto proisxodit*, serves as an antecedent of the reflexive *svoego*, and precedes the predicate *stydno*; by this last feature, it meets the requirements of one of the coding tests (since it is clause-initial, the position most frequently occupied by subjects in Russian despite the relatively free word order), but only one: as in Hindi, the agreement and case requirements are not met, so that in both languages, we are left with a situation in which the dative NPs have certain behavorial, and only one of the coding, properties. Are there cases, then, where both requirements are met?

Such cases, although relatively rare, are documented. In Old Georgian as well as in Modern Georgian, the behavior of dative experiencers is typical of subjects rather than of indirect objects, but in Old Georgian, there was no number agreement between the verb and the sentence-initial dative NP: in

(125)   *me mi-q'var-an isini*
           (I~DAT me-love-3PL they(NOMIN)),

literally "to me are loved they", i.e., "I love them", the 3PL.SUFF -*an* refers
to *isini* "they". This still holds true in Modern Literary Georgian whenever,
the experiencer being 3PER, the "affecting" NP is 1 or 2 PER, e.g.,

(126)   *mas vu-q'varvar-t čven*
           (he~DAT him-love(redupl.=1PER)-1PL we(NOMIN)),

literally "to him are loved we", i.e., "he loves us". However, there is an
interesting restriction: a structure unknown in Old Georgian appears in
sentences where both the affecting and the experiencer NP are 3PER. In
such cases, the verb agrees in number with the dative, not the nominative,
NP: in

(127)   *mat u-q'var-t is*
           (they~DAT him-love-3PL he(NOMIN)),

literally "to-them him-love-they he", i.e., "they love him", -*t* is plural, like
mat and unlike *is* (Tschenkeli 1958, Cole *et al.* 1980:739-740). Number
agreement is only one of the formal properties of subjects, and contrary to
Keenan's (1976:324) claim, illustrated in the formula given at the beginning of the present section, it is not true, as far as Georgian is concerned,
that an NP which triggers number agreement must also acquire the properties referring to case marking and position: in (127), *mat*, although it
controls verb agreement, remains in the dative, and it is not necessarily
sentence-initial, since a sentence like *uq'vart mat is* (or *igi* in Western
Georgian) is at least as frequent as (127). It is true, however, that verb
agreement, as a concrete material phenomenon by which one part of an
utterance is tightly linked to another, must be considered an important
criterion, not to mention the possibility that Georgian NPs like that in (127)
may some day acquire position and case marking properties. At any rate,
number agreement is already gaining wide acceptance, since, according to
Tschenkeli (1958), the restriction valid for literary Georgian does not exist
in the colloquial language, where the dative experiencer controls number
agreement whatever the person. If case marking properties were acquired
in addition to verb agreement, then we could really speak of *subjects*.

The importance of verb agreement is often forgotten: it is frequent in modern work on syntax, known for its wide use of the notion of subject, to treat as subjects many NPs that do not agree, as if the behavioral properties were sufficient criteria for subjecthood. Thus, in ergative languages, a certain NP (whether bearing an ergative (or other) case affix or coindexed in the VP) is often considered to be a subject, when, in fact, it only expresses a semantic notion, that of agent. Similarly, following Dixon (1979), many linguists have become accustomed to calling the "transitive object" the object (O), although it is the grammatical subject, since it controls verb agreement and is ordinarily not marked, or stands in the absolutive (or nominative, depending on the language) in sentences where, semantically, it represents the patient, and where the other NP, the agent, is marked by the ergative. The English equivalents of ergative sentences of many languages have probably exerted a strong influence on the choice of such an analysis. However, theoretical justifications have been provided, of course. Thus, it has been claimed that the assignment of the NP representing the patient to "transitive subject" might find support in transformational arguments, corresponding in part to Keenan's behavioral and control properties. Rules like Equi NP deletion, subject raising, reflexing, conjunction formation (Anderson 1976), as well as coordination and subordination rules (Dixon 1979) are claimed to establish that languages with morphological ergativity are in fact "syntactically accusative" (like English), the often mentioned example of Dyirbal being, allegedly, "the exception which proves the rule" (Anderson 1976:23). Other languages may in fact be added to Dyirbal, among them Lezgian, in which, according to Mel'čuk (1988: 212-223), it is the NP in the nominative, not the NP in the ergative, which possesses the following subject properties: it is non-deletable, gapping-collapsible, and it controls the agreement of the predicative complement participle. Taking behavioral properties and other transformational arguments as justifications for the assignment of subjecthood to agent NPs in ergative languages amounts to not recognizing that behavioral and coding properties constitute two disjunct sets, with cases of conflicting evidence, as we have seen above for Hindi and Kannada.

The question then arises whether it would not be useful to know exactly what is reflected by behavioral and control properties. The answer is clear: they reflect various types of operations. In early Generative Grammar, these operations have been claimed to belong to the speaker's competence. Whether this is true or not, what is certain is that these operations constitute a methodological approach *used by linguists*. As opposed to that, respecting verb agreement implies using, in order to establish a relationship between two parts of a sentence, linguistic material, i.e., morphemes, that are part of the concrete elements every speaker of a language knows. There is no reason why we should consider overt material phenomena as merely "surface" events, as has constantly been and continues to be the case, not without condescending implications, in Generative Grammar and current models of formal linguistics. Once more, we are forced to remark that Generative Grammar talks about linguistics, not about language(s).

In the light of the above considerations, it appears that the acquisition of certain characteristics of subjecthood by dative NPs in Modern Colloquial Georgian testifies to the anthropocentric nature of syntax. Among the two markers, one points towards a subsequent stage and the other recalls a prior stage: in (127) above, the *-t* in *u-q'var-t* bears witness to the fact that the language has finally assigned subjecthood to *mat*; but at the same time, since *mat* is dative, we have a concrete trace of a partial resistance, on the part of LBs', to this same treatment: the dative is retained even though verb agreement shows that *mat* no longer functions as an indirect object[4]. Thus (127) is a live illustration of the fertile contradiction which characterizes LBs' activity.

If it is true that they cannot easily free themselves from the pressure of an existing structure, since they retain material traces of prior syntactic status, the data of various languages show that this does not prevent them from imposing their presence, by their permanent shaping activity, on grammatical constructions. In an example such as (127) above, there is a tendency, but only a tendency, towards a kind of coincidence between grammatical subjecthood and LBs' subjectivity. In other words, the same NP appears as the point at which two dimensions converge: the highest syntactic function, namely subject, as manifested by one of its defining features (agreement), and the humanized vision of the world. In cases where there are only behavioral criteria, we may take into account the importance of the operations on which they are based, but having recourse to such operations suggests, rather than demonstrates, the psychological reality of various mechanisms. In that case, we will therefore even less agree to speak of "dative subjects". At any rate, speaking of "dative subjects" is quite confusing. It is even syntactically senseless, since the notion of subject is a grammatical notion (viewpoint 1 in terms of the three viewpoints theory, cf. 3.1), while dative is a semantic notion (viewpoint 2).

But the interesting aspect of the issue is the light it brings on humans' place in morphosyntax.

So-called "dative-subjects" are, in the real world, experiencers confronted with something that happens to them rather than voluntary initiators. It is interesting to note that this special status is reflected in various syntactic constraints, showing that experiencers do not cover the same domain as agents-patients, but a more limited one. Thus, in Hindi, experiencers with the imperative are generally rejected by informants; in this respect, experiencers are analogous to the agents of verbs implying no voluntary activity, like *girnâ* "to fall". In Kannada, experiencers may appear with the imperative, but in such cases the sentence expresses a wish, or a prayer addressed to some unspecified controlling force; moreover, experiencer sentences may neither contain adverbial phrases implying volition on the part of the experiencer, nor refer to an inherently volitional action (such as suicide for instance): only nominative subjects are possible in both cases (Sridhar 1976:584).

As noted in the beginning of this section, the predicates of experiencer sentences may express possession. The coincidence between subjecthood and subjectivity is clearly illustrated in (128) below, from Preclassical Latin, and, negatively, in (129), from Classical Latin (Fruyt 1987:217):

(128)   *neque praeter se unquam ei servus fuit* (Plautus: *Captivi*, 580)
          (nor except himself ever he-DAT slave was)
          "nor did he ever have any slave except himself"

(129)   *liberi [...] mihi et propter indulgentiam meam et propter excellens eorum ingenium, vita sunt mea cariores* (Cicero: *Oratio post reditum ad Quirites*, 2)
          (children I-DAT and due~to mildness my and due~to excellent their nature life~ABL are my dearer)
          "due both to my natural mildness and to their being very good-tempered, I love my children even more than my own life".

In (128), the reflexive pronoun *se* refers to the dative *ei*, expressing the possessor, although the grammatical subject of the sentence is *servus*; in (129), the anaphoric pronoun, although it refers not to the dative pronoun *mihi* but to the grammatical subject *liberi*, is not the reflexive *suum*, but the non reflexive *eorum*, because *mihi*, being the semantic center, controls cross-reference.

Although the notion of "dative subject", strictly speaking, is normally applied to languages with a case system, it is interesting to note the analogy between "dative subjects" and a beneficiary promoted to subject function in a language without a case system, but with an inflected pronominal paradigm. In Classical Nahuatl, the only way of passivizing

(130)   *ni-mic-tla-maka*
          (I-you(OBL)-INDEF.OBJ-give)
          "I give you something",

when the agent is deleted, is to confer subject status to the (human) beneficiary, hence

(131)   *ti-tla-mako*
          (you(SUBJ)-INDEF.OBJ-give(PASS))
          "you are given something",

where *mako* is from *maka-l-o*, with *-l* = causative and *-o* (from *wa*) = impersonal (Launey 1979:45). In English one can also say

(132)   *something is given to him*,

whereas the corresponding Nahuatl structure is impossible.

CHAPTER 4

The presence of LBs
in creologenesis

Creologenesis is an important illustration of the LBs' presence in the construction of languages. I will begin (4.1) with the study of certain interesting characteristics of borrowing, the general activity to which creologenesis is related. I will then present (4.2) two of the features that define the specific process of pidgino- and creologenesis. Finally, I will examine (4.3) the issue raised, in modern linguistics, by the nature of creoles: are they the results of substratum influence, or the products of an innate program, and what does the answer tell us about the human being as a language builder?

4.1 Borrowing and the opposition between grammar and lexicon

As stated in 1.4, the opposition between grammar and lexicon can be measured in terms of time-sharing and rate of energy expense. This does not prevent the relation between the two from being a rather flexible one, as we have seen in 2.1.2. Nor does it mean that grammar and lexicon are opposed with regard to the possibility of transferring some of their features from one language to another one. It will become apparent in 4.3 that pidgins and creoles are good examples, since most of them blend some grammatical features of the source-language with the lexicon of the target-language. It is useful, before studying the process of creologenesis, to examine its framework, i.e., borrowing.

There is no opposition between grammar and lexicon with regard to borrowing: any linguistic feature can be borrowed, whatever the component it belongs to. Grammatical features, therefore, are open to borrowing, contrary to a widely-shared opinion, still expressed in the 20th century by a number of linguists, from Meillet to Bickerton. Meillet claimed in 1914 that "borrowed elements are basically those which belong to the vocabulary", unless we are dealing with dialects of the same language (1958:87). As for Bickerton, he asserts (1981:50) that "languages, even creoles, are systems, systems have structure, and things incompatible with that structure cannot be borrowed: SVO languages cannot borrow a set of postpositions, to take an extreme and obvious case". This claim is flatly belied by a creole which, perhaps for the very reason that it is "aberrant", has not attracted much attention so far: Sri Lanka Portuguese, which I will present first, along with other cases of word order borrowing. Nominal and verbal modifier borrowing will then be examined, thus leading us logically to pidgins and creoles, the most spectacular cases of linguistic borrowing. This study will therefore contain two parts: *sequential* borrowing (4.1.1); *nominant* and *verbant* borrowing (4.1.2).

4.1.1 Sequential borrowing

By *sequential* borrowing, I mean the borrowing of a certain type of word order from a language into another, which however, in this process, does not necessarily borrow the words themselves. Sri Lanka Portuguese, after an initial stage, in which it had, like Portuguese, prepositions – a fact generally linked to SVO word order – has, in a new stage, acquired postpositions, according to the word order of Tamil, with which it was in permanent contact. Thus, we have (Stolz 1987a:21) the following paradigm (SLP = Sri Lanka Portuguese):

(133)

Case	Portuguese	SLP (Old)	SLP (New)	Tamil postpositions	
NOMIN	*o homem*	*(o) home*	*fiju-ø*	*-ø*	
GEN	*do homem*	*de (o) home*	*fiju-su(wə)*	*-r'a*	
DAT	*ao homem*	*per (o) home*	*fiju-pə*	*-ukku*	
ACC	*(a)o homem*	*(per)(o) home*	*fiju-pə*	*-a(y)*	(+hum)
			fiju-ø	*-ø*	(-hum)
LOC			*fiju-ntua*	*-iTTa(y)*	(+hum)
			fiju-ntu	*-ila(y)*	(-hum)

Such contact-induced borrowing of word order, by which a prepositional language acquires postpositions while keeping the etyma of its source, is not an isolated case, nor is it found in creoles only. I will just recall, among others, the example of Lithuanian, in which (cf. 2.3.1) the Finnic influence has resulted in the adjunction of three new cases, illative, allative and adessive, "of which at least the last two are expressed by suffixes developed from an original Lithuanian preposition" (Thomason 1986:262).

Contact-induced *sequential borrowing* is also illustrated by the borrowing of clitics. It will suffice here to mention two examples, in both of which the material form of clitic morphemes is itself also borrowed: Central Siberian Yupik, due to widespread Chukchee-Eskimo bilingualism, has borrowed more than one hundred sentence adverbials and conjunctional clitics (de Reuse 1989); Lappish has borrowed as semi-clitics, for the same reason, at least five Finnish clitics (Nevis 1985). Since the material forms of the morphemes are also borrowed here, Yupik and Lappish are not strictly cases of *sequential borrowing,* as are Sri Lanka Portuguese and Lithuanian. The latter show that LBs in contact situations are able to differentiate, by an implicit metalinguistic operation, linguistic facts whose separate identification is a rather technical matter, such as order of units and units themselves. If the order is the same, as is the case for Eskimo-Yupik and Finnish-Lappish, the process of borrowing will of course be a global one.

4.1.2 Nominant and verbant borrowing

Besides an abstract feature like word order, borrowed, as the case may be, along with or without the words it characterizes, the bound modifiers of the noun and the verb, which I have called *nominants* and *verbants* respectively (cf. 2.3.3), provide one more illustration of the fact that grammatical features can also be borrowed. As far as *nominants* are concerned, entire systems are open to borrowing. A famous case is Ma'a (Mbugu), a Cushitic language, which, as a result of widespread bilingualism and continuous contact with neighboring Bantu languages, has adopted the Bantu noun-class prefixes and agreement system, extending it even to some of the original Cushitic vocabulary (Welmers 1973:8-9). The way things occurred, however, is interesting to examine since it shows, as far as grammatical elements are concerned, how LBs in fact behave in the course of the borrowing process. LBs are not professional linguists, even though they are able, as shown in 4.1.1 above, to borrow word order alone without borrowing the words it organizes. But word order is a grammatical device which has no necessary link with any specific word-type. As opposed to that, *nominants* are by definition linked to the noun, which both gives them access to the sentence and is identified as noun by their presence. Since we note, precisely, that Ma'a LBs adopted a vast Bantu nominal vocabulary, we must conclude that they did not adopt Bantu noun-classes in the abstract, but as incidentals to this borrowed vocabulary, whose introduction itself resulted from extensive bilingualism.

With regard to *verbants*, the situation is quite comparable. Contrary to a widely-held belief, they are also open to borrowing. But like *nominants*, they often follow in the wake of the verbs which have themselves been borrowed. Moreover, *verbants* are not necessarily borrowed by an automatic process which would result in the introduction of whole unaltered systems. It may happen that LBs leave their signature through the manner in which they seem to make choices when, by maintaining some autochthonous features, they secure a certain parallelism in the borrowed paradigms. An interesting illustration of this phenomenon is found in the Romani dialect of Ajia Varvara. Its speakers left Turkey in the twenties, not without keeping heavy traces of a long period of Turkish-Romani bilingualism. As a result, the Turkish verbal etyma borrowed in Romani are inflected with Turkish personal endings. The whole VP, then, root as well as suffix, would appear as totally Turkish, were it not for one interesting point. Compare (134) with (135) and (136), i.e., three different paradigms for the preterite (cf. Stolz 1987a):

(134)   Personal endings of the Romani verbs whose roots are borrowed from Turkish:
        Singular   Plural
        1 -*d-um*   1 -*d-***umus**
        2 -*d-un*   2 -*d-unus*
        3 -*d-u*   3 -*d-ular*

(135)   Personal endings of verbs in Turkish (if the root has an *ü* vowel):
        Singular   Plural
        1 -*d-üm*   1 -*d-ük*
        2 -*d-ün*   2 -*d-ünüz*
        3 -*d-ü*   3 -*d-üler*

(136)   Personal endings of the Romani verbs belonging to the vernacular lexicon:
        Singular   Plural
        1 -*l-em*   1 -*l-am*
        2 -*l-an*   2 -*l-en*
        3 -*l-as*   3 -*l-e*.

While (136) is vernacular Romani, including with respect to the preterite marker, *l*, (134) results from borrowing of both the Turkish preterite marker *d* and the Turkish personal endings. However, since Romani, unlike Turkish, has no vowel harmony, we note that Romani LBs have adopted a uniform back vowel *u*, and *a* in 3PL, whatever the vowels of the root; hence the difference between the vowels of the personal suffixes in (134) and (135). More importantly, while all other persons are almost identical (were it not for vowel harmony), a striking difference appears between (134) and (135) in 1PL: -**umus** in (134) but -*ük* in (135). Thus, the Romani LBs have combined two systems which they commonly used as bilinguals: by analogy with both Turkish 2PL -*ünüz* and Romani 1SG/PL -*m* and 2SG/PL -*n*, they have made 1PL -*umus*, instead of Turkish -*ük*, thus maintaining parallel formations SG -*m*/-*n*, PL -*mus*/-*nus*, the -*s* instead of -*z* being probably introduced on the analogy of Romani 3SG -*as*.

Another illustration of LBs' presence even in massive borrowing of *verbants* is provided by a comparison between two Aleut dialects (Menov-ščikov 1969). On Beringa island, the Aleut population was much greater than that of the Russian settlers, so that it was on the neighboring island, Mednyj, that the Aleut bilinguals in permanent contact with the many Russian settlers gave up the impressing array of Aleut verbal endings, which amount to several hundreds, and adopted the Russian personal suffixes in the present, as well as Russian -*j* in the imperative. But in both cases, unlike the Romanis, they combined these suffixes with autochthonous Aleut roots. Moreover, in the past, a tense in which Russian does not show person, they combined Aleut roots with preposed Russian personal pronouns and with the postposed Russian past marker *l* (diachronically, a participial suffix); and in the future, they combined the Aleut verbal roots with the two Russian markers of the imperfective future: the prefixed "be" auxiliary *budu*, *budeš*, etc., and the suffixed infinitive marker *t'* (cf. 2.2.2). If we recall that in the present tense, they add Aleut morphemes in order to express the dual, it appears that despite this large scale borrowing of foreign markers on vernacular roots, LBs again are far from blindly digesting whole important paradigms of personal morphemes. They leave their signature through the choices they unconsciously make. And borrowing of *verbants* along with the verbs themselves is by no means a law, frequent though it may be: Yucatec adds its vernacular transitive marker -*t* to transitive verbs borrowed from Spanish, hence *mostrar-t* "to show (it)", as well as to those belonging to the autochthonous verbal lexicon, hence *bo?ol-t* "to pay (it)".

To sum up, the borrowing not only of word order, as shown in 4.1.1, but also of *nominant* and *verbant* systems testifies to the fact that grammatical features are more often borrowed than has generally been assumed. But we have seen that even in cases of impressive phenomena like the large scale borrowing of verbal morphemes in Romani or in Aleut, LBs leave the traces of their subliminal reshaping activity, no matter whether applied to major or minor points. This permanent presence of LBs in the construction of languages is even more perceptible in a case which, if compared with those examined above, is by far the most spectacular, i.e., in creoles. Interestingly enough, creoles are built on a component which is not the result of partial borrowing as in the case of Ajia Varvara Romani or of Aleut, borrowing as they do one among other morphological paradigms. In the case of creoles, there is total, not partial, borrowing. And the component thus borrowed in its entirety is not the grammar but the lexicon. The question whether or not there are parts of the grammar that are inherited from a vernacular language is an object of debates among creolists, as we will see below after having defined the main notions.

4.2 On two defining features of pidginogenesis

Certain situations raise the problem of crosscultural communication. This is the case, in particular, when a social group does not speak the language of another group with which it comes into contact, or has an imperfect grasp of it, having begun to acquire it at the first stage of contact. This situation produces *jargons*, characterized as unstable, individual solutions, not excluding ingenious modes of expression invented by some gifted people. But jargons are then replaced by *pidgins*, i.e., a stabilized form, which tends to become the fixed, conventionalized mode of expression between communities. When a pidgin becomes the native language of a speech community, specialists generally consider that a *creole* language has arisen. Furthermore, when a pidgin nativizes itself, its vocabulary and morphosyntactic devices tend to develop and to meet all the communicative needs of its speakers (Hall 1966, DeCamp 1971).

These definitions are, with some nuances, more or less accepted by creolists. In what follows, I would like, in the perspective of this chapter devoted to the LBs' presence in creologenesis, to examine two points which are less commonly studied. The first one is even practically un-known, while the second one does not attract the attention it deserves. The study will therefore contain two parts: pidginogenesis and the continuation of vernacular usage (4.2.1); pidginogenesis as a rapid process (4.2.2).

4.2.1 Pidginogenesis and the continuation of vernacular usage

Not all pidgins are the products of slavery imposed on African tribes. This scheme does not apply, for instance, to the many pidgins spoken in New Guinea, Melanesia, the Philippines, China, the Deccan Plateau; nor does it apply to those used in a large number of African towns and in some American Indian reservations. Despite this diversity, which is not enough taken into account, most discussions in creolistics center around Caribbean creoles and the pidgins from which they have developed. The important claim I would like to discuss is related to these languages.

It is often believed that plantation owners in the Caribbean "deliberately acquired slaves with the greatest possible variety of language in order to make native-language communication among slaves impossible and thus reduce the risk of insurrection" (DeCamp 1971:20). Consequently, it is supposed that slaves were in a state of linguistic deprivation which would explain the advent of pidgins as instruments allowing them to meet the requirements of communication. A careful scrutiny of texts of the 17th and 18th centuries describing exactly the historical situation (Debien, Poyen de Sainte-Marie, Fathers Dutertre, Labat and Pelleprat, all abundantly cited in Cérol 1991) shows this to be no more than a long-lived prejudice: in fact, evangelizing was initially done in African languages; and the masters, far from scattering the tribes, strived to make the members of the same tribe live together and to facilitate the training of the younger and the new-comers by the more experienced workers, given the very hard type of work that was imposed on slaves. What the plantation owners feared above all were maroons, not newcomers from tribes already represented in the plantations. The need for renewed fresh labor made it necessary for the owners to import, almost uninterruptedly, African slaves bought from blackbirders. It also happened, of course, that these were speakers of African languages not yet present in the colonies: in that case, something at least of these languages was introduced. And when the new slaves spoke languages already present, these were thereby maintained and spread over to new families. Thus, we may safely assume that the vernacular African languages remained fairly long in use. This does not mean, of course, that pidgins had not already been created during the first years of plantation life, if not sooner (in Portugal (cf. Naro 1978) or elsewhere). Thus, the slaves, in all likelihood, remained bilinguals during a long period. Not before the middle of the 19th century was this process brought to a close, along with the effective end of slavery (officially abolished, in France, in 1794, but reestablished, and abolished again in 1848). Only then did the slaves adopt stabilized and increasingly expanded pidgins (cf. Mühlhäusler 1979:16,83), soon to become their mother tongues, i.e., creoles.

These observations, although restricted to the Caribbean area, have implications valid for the whole of pidginogenesis. They mean that this process is not quite the purportedly natural laboratory experiment that offers linguists an exceptional opportunity to observe the conditions of language birth. Complex social factors must also be taken into account, which show the importance of the role played in this process by the linguistic history of LBs, as will appear again in 4.3.

4.2.2 Pidginogenesis as a rapid process

Pidginogenesis occurs at an exceedingly rapid rate if compared with the ordinary evolution rhythm in most non-pidgin languages. Thus, the process by which a deictic pronoun or adverb meaning "this" or "like this" yields a complementizer after verbs of saying, thinking, etc., is well documented (cf. Hagège 1990a). But what in English, for example, took several centuries has taken three generations in Tok Pisin. Just as *that*, depending on the context and the intonation, is, as a result of a gradual process taking place during the history of English (Coulmas, 1986:20), either a deictic (as it already was long ago) or a complementizer, Tok Pisin *olsem* (from English *all (the) same*) can, according to Woolford (1981:132-133), be used either as an adverb or as a complementizer. The major difference between the two languages, however, is that in Tok Pisin, this evolution is observable today as an extremely rapid ongoing process. Compare (137) and (138) (Woolford, *ibid.*):

(137)   *olsem nau bai yumi tok wanem ?*
          (thus now FUT we(INCL) talk what)
          "so now what will we say?"

(138)   *na yupela i no save olsem em i matmat ?*
          (and you(PL) PER NEG know COMP this PER cemetery)
          "and you did not know that it was a cemetery?"

(137) is similarly used by old, middle-aged and young people, whereas (138), in which, according to the author, "it is fairly clear from the intonation that *olsem* is being used as a complementizer", has been uttered by a young urban speaker. Thus we see, or hear, LBs in the very process of creation of new grammatical categories.

Another example is Kituba. In this Kikongo-derived pidgin, the inflected Kikongo auxiliary *imene*, indicating the perfective, keeps this form in the speech of the oldest generation ((139)), but it has become a monosyllabic morpheme in the speech of the middle-aged generation ((140)); and in the youngest generation ((141)), it has been eroded, yielding a proclitic, which follows an equally eroded and proclitic form of the personal pronoun (Fehderau 1966:116)[1]:

(139)   *munu imene ku~enda*
          (I PERF INF~go)
          "I have gone"

(140)   *munu me ku~enda*
          (I PERF INF~go)
          same meaning as (139)

(141)   *mu-me-ku~enda*
          (I-PERF-INF~go)
          same meaning as (139).

Comparable phenomena are found with respect to other auxiliaries, such as the two aspect markers *ikele*, progressive, and *lenda*, potential. This is shown by comparison between the speech of the oldest generation, exemplified by (142) for *ikele* and (144) for *lenda*, and the speech of the youngest generation, exemplified by (143) for *ikele* and (145) for *lenda*:

(142)   *munu ikele ku~enda ku~sosa*
          (I PROGR INF~go INF~search)
          "I am going about searching"

(143)   *mu-ke-kwe-sosa*
          (I-PROGR-go-search)
          same meaning as (142)

(144)   *munu lenda ku~sala*
          (I POT INF~work)
          "I may work"

(145)   *mu-le-sala*
          (I-POT-work)
          same meaning as (144).

With respect to the speech of the youngest generation, we note that, in addition to the reduction of the aspect markers to monosyllabic affixes, the Bantu infinitive prefix *ku~* is either dropped ((145)), or ((143)) retained along with only a part of the first verb, i.e., its first syllable *e*, with which it blends into a single syllable *kwe*; due to the frequency of this verb, which means "to go", such a reduction could appear as a step towards its freezing as an *itive* marker (cf. 3.2.1) in this context of verbal series.

Thus, these reductions have taken no more than two generations. This remarkable shortening of the time ordinarily required by such evolutionary processes may be explained by a general tendency: as long as they have not yet developed into creoles, pidgins are used as means of communication by bilinguals or trilinguals who do not have them as mother tongues; provided these pidgins meet the requirements of what I propose to call Communicative Pressure (CP), their users do not care to abide by a norm which would reflect their identity as native speakers. As pidgins turn into creoles, LBs tend to identify themselves much more with their language as one of their defining characteristics, and concomitantly the latter tends to acquire a certain amount of grammatical diversification into distinct categories. This psychological phenomenon can account for what is generally referred to in ambiguous terms, namely the "simplicity" of pidgins as opposed to the relative complexity of creoles.

4.3 Substratum, bioprogram and the nature of LBs' activity

It appears from the above that pidginogenesis is a most spectacular type of contact-induced phenomenon: other cases of borrowing, impressive as the transfer of morphological paradigms may appear (4.1), are much more restricted; in addition, pidginogenesis associates two features which, although not at all contradictory, are rarely associated, i.e., continuation of vernacular usage and rapid changes (4.2). Some specialists, rejecting this evidence, prefer to resort to a nativist hypothesis in order to explain pidginogenesis. There are, however, plenty of facts pointing to the importance of input languages. LBs, thus, build pidgins and creoles from a variety of sources. These three points will be treated in the following subdivisions: the bioprogram hypothesis (4.3.1); pidgins and substratum (4.3.2); humans' place in pidgino- and creologenesis (4.3.3).

4.3.1 The bioprogram hypothesis

Contact-induced evolution is a defining feature of human societies. Its application to linguistics through creolistics, before gaining renewed interest in recent years, had already been stressed at the end of the 19th century in such pioneering work as Schuchardt 1979. This does not mean that internal factors are neglected, since it is, on the contrary, a methodological habit in linguistics to examine them first. However, internal factors may be conceived of in various ways. Thus, according to Bickerton (1981:XIII), "all members of our species are born with a bioprogram for language [...] which [...] comes partly from the species-specific structure of human perception and cognition, and partly from processes inherent in the expansion of a linear language." At this level of generality, any linguist would feel in agreement with Bickerton.

But later in his book, he applies this hypothesis to creoles: "[...] a creole language", he writes (1981:50-51), "has to have certain types of rules [...]; the creole will acquire such rules, not because they are in the input [...] but because they are required by the structure of the emerging language." There are important rules, however, which are not particularly required by the structure of the emerging language; this does not prevent them from being acquired by it, as we will see in 4.3.3 section a.) for verb focalization and serial verb construction. If we add that such rules, as far as Caribbean creoles are concerned, are abundantly represented in the African languages whose use (cf. 4.2.1) has in all likelihood lasted much longer than is generally assumed, we are obliged to conclude that internal motivations, important though they are, cannot explain everything. The rate of linguistic retention appears to be directly proportional to the degree of contact.

4.3.2 Pidgins and substratum

Not convinced by this line of reasoning, Bickerton dismisses the arguments of those for whom the similarity between many Caribbean creole structures and their equivalents in the African languages spoken in the countries where the slaves were bought is not quite irrelevant. He writes (1981:48):

> Substratomaniacs, if I may give them their convenient and traditional name, seem to be satisfied with selecting particular structures in one or more creole languages and showing that superficially similar structures can be found in one or more West African languages.

Bickerton does not quite exclude the possibility of a substratum; he simply thinks it is irrelevant; thus he adds (p.51):

> even if we accept the entire substratum case, the situation is not substantively changed; the first creole generation has merely acquired the kind of rule that it was programmed to acquire, and saved itself the trouble, so to speak, of having to invent something equivalent.

The best way to assess this view is to examine how it applies to particular systems within the creole languages. As early as 1974, Bickerton had attempted to account for the similarities between the verbal morpheme systems of creoles by appealing to innate features of human perception which, according to him, make up a part of the universal characteristics determining the form of human language. He observed that, in most cases, the Tense-Modality-Aspect (TMA) system was so organized that the morphemes expressed (retaining only the "+" value for simplicity's sake) +Anterior, i.e., very roughly, past (tense), +Irrealis, i.e., future, conditional, optative (modality), and +Nonpunctual, i.e., progressive-durative, habitual-iterative (aspect). Attempting to justify this organization, Bickerton (1975:124) writes that a speaker needs to be able (a) to know the order in which past events occurred (b) to distinguish between sensory input and the product of his imagination (c) to tell whether something happened once only, or was either repeated or protracted in some way (d) to distinguish states from actions. The first three capacities underlie the anterior, irrealis and nonpunctual categories respectively.

This universalist interpretation calls for some remarks. First, we do not know enough, as yet, about the functioning of the brain to be able to evaluate Bickerton's claim. It remains therefore gratuitous at the present stage of research, even though many would be happy if a serious biological basis were some day found to underlie the linguistic properties that are recognized to be an endowment of the human species. Second, the author leaves some points unexplained. We do not know, for instance, why the TMA morphemes, both as regards their sequence and their position with respect to the verb, which they are said to precede, should be ordered the way the author claims and not otherwise, nor does he show why their material realization is that of separate units. Third, Bickerton's assertions are mostly founded upon English- and French-based creoles, such as Jamaican, Sranan, Hawaiian pidgin and Hawaiian creole, Haitian, Guyanese, etc. But if we extend the examination to other pidgins and creoles whose study he neglects or explicitly rejects for such reasons as (alleged) lack of dependable or relevant data (1981:73 ff.), we see that their TMA systems are very different from his model. This applies, among others, to the by now well-studied Portuguese- and Dutch-based creoles: Senegal Kryol, Guinea-Bissau Crioulo, Portuguese creoles of the Cape Verde Islands and of the Gulf of Guinea Islands (Annobon, São Tomé, Príncipe), Sri Lanka Portuguese creole, Damão, Goa, Macao and Malacca Portuguese creoles (Stolz 1987b), as well as Berbice Dutch (Guyana) and Negerhollands (today on the Virgin Islands) (cf. Stolz 1986 and references cited there), let alone Afrikaans.

Bickerton does not quite ignore the data provided by Portuguese- and Dutch-based creoles. But while he discusses at length the problem raised, for his theory, by the fact that the Crioulo anterior marker *ba* contradicts his predictions since it "follows rather than precedes the main verb" (1981:77), he dismisses Senegal Kryol, which also has postverbal TMA markers, for the reason that it has a "checkered history" which makes its data irrelevant (p.74), – the linguist thus giving himself the comfortable possibility of making a decision as to which data fit the theory and which ones do not and consequently must be rejected. Furthermore, there is another creole, Berbice Dutch, which is unique among the Caribbean creoles, since it possesses both preverbal and postverbal TMA morphemes; Bickerton may not have had access before 1981 to Robertson 1979, the most detailed modern description of this language; anyway, Berbice Dutch is not even mentioned in the discussion. Now if we examine certain African languages, we immediately note that the position of TMA markers in Senegal Kryol is comparable with that observed in Mandinka and Fula, spoken in the same area as it, and that the Berbice Dutch TMA system is very reminiscent of that of Ijo, the language of most first speakers of Berbice Dutch (Smith *et al.* 1987). In addition, the TMA system, important though it is in Bickerton's theory, is of course not the only argument he uses against the "substratomaniacs". Now it so happens that the Portuguese- and Dutch-based creoles are also interesting in this inquiry. Some of them, contrary to the predictions, display a rich morphology, whose necessity in terms of bioprogram is far from obvious. One does not see what internal motivation may have brought about diminutive prefixes in Annobon (while Portuguese, the target language, has suffixes in this case), nor why Crioulo has a synthetic causative *-nta*: it is difficult not to compare these morphemes with those found, respectively, in Bantu (class prefixes) and in Malinke, i.e., the languages known to have been spoken by the ancestors of present speakers of Annobon and Crioulo (Stolz 1989). Besides, the case of Negerhollands deserves to be recalled: Stolz has shown (1986:29 ff.) that, in contradistinction to Bickerton's (1981:74) assertion, this creole is not quite extinct, and that the available data are more dependable than is believed; thus, it is not irrelevant to draw attention to the fact that besides comparatives whose structure follows the Dutch model, it also possesses some that resemble very much those of Ashanti-Twi, whose speakers are the ancestors of the present speakers of Negerhollands.

If we extend the inquiry, now, not only beyond the TMA system, but beyond the Portuguese- and Dutch-based creoles, and examine the Caribbean, African and American creoles that constitute the main material of many works, including Bickerton's, we cannot but note with other researchers the many morphological and syntactic similarities between these creoles and various African languages belonging to such stocks as West Atlantic, or Mande, or Benue-Congo, whose speakers invented the first pidgins some centuries ago. The following are some of the most often mentioned similarities (cf. Holm 1987); they belong to various fields of morphosyntax: nouns, verbs, nominal and verbal modifiers, relators, conjunctions:

- the noun is pluralized by adjunction of the 3PL personal morpheme: Jamaican, Papiamentu; *id.* in Ewe;
- the possessive and personal pronouns are materially identical; they are distinguished by the fact that the element they modify (mostly an element they precede) is a noun in one case, a verb in the other case: Haitian; *id.* in the Mande languages;
- adjectives and state verbs are functionally similar: Sranan; same thing in Yoruba;
- the (habitual and punctual) present is unmarked, as opposed to other tenses and to the moods and aspects: Jamaican, etc., like Yoruba, etc.;
- there is little or no passive morphology: Jamaican, etc.; same thing in the Kwa languages;
- "give" is grammaticalized into a dative or beneficial relator meaning "to", "for", "in favor of", "for the sake of": Haitian, Saramaccan; *id.* in Twi;
- "pass", "go beyond" is grammaticalized into a conjunction meaning "than" after a word or phrase expressing a comparison: Príncipe, Gullah; *id.* in Ewe;
- the same element, according to the context and to the functions of the units it links together, means either "with" or "and": Papiamentu; same thing in Yoruba.

For Bickerton, this massive body of evidence based on substratal influences is not convincing. His main argument in favor of a universalist and nativist hypothesis is in fact an indirect one: it is because neither contact nor substratum can, according to him, account for the similarities between creoles that he sees his bioprogram as the only possible explanation. In his view, therefore, using substratal evidence is no more than following an old recipe which resorts to accumulation. But in fact, the arguments of most authors pointing to structural correlations between creoles and African languages are just as solid, and their method just as well founded, as those used by 19th and early 20th century comparatists in order to set up the world's largest linguistic families, on whose basis most linguists, including Bickerton, go on working today. Bickerton's eagerness to dismiss substratal influence is based on the conviction that if it were a good explanation, it should explain everything, as he thinks his strong nativist hypothesis does.

According to such a view, in other words, for a language to be considered as the substratum of another language, there should be complete correspondence between their systems (Bickerton 1985). In fact, most studies devoted to the subject (starting from Weinreich's (1964) classic) have shown that the normal situation here is interference and partial retention. This reflects the complex process by which human languages are formed. This complexity casts some doubts on *the metaphysical attitude which consists in believing that a single theoretical framework must account for everything*, and that all other frameworks must consequently be rejected, as if they were themselves inspired by the same metaphysical approach. Such an attitude, it is true, may lead one to a strong and explicit formulation of a theory, thus making this theory easier to falsify, but it also results in concealing a part of the facts.

4.3.3 The place of humans in pidgino- and creologenesis

Given the specific conditions in which pidginogenesis occurred in the Caribbean, the slaves could neither forget their African languages completely, nor remain monolinguals using these languages. There is no reason either to reject the substratum entirely, or to deny any participation of the (still largely unknown, but no doubt important) biological factors which account for a part of the process of linguistic morphogenesis. The substratum does not have the power of explaining everything, but even if we do not accept as sufficient proofs the striking similarities between various African languages on the one hand, and, on the other hand, Gullah (Turner 1949) or English and French creoles of the Caribbean such as spoken in Jamaica, Guyana, Trinidad or Haiti (Allsopp 1977, Wingerd 1977), we cannot easily dismiss substratal factors in favor of a totally antisubstratist view inspired by universal grammar. This is particularly the case when the features found in creoles and likewise in African languages, far from being a natural answer to the common requirements of human communication as defined by the bioprogram, are not expected at all. Two often discussed examples of this situation are verb focalization and serial verb constructions. It is even more difficult to deny the substratum when the source language is still perfectly alive and spoken as a mother tongue by bilinguals. These three points will be treated in the following sections:

a. Verb focalization in creoles and African languages
b. Verb serialization in creoles and African languages
c. Pidgins, bilinguals, and the notion of substratum.

a. *Verb focalization in creoles and African languages*

Focalization is an operation by which a word or a phrase within a sentence receives emphasis. In order to focalize a noun or NP, all human languages possess intonational devices, and many have structural devices in addition. Creoles do not differ from other languages in that respect. In Seychelles Creole, for example, we find such sentences as

(146)   *sa divâ ki n kas ban brâs*
          (DEM wind REL PERF break PL branch)
          "it is the wind which has broken the branches" (Corne 1987:94).

Here the focalized NP is the subject. The same device is used if the NP to be focalized is not the subject; thus, in English, if the object is focalized, we get, instead of the translation of (146),

(147)   *it is the branches which the wind has broken.*

But most Indo-European languages do not have comparable devices to focalize the verb; they resort, in that case, to an intonational strategy, or to adverbs, like English *actually*. In contradistinction to that, many creoles possess a very specific structure, in which the verb appears twice, i.e., first, fronted, often with a focalizer morpheme or a copula, and then in a complete structure, i.e., along with its *verbants*, if any. Although some creoles, like Haitian, also use this structure, on occasion, with an adverbial (temporal, causal, concessive) meaning, it is mostly a focalization device. Here are some examples, from Haitian ((148)), Djuka ((149)), Papiamentu ((150)) and Jamaican ((151)):

(148)   *se malad tifi-a malad*
          (FOC ill girl-ART ill)
          "the girl is ill" (Piou 1982:123)

(149)   *na kii mi dda kii tu pakila*
         (FOC kill my father kill two peccary)
         "my father killed two peccaries" (Huttar 1975:15)

(150)   *ta kôre e ta kôre baj*
         (FOC run he PROGR run go)
         "he is running away, actually" (Taylor 1977:183)

(151)   *a no tiif kofi tiif di manggo*
         (FOC NEG steal K. steal the mango)
         "Kofi did not *steal* the mango" (he *bought* it) (Bailey
                                                          1966:95).

Such structures are abundantly represented in Kwa languages of West
Africa like Twi ((152) below, from Alleyne 1980:172) or Yoruba ((153),
from Bamgbose 1966:56):

(152)   *hwe na kwasi hwe ase*
         (fall is K. fall down)
         "Kwasi actually fell"

(153)   *mi~mú ni wón mú mi*
         (NMLZ~take COP they took me)
         "they actually arrested me".

(153) shows that in order to be focalized, the verb must, at least in Yoruba,
be nominalized; thus, the question remains open whether the element
appearing after FOC or NEG in (148)-(151) is a verb or a noun, since in
most creoles, there is no *morphological* distinction between verbs and
nouns. But asking this question implies that the Atlantic creoles must be
structurally related to the Kwa languages, which leads us back to the main
issue: are the Kwa languages the substratum? To those whose answer is
yes, Bickerton objects (1981:48-49) that in order for that to be true, we
must assume that a given rule of, say, Yoruba syntax

   passed from Yoruba into the antecedent pidgins of a number of creoles, and
   thence into those creoles. For this to have happened, a substantial number of
   Yoruba speakers must have been present during the pidgin phase in each

area, or at least no later than the earliest phase of creolization. If not, if a substantial number did not arrive in a given area until after the creole had been formed, then previous speakers would hardly abandon the rules they themselves had arrived at and replace them with new rules, unless the number of Yoruba was so great as to constitute an absolute majority – and that, to the best of present knowledge, was never true at any time for any Caribbean territory.

This line of reasoning may well be valid with respect to Caribbean creoles. But if Bickerton's requirement is not met in this case, it is met in another case, which he could not mention in 1981: Mauritius and Seychelles creoles, thoroughly studied in Baker 1982. Like the Caribbean creoles, Mauritian creole has verb focalization; the fronted verb may be followed by the relative *ki,* like the focalized noun in Seychelles creole (cf. (146)):

(154)   *âraze ki mo ti âraze*
          (furious REL I PAST furious)
          "I was hopping mad" (Corne 1987:95).

This structure is unattested in French: contrary to Corne's (1987:103) assertion,

(155)   *pour (ce qui est d') être malade, il a été bien malade*
          "he was as sick as a dog"

is not simply a case of focalization, but of topicalization followed by focalization: something is predicated about *être malade,* i.e., its high degree of realization. But this structure is well-attested in Bantu, as is shown by (156) and (157), from Haya and Makuwa respectively (Corne 1987:101):

(156)   *oku~lya tu-ka-lya*
          (INF~eat 1PL-PAST-eat)
          "we really ate"

(157)   *o~khoma ki-ā-na-khoma*
          (INF~hit 1SG-PAST-PROGR-hit)
          "I was really hitting hard".

In addition, there is a high incidence of (French etymological) article + noun agglutination in Mauritian creole: whereas Haitian and Lesser Antillean have been found to contain, roughly, about 100 nouns having an initial syllable wholly derived from a French article, the number of such nouns amounts to 450 in Mauritian creole, according to one of its best specialists, C. Corne, who adds (1987:104): "The high incidence of agglutination is undoubtedly due to the perception by Bantu speakers of French articles as elements akin to the class markers which obligatorily co-occur with nouns in Bantu languages".

These two facts would not by themselves be sufficient to prove that Mauritius and Seychelles creoles come from a Bantu substratum, were it not for the existence of another decisive fact: Baker 1982 has shown that the last third of the 18th century "saw an overwhelming majority of East Africans among all arrivals [...], this period of massive numerical preponderance of Bantu speakers coinciding with a crucial period in the emergence of Mauritian creole." After presenting in these terms Baker's results, Corne writes (1987:102):

> An earlier period of pidginization (inadequate second-language learning by adults) and creolization (first-language learning with variable input according to the individual's position in ethnosocial space) must have been ending around 1774, when the number of locally-born slaves exceeded, for the first time, the number of members of the French-speaking 'ruling-class'. The period of the rapid development of a homogeneous creole language, the jelling of Mauritian creole, must have been from about this time (1774) to around 1810, when an end was put to the regular introduction of foreign-born slaves.

In Bickerton's view, however, even this argument is not sufficient, since he considers (cf. 4.3.1) that a creole acquires certain rules not because they are in the input, but because the structure of the emerging language requires them. According to Bickerton, if verb focalization is required here, it is because most creoles have VP, but not V, as a major category. If no copy were left at the extraction site when V is fronted, interpretation difficulties would arise, so that "any language with movement rules that involve V only, rather than VP, must develop a copying rule [...]. No borrowing from any other language would be required." (1981:55). But Bickerton does not demonstrate that Guyanese creole, the language on which this reasoning is based, actually has V, rather than VP, as a major category; he only writes (p.54) that this is "highly probable". In addition, he does not define what he exactly means by "major category", nor does he show to what extent he is justified in treating verb focalization as a transformational rule in the Chomskyan sense, with all the implications of such a treatment. Moreover, he does not wonder whether the absence of verb focalization in Hawaiian Creole English – which, according to him, has VP as opposed to Guyanese creole, which has V (p.53) – could not be brought into correlation with the absence of African input. Finally, no data from child language acquisition is provided here, as should be done in order to show that verb focalization belongs to the bioprogram. Consequently, there are no compelling arguments here to show that verb focalization was required by the structure of the emerging language, and that the African input has played no role.

b. *Verb serialization in creoles and African languages*
    Serial verb construction is another interesting feature which is widely found in Caribbean creoles as well as in the Kwa and Kru languages of Africa, from Liberia to Cameroon. By juxtaposing two or more V(P)s, or two or more V(P)s + N(P)s associations, this construction serves to express a variety of meanings: the splitting up, into successive steps, of an action, as in Sranan (158) and Yoruba (159); an action followed by its result, as in Saramaccan (160) and Ewe (161); an action and its instrument, as in Jamaican (162) and Fanti (163); an action and its (mostly human) beneficiary as in Jamaican (164) and Yoruba (165); or an action and the concrete or abstract participant that accompanies it, as in Gullah (166) and Ewe (167):

(158)   *a pitjin e teki skropu tjar go na atrasee*
          (the child is taking shells carry go to other-side)
          "the child is carrying shells to the other side" (Alleyne 1980:92)

(159)   *ó mú ọbẹ wá*
          (he pick~up knife come)
          "he brought a knife" (Welmers 1973:375)

(160)   *de suti en kii*
          (they shoot him kill)
          "they shot him to death" (Alleyne, *ibid.*:93)

(161)   *e no tsi ku*
         (he drink water die)
         "he died because of the water he had drunk"
         (Alleyne, *ibid.*:169; tones not provided)

(162)   *im tek naif kot mi*
         (he take knife cut me)
         "he cut me with a knife" (Alleyne, *ibid.*:93)

(163)   *me de sekan twaa nam*
         (I take knife cut meat)
         "I cut the meat with a knife" (Alleyne, *ibid.*:168; tones not
         provided)

(164)   *kya di buk kom gi mi*
         (bring the book come give me)
         "bring the book for me" (Alleyne, *ibid.*:94)

(165)   *gbé wá fún mí*
         (lift come give me)
         "bring it for me" (Alleyne, *ibid.*:170)

(166)   *dɛm gain tɛk dɛm go bak*
         (they going take them go back)
         "they are returning with them" (Alleyne, *ibid.*:93)

(167)   *è tsɔ dɔmè gegi yi afé*
         (he take empty belly go home)
         "he went home hungry" (Alleyne, *ibid.*:168).

We will return later (7.4.1) to this structure, which, in cases like those
illustrated by (162), (164), (165), (166) and (167) often provides the
framework for the genesis of relators. According to Bickerton (1981:120),
one may suppose that "creoles and West African languages invented verb
serialization independently, but for slightly different reasons". Later (p.
130-131), he adds: "Verb serialization is the only answer to the problem
of marking cases in languages which have only N and V as major categories", meaning that creoles necessarily had to resort to this device since

they have no relators (prepositions) at their early stages; they are only beginning to acquire them, like Sranan, which "this process serves to bring [...] structurally closer to the high-prestige language, Dutch". But even if it were true that creoles acquire relators because LBs are in a hurry to make them look as much as possible like their prestigious models, why is verb serialization, while present in many non-creole languages of South-East Asia, New Guinea, etc., absent from *bona fide* creoles which also lacked prepositions before beginning, at a recent stage, to acquire them, i.e., Mauritian, Reunion and Seychelles creoles? Strikingly enough, we are dealing there with those very creoles whose speakers, as recalled above, were still, at the early period of pidginogenesis, users of Bantu languages, i.e., languages in which verb serialization is not found either: in Bantu languages, by a particular application of the principle according to which there is a crosslinguistic division of labor (cf. 2.1.2), the indication of nominal functions is dealt with not by verb serialization, but by another type of VS (cf. *ibid.*), i.e., a rich verbal morphology, with various affixes in correlation with nominal complements.

c. *Pidgins, bilinguals, and the notion of substratum*
    There are cases in which the influence of the source language, whether we call it substratum or not, is obvious, simply because, far from having been replaced by a creole, it is the living mother tongue of bilinguals, as African languages were in the Caribbean before the beginning of creolization. In one of the cases referred to here, which is represented by Bichela-mar, a pidgin spoken in Vanuatu, the Melanesian languages are not threatened with extinction, because the social situation is quite different. Bichela-mar speakers are not slaves bought and transferred to plantations. The pidgin is simply a useful means of communication for them, since their Melanesian mother tongues are fairly diverse, from one island to the other as well as on the same island. Bickerton dismisses Tok Pisin, whose structure, lexicon and social environment are, in several respects, fairly close to those of Bichelamar. The reason he gives to justify this dismissal is that Tok Pisin has "arisen under circumstances so vastly different from those of the classic creoles that the fact that it is now some people's native language – hence, nominally a creole – has no bearing on the present discussion" (1981:74). Such a selection of data is of course alien to the very inspiration of the present book, in which LBs' conscious and unconscious activity is examined in all its complex manifestations, not in order

to confirm a preconcerted theoretical project, but in order to reach a general characterization which tells us something about the relationship between man and the languages he builds.

To mention just one particular example of substratal pressure, we know (Charpentier 1979) that -*im*, the marker of transitivity characteristic of Bichelamar (and of Tok Pisin), is substantially English (*him*) but structurally Melanesian (a type of hybridization typical of pidgins): all the Melanesian languages spoken by the bilingual inhabitants of Vanuatu possess a verbal affix which marks transitive verbs as such. Charpentier has even noted that the variations he observes within Bichelamar faithfully reflect the features of the various Melanesian languages spoken throughout the archipelago.

4.4 Conclusion

LBs have built new languages by using human capacities to fulfil human requirements in the process of communication. In the case of Caribbean creoles, LBs have both been inspired, in their subliminal building work, by universal tendencies thanks to which they have resolved various problems of expression, and influenced by the structures of their former African tongues, to which they have adapted the lexicon provided by the social (European) environment. This conflation of universal and local forces is precisely what makes pidgino- and creologenesis: a single theoretical model is unable to explain everything. Bickerton's 1981 dedication credits creole speakers with the merit of having fought "for decency, dignity and freedom against the Cartesian savagery of Western colonialists and slavemakers", and thus offering us "indispensable keys to the knowledge of our species". But this does not take into account the dignity and freedom with which creolophones preserved and continue to preserve their identity by combining, in their languages, inherited structures and European elements. Far from that, Bickerton uses, as have many others, the concept of decreolization (1981:46-47, 191 ff., etc.), which, like DeCamp's 1971 "post-creole continuum", implies that creole speakers are eager to lead their languages back to respectable models, as if their dignity and freedom did not consist in claiming their mother tongues as parts of their identity whatever the origins of these tongues, but in making them closer to English and other European languages. Jamaican, for instance, is often mentioned as a case of post-creole continuum. In fact, in Jamaican, as in other languages, there are various styles, and no indication that the style which is closest to English as for the rate of lexical and syntactic borrowing represents the future or destiny of the whole language. As Lawton writes (1985:75), Jamaican creole, "far from lapsing into a post-creole situation (DeCamp 1971:29), is alive and well".

The constant morphogenetic work of LBs must be studied as it is, and it was my aim in the foregoing to show the variety of factors which contribute to it in the specific field of creologenesis.

CHAPTER 5

LBs and the
linguistic cycle

If linguistic evolution is commonly thought to follow a linear path, this is simply an illusion produced by the shallowness of most people's perspective on language change. In the known cases of languages whose history is documented over a very long period of time, we observe the regular return of phenomena which, as an effect of short-sighted intuition, were believed to be buried forever in a remote past. The reason for the cyclical nature of linguistic evolution is not far to seek: as shown above in 2.3 and schematized in (49) there is a dialectical relationship between various needs felt by LBs in communicating. The action of opposite tendencies such as ease of production and search for expressiveness results in a permanent conflict which is resolved, depending on the period, in one or the other direction.

In order to characterize the LBs' presence in the cyclical processes which are typical of the evolution of languages, I will begin with a definition of the notion of cycle (5.1). I will then study the role played by expressiveness in the cyclical renewal of linguistic systems (5.2). After that, I will examine certain curves within cycles (5.3), and finally, complete cycles when they are documented (5.4). It will thus appear in this chapter that attention to the cyclical nature of language evolution as reflecting LBs' needs and tendencies is more revealing than mechanistic conceptions.

5.1 Cycle and spiral

The study of the linguistic cycle comes as a natural conclusion to that of creologenesis just presented in chapter 4. The alternation of analytical and synthetical phases shows it clearly. We know that pidgins tend to have an analytical structure, like isolating languages, whereas in creoles, we often see the first steps of a fusional morphology. A simple illustration is provided by the following evolutionary scheme of the 1SG.FUT in Romance:

(168)   Classical Latin *cantabo* → Late Latin *cantare habeo* → Early
            Romance **cantar(e) ávyo* → French *(je) chanterai* → Haitian
            Pidgin [*mo apye šãte*] → Haitian Creole *m'ap-chanté* "I will
            sing" (Hagège 1988a:277).

This evolution is an illustration of the cycle which leads from a synthetical to another synthetical structure across an analytic phase. But things are
in fact less simple. First, because this evolutionary scheme involves different languages rather than the history of a single one: French is not simply
a phase in the history of Latin, but another language; and Haitian pidgin
and creole have developed (partly) from French, but do not represent its
contemporary stage. Furthermore, the *-b-* of *cantabo* is the Latin reflex of
an Indo-European verb "to be", **bhʷ*; thus *cantabo* follows a retraceable
analytic stage **canta-fu-o*; but *cantabo* itself would not have been systematically replaced by *cantare habeo* if the Christian theologians who widely
spread this form (already present, but sparsely, in Classical Latin) had not
needed it in order to render the notion of predestination: for such a notion
the Latin future, mainly expressing an intentional or potential sense, was
inadequate (Benveniste 1968). Thus, the LBs made a periphrastic form
corresponding to a sociocultural need. It also corresponded to a general
trend towards analytic formation in both verb and noun. At the end of a
period of coexistence between the classical synthetic and the new analytic
future, the latter eventually replaced the former in all its uses, and *cantabo*
disappeared. In Haitian pidgin, [*mo apye šãte*], literally "me after sing",
results from the prefixation of the adverb *apye* "after" to the verb stem, an
analytic process reminiscent of the one used in West African languages,
many of which have separate tense-aspect morphemes. Finally, the reduction and fusion of the personal pronoun and future marker in Haitian creole
as shown in (168) illustrate the return to a synthetical stage, thus completing the cycle.

The notion of cycle has undergone various criticisms. Thus, Jespersen
reacted against the formulation of a cyclical conception which was preva-
lent in the end of the 19th and beginning of the 20th centuries, and according to which the inflectional structure resulting from the fusion of the root
with the grammatical element previously agglutinated to it had been
followed by a stage of disintegration leading to the decay of the old Indo-
European architecture. Commenting on his reaction, he writes later (1941:7,
quoted in Hodge 1970:2): "To this, I objected, trying to show that viewed

from the point of view of human energetics so far from being retrogressive the tendency in historical times has on the whole been a progressive one." If he means thereby that there is an uninterrupted constructional work done by human beings on their languages, we can only agree, of course, given the conception which underlies the present book. In fact, there is no reason to interpret the successive phases in terms of progress and degeneracy. The problem with the notion of cycle would rather be this: it seems to imply that the same process recurs once the last curve of the cycle is completed and a new cycle starts. Moreover, "the introduction of new for frozen lexical material usually takes place before the existing grammatical element has disappeared" (Heine & Reh 1984:70). Therefore, the notion of spiral, already used in Gabelentz (1891:251), would seem to better reflect the facts. But it is no less metaphoric than the notion of cycle, and much less usual. Consequently, the notion of cycle, imperfect though it is, will be retained here.

The passage from one linguistic type to another may be hastened by cultural habits such as articulatory gestures. Stress shift, affix erosion, assimilations and the requirement for equal phonetic weight, in particular, must be mentioned as some of the important factors that trigger typological evolution. The general scenario is as follows: at a given stage, there is an association of full words in the sense of Chinese grammarians as recalled in Hagège (1975:23-25), and these words indicate their interrelations by their very meaning (semantics); as the boundary between stem and affixes is more and more blurred in those which are complex units, these units are less and less distinguished by morphological marks, and the role of word order increases, the result being an isolating type of language; at the following stage, grammatical words begin to appear, which distinguish themselves from lexemes by their function in the sentence (syntax); then grammatical and lexematic words tend to combine into unified complex words, a new kind of association appears, and the language becomes agglutinative; at a subsequent stage, this organization itself yields, in many languages, complex units, in which the indication of syntactic relationships becomes frozen (morphology); the unstressed parts of the words undergo conditioned sound changes, which eventually become phonemic as the conditions disappear; at that stage, a formerly agglutinative language is already in the process of acquiring stem-internal phoneme alternations, which means that it is becoming inflectional; its words then split into independent units, and a new cycle begins.

5.2 Expressiveness and the cyclical renewal of linguistic systems

The search for expressiveness, which appears as a leading force in the evolution of languages, is often responsible for the revival of a frozen structure. But its scope is much broader than the synthesis-analysis dialectics illustrated in most of the cases studied in 5.4. Even when linguistic systems seem to have reached a kind of balance, the demotivation of many formulations brings about the need to remotivate them. The result is often an analytical stage in a cycle, but analysis and synthesis are just terms used by linguists in order to characterize the structure at a given stage. LBs are unconsciously striving to make their speech clearer, by splitting words into elements or adding new elements. Speakers of Late Latin who said *cantare habeo* were doing just that; they were not "practising an analysis". From the LBs' viewpoint, using, without metalinguistic knowledge, what professional linguists call separate words, instead of bound morphemes, rule-governed clitics, obligatory affixes, or *a fortiori*, fused elements whose form and meaning cannot be traced back short of researching their etymology, has three advantages: first, it provides speakers with a mode of expression that seems sharply articulated; second, it stresses the speaker's message and makes it appear more important; third, it has a stronger effect on the hearer. The prepositional phrases of Late Egyptian (5.4.2 below), the predicative participles of Aramaic (5.4.3 section a.), the directive verbs of Tibeto-Burman languages (5.4.4) have replaced conjugated forms or independent lexemes which, becoming more and more frequent and unanalyzable, were losing most of their strength.

Thus, the synthesis-analysis dialectics is only one aspect of the competition between various forces. In order to show the importance of the search for expressiveness as one of these forces, I will study two of the main fields in which it manifests itself; one is related to phonology, the other to morphology. I will, therefore, successively deal with the following two cyclical phenomena: reduplication (5.2.1); negation (5.2.2).

5.2.1 Reduplication. The enrichment of phonemic systems

It is a natural tendency for LBs to use partial or total reduplication as an expressive device. Ideophones (1.3.1 section e.) are a typical illustration. But reduplication is also used, in many languages, to render such meanings as plurality, distributivity, intensity, iteration. Probably one of the oldest word formation devices in language, reduplication is often considered iconic (e.g., in Haiman 1980:530), because the formal phenomenon seems to mimic the semantic content: the repetition of linguistic material seems to reflect the repetition of states or actions denoted by adjectives and verbs, as in Lahu (Matisoff 1973:292), or the plurality of participants (in syntactic terms, subject or object), as in Comox (Hagège 1981c:116); in the noun, reduplication reflects the multiplication of things or notions, i.e., plural or iteration; in Malay, plural nouns are formed by total reduplication; some cases of total reduplication in Japanese also correspond to the plural, or to an iterative meaning, e.g., *hito* "man" → *hitobito* "men, people", *toki* "time" → *tokidoki* "sometimes": in these two examples, a voicing process known as *rendaku* applies, according to which the initial consonant, if any, of the second member of a compound generally gets voiced, unless there is, already, a voiced obstruent. In several Micronesian languages, such as Marshallese, Trukese, Woleaian (Harrison 1973) there are verb inflections by reduplicative derivation, yielding various results, aspectual and others: imperfective, distributive, stative, intransitive (often in association with an incorporated object), plural (indicating plurality of the subject or the object), etc. Comparable facts exist in Indo-European, where the perfect of Classical Greek, referring to the still lasting result of a past event, is formed by the reduplication of the first syllable, a device originally expressive but already demotivated and frozen, in the 5th century B.C., into a mere morphological mechanism.

In all the cases mentioned so far, reduplication, although used on a large scale, has not modified the phonemic system. But in four Melanesian languages, the process has resulted in the enrichment of the phonemic system by the creation of new aspirated consonants: a consonant-initial word gets expressive reduplication; the interconsonantic vowel thus created is then lost; the two consonants thus put into contact yield a single *fortis* consonant, often becoming aspirated. The process sometimes goes even further: a high tone appears on the following vowel, due to the laryngeal tenseness of unvoiced initial consonants, just like in languages of South-East Asia (Hagège & Haudricourt 1978:94-100). In the four Melanesian languages presented below, the line of evolution, given initial syllables like *pa-* and *no-*, is as follows (Hagège & Haudricourt 1978:117-122):

(169) a.   1) *pa-*   2) *papa-*   3) *pha-* 4) *pá*
       b.   1) *no-*   2) *nono-*   3) *nho* 4) *nó*.

The four languages are Cèmuhî, spoken in New Caledonia, and three languages spoken in the neighboring Loyalty Islands: Iaai, Drehu and Nengone. Stage 4) in (169)a and b is illustrated by Cèmuhî. Stage 3) is illustrated by Iaai and, to a lesser extent, by Drehu and Nengone. In Iaai, the process has created unvoiced aspirated consonants, such as *x*, *hl*, and *hn*; these appear in (170)b, as initials of verbs used in association with an incorporated object (recall Micronesian above) and showing complex vowel inflections; the first stage in the development of these verbs were expressive reduplicated forms derived from the simple transitive verbs in (170)a:

(170) a. *kap* "to lift" b. *xöp*
       la   "to burrow"   *hle*
       naŋ "to wave"   *hnöŋ* (Ozanne-Rivierre 1986:30).

In Drehu and Nengone, the last syllable is sometimes also reduplicated, along with the first one; this, here again, has brought about a new series of aspirated consonants; reduplication corresponds, in this case, to an intensive meaning:

(171) | Drehu | Nengone | |
|---|---|---|
| *mano* | *nono* | "to breathe" |
| *hmanono* | *hnenono* | "to get out of breath" |
| *mek* | *(wa)nec* | "to close one's eyes" |
| *hmek* | *hneco(n)* | "to sit up late". |

(Ozanne-Rivierre 1986:31).

This fossilization of expressive forms by syllable reduction has enriched the phonemic systems of the languages in question, but it has also resulted in an impoverishment of the means of morphological distinction. However, interestingly enough, LBs have renewed the expressive process, as is shown in the three languages of the Loyalty Islands, by applying reduplication not only to original words, but also to words already derived from original roots by reduplication. The second reduplication is either partial or total. It is partial in (172), from Drehu, and total in (173), from Iaai. In both, we have an aspirated nasal initial, whose genesis is as schematized in (169)b 1)-3), and the second reduplication corresponds to the beginning of a new cycle. (174)a and b, from Iaai, are even more revealing: in these two examples, the three stages are all represented (Ozanne-Rivierre 1986:44):

(172)   *hmakaany* "morning"   *hmaahmakaany*   "early in
                                                the morning"

(173)   *hŋele*   "to watch"   *hŋelehŋele*   "to watch all
                                                around"
(174)

a. *ken* "to twist" *xin* "to twist (with INC.OBJ)"   *xixin* "to have
                                                         crooked legs"
b. *mëtr* "ripe"   *hmëtr* "ripe (banana)"   *hmëhmëtr* "quite
                                                         ripe".

5.2.2 Negation and Expressive Renewal (ER)

Expressive reduplication, which thus results in the enrichment of phonemic systems, is also a frequent phenomenon in the field of negation.
Negation changes the meaning of a sentence into its contrary. Due to this
semantic importance, the speaker often stresses it strongly, both to mark its
role and to make sure that the hearer will perceive it clearly. This is the
reason why it is often open to ER.

The ER of negation was already emphasized by Jespersen who, in a
passage (1917:4) presenting what Dahl 1979 calls "Jespersen's cycle",
wrote:

> The history of negative expressions in various languages makes us witness
> the following curious fluctuation: the original negative adverb is first weak-
> ened, then found insufficient, and therefore strengthened, generally through
> some additional word, and this in turn may then in course of time be subject
> to the same evolution as the original word.

This process is well-known in French and in Afrikaans (the latter being
similar in that respect to Middle Dutch, which had an embracing negation).
The strengthening stage of the evolution may result in a discontinuous
negation, as shown by Modern Written French, Moore and Burmese
(Hagège 1982:86).

Much less studied is the ER which opposes not a continuous and a
discontinuous negation, but two distinct negative structures whose difference consists in the addition of a strengthening element. In Modern Literary Arabic, the negation of the perfective is a morpheme *lam*, which

appears not before the perfective itself, but before a form of the imperfective, i.e., the prefixal form characterized by the apocope of the final vowel, and also used to express the imperative. In Preclassical Arabic, represented by the Qor'an, another negative structure was also used, consisting of the negation *mâ* plus the imperfective, itself a suffixal form. This choice has almost disappeared in Modern Literary Arabic, despite its close resemblance with Preclassical Arabic; modern writers normally use the first structure, reserving the second one to very specific contexts, or to the fairly rare cases in which they cultivate archaic formulations. However, Western specialists often claim that "the choice between *mâ* with perfect and *lam* with jussive is one of style" (Abboud & McCarus 1983:II, 241).

Even if applied to Preclassical Arabic, this claim would remain false. It is contradicted by the Arabian grammatical tradition. For example, Al-Zamaḫšarî (12th century) writes (1981) that "*mâ* is used to negate the present [...] and to negate the past which is close to the present". The same view is to be found in the main commentary on Al-Zamaḫšarî, written one century later by Ibn Yaʕîš (Kouloughli 1988:53-54). Thus, with *faʕala* "he did" (the verb taken as a model in the grammatical tradition), *lam yafʕal* is "he did not do", whereas *mâ faʕala* is "he has not done", and always implies a modalization of the sentence, i.e., the personal involvement of the speaker, referring either to a non-distant past or to a distant past which, however, is considered still valid in the present. Therefore, *mâ faʕala* has the properties of a perfect. In fact, along with *lam yafʕal* and with *faʕala*, the positive corresponding to these two negative structures, *mâ faʕala* represents one of the stages of a historical process which is schematized in (175):

(175)

Affirmative perfective		Negative perfective
a. 1st stage *yafʕal* (AO and PERF) (Prehistoric)		*lam yafʕal* (AO and PERF)
b. 2nd stage *faʕala* (Preclassical Arabic (Qor'an))	"	*mâ faʕala* / *lam yafʕal* (PERF) (AO)

c. 3rd stage *faʕala*   "   *mâ faʕala* (AO and PERF)
   (Middle Arabic)
d. 4th stage *faʕala*   "   *lam yaffal*   "
   (Modern Literary Arabic).

We may hypothesize (cf. Kouloughli 1988:64-65) that originally the perfective *yaffal* expressed both observed events and evoked events. Observation is the basis of evocation, at least in its first stages. But forms referring to observed events constantly tend to acquire an evocatory content. We may call Aoristic Drift Principle (ADP) this tendency, which is dialectically opposed to ER. As examples (cf. Boulle 1987), we may mention the French simple present, which often takes a narrative value referring to past events; as for Koine Greek, just like Sanskrit when compared with Vedic, it had lost the Classical Greek perfect, which, however, reappeared in Modern Greek; most Slavic languages lost the Old Slavonic aorist, but it survived in Serbo-Croatian and Bulgarian.

In Arabic as represented by (175), a remarkable phenomenon occurred between the 1st and the 2nd stages. This phenomenon characterizes the verbal system of many languages, and is an important one in the perspective of the present book. Given the ADP, *yaffal* progressively lost its modal value. So a new form was needed. As often happens, the one which was chosen was a nominal form, meaning an acquired state that results from a certain event: *faʕala* is originally a nominal form which, by its static-resultative meaning, makes it possible to gear the sentence with the present situation of the speaker, thus recalling similar effects of other means of ER, like "be" and "have" auxiliaries. However, expressive forms get frozen in the long run: the first phase of stage b in (175) is innovative; *faʕala* is a newly introduced expressive form with the modal meaning of a perfect; but later, it eliminates *yaffal* and therefore takes over its aoristic value, adding a tense indication to a mood indication; thus, in a second phase of (175)b, it becomes, in its turn, the unmarked form; but in the negative perfective, *mâ faʕala* still keeps the meaning it had when it appeared as a marked form: thus it stands in opposition, as a perfect, to *lam yaffal*, the unmarked form. This opposition disappears in the third stage, where *mâ faʕala* becomes the only negative form, with both perfect and aoristic values. This has provided the basis of the negative perfective in the Arabic dialects. However, in most of them, the need for ER has brought about the adjunction of *š(i)* "thing" after the verb, strengthening the negation into the discontinuous *mâ... š(i)*, characteristic of Western and many Eastern dialects of Arabic.

The interesting aspect of the final stage (175)d is that, while in the positive *faʕala* continues to exist as the unmarked form, meaning both aorist and perfect, in the negative *lam yaffal* comes back again. Kouloughli (1988:68) tries to explain this situation, which he calls "a case of linguistic teratology", by the artificial character of Modern Written Arabic, which is generally considered as not corresponding to any really spoken language. In fact, a literary language which has continuously been used in all written styles is a concrete linguistic object, just as much as any of the dialects. In this light, the return of *lam yaffal* can appear as the beginning of a new cycle, since it reproduces the first stage, represented by (175)a. It is true that this stage is not attested but reconstructed. But comparison of stages 2 and 3 makes it very likely, let alone that, as expected in a cyclical process, it is the originally unmarked term, not the one newly introduced in stage 2 as being marked, which comes back.

5.3 Curves within cycles

Such evolutions as those described in 5.2 usually extend, except in special cases like that of pidginogenesis (cf. 4.2.2), over huge periods amounting to several millennia. Unfortunately, the available material often shows us only one curve of the cycle, leading from a synthetic stage to an analytic stage, or the reverse. We can see this when we compare, for instance, the present states of Indo-European and Uralic languages. While many of the former have reduced or lost their declension cases, the latter have often increased the number of theirs, and still go on increasing it, as is witnessed, among other illustrations, by Modern Hungarian (cf. 7.3.1). Within Uralic languages, Zyrian and Votjak are clearly agglutinative, whereas Estonian, Livonian, and Lappish present stem-internal alternations, portmanteau morphs, and fused boundaries which make them fairly close to the inflectional type (Korhonen 1982). An important factor, in Estonian for example, was the loss of the final marker of the genitive *-n*, which, before disappearing, had brought about a weakening, often followed by the deletion, of the first consonant of the syllable closed by this *-n*. Thus, the balance between syllable weights is preserved by the deletion of elements which make a word quantitatively heavy. When, due to this deletion, two vowels originally belonging to two distinct syllables separated by a consonant became contiguous, high vowels were lowered by assimilation to a preceding or following *a*, as in (176)a, and two adjacent high vowels were both lowered by analogy with the general lowering of high vowels, as in (176)b. Thus, we have in Estonian (Hagège 1990c:302-303):

(176) a.   NOMIN.SG *madu*   "snake"   GEN.SG *mao*
           NOMIN.SG *viga*   "error"   GEN.SG *vea*
       b.   NOMIN.SG *tigu*   "snail"   GEN.SG *teo*.

Palauan is an even more striking case of a language acquiring fusional features, while the languages of its stock (Austronesian) are mostly agglutinative. Consider (177) (Hagège 1986:29, 42-43, 80):

(177) a.   *ʔjull*   "cushion"   *ʔill-ék*   "my cushion"
           ker   "question"   *kər-íδ*   "our (INCL) question"
       b.   *mə-ŋímδ*   "to trim"   *kmuδ-l*   "having to be trimmed"
           mə-lésəb   "to burn"   *səsób-l* "having to be burnt".

Here, complex changes have obscured the internal structures as well as the boundaries. In the possessive NPs (177)a we see that the stem vowels, becoming unstressed because the stress shifts to the possessive suffixes, are either centralized, as in *kər-íδ*, or deleted, as in *ʔill-ék*, which shows vocalization, and consequently syllabification, of the glide. In the verb system, the shift of the stress also brings about considerable differentiations. The final nasal consonant of the common Austronesian verb marker *məN-* is prefixed to the verb stem to form the imperfective conjugation, here translated ((177)b) by an English infinitive. This nasal nasalizes the first consonant of the verb stem if it is a velar, and fuses with it, hence *ŋ* as in *mə-ŋímδ*. But since Austronesian *n* became *l* in Palauan (Hagège 1986:12), the verb marker, by assimilation of its final consonant to the first consonant of the verb stem, will be *məl-*, instead of **mən*, when the verb stem begins with a dental, hence **məl-sésəb*, which yields *mə-lésəb* by absorption of *s*. We see, then, that the prefixation of the verb marker results in masking the first consonant of the verb stem. But this consonant is recovered in suffixed forms, such as the two passive obligative participles in (177)b. Since these participles are formed by adjunction, to the stem, of an enclitic *-l*, which attracts the stress on the last syllable of the stem, and since unstressed vowels, i.e., the vowel of the first syllable in the participle and that of the second syllable in the imperfective, are, as in the possessive NPs, either centralized or deleted, we can understand the formation process of the four complex words in (177)b, including the one in which the stem becomes monosyllabic.

This exuberant allomorphy of the nominal and verbal forms of Palauan gives it a physiognomy which is reminiscent of that of highly fusional languages like Hebrew (Hagège 1986:90-92). Such a situation bears witness to the present cultural habits of Palauan LBs: they strongly stress stressed syllables and speak very fast, as is immediately clear to any careful observer as soon as he arrives in the country. This has a devastating effect on the unstressed vowels. Should we consider, then, that Palauan LBs, faced with the blind force of phonetic laws, are the powerless users of a language in which nominal roots are made unrecognizable by the shift of stress on possessive suffixes? In fact, the present state of Palauan is a stage within a cycle. The articulatory behavior of Palauan LBs results in stem-internal vowel alternations which are typical of an inflectional language, an exceptional situation in the Austronesian stock, known for the agglutinative nature of most of its members. The tendency towards ease of production may be held responsible for this situation. At a following stage of the cycle, in the (very distant) future, the search for expressiveness, combined with the tendency towards ease of production, may lead to a renewal of the nominal and verbal paradigms, and to more resemblance between the various, context-conditioned, forms of the same unit.

5.4 Complete cycles

In some fortunate cases, a very long and uninterruptedly documented history allows us to observe not simply curves within cycles, but the whole cycle itself. Moreover, interdialectal comparison sheds light on diachronic evolution. The various types of cycles that can thus be studied will be presented in the forthcoming four parts, i. e., from morphology to morphology: Chinese (5.4.1); the synthetical stubbornness of conjugation: Egyptian (5.4.2); two types of cycles in Semitic: verbal paradigms; definite article (5.4.3); relexicalization of directive markers: Tibeto-Burman (5.4.4).

5.4.1 From morphology to morphology: Chinese

According to Jaxontov (1965:36-37), Archaic Chinese possessed a component which is almost totally absent in Classical Chinese: morphology. Karlgren (1920), based on a very thorough work of form reconstruction, provides fairly convincing arguments showing that Proto-Chinese must have been inflectional. Initial consonants and tone modifications are assumed to be vestigial prefixes that served to form causative and denominative verbs. The 3SG pronouns *yī* (NOMIN), *qí* (GEN) and *zhī* (ACC) were members of a declensional paradigm, and so were the 1SG pronouns *wú* (NOMIN and GEN) and *wǒ* (ACC), and the 2SG pronouns *rǔ* (NOMIN and GEN) and *ěr* (ACC). Later, in Classical Chinese, *qí* and *wǒ* tended to extend their uses beyond the domains to which they originally corresponded, and to become the usual personal pronouns. Be that as it may, the difference we know best, namely that between Classical and Modern Chinese, is that Modern Chinese has an agglutinating tendency: it contains many nominal and verbal compounds, contrary to what the isolating script in separate characters could lead one to believe (Hagège 1975:153). We can thus say, especially when we consider the increasing number of disyllabic words with tonal reduction on unstressed vowels, that Chinese illustrates a "complete cycle, beginning and ending with a heavier morphologic stage" (Hodge 1970:3).

5.4.2 The synthetical stubbornness of conjugation: Egyptian

The successive known stages in the history of Egyptian also span several millennia. Hodge (1970:3-5), drawing on Korostovcev's (1963:225) statement that "the Old Egyptian synthetic verb of the suffix conjugation changed into the analytic Late Egyptian verb, and finally into the Coptic synthetic verb of the prefix conjugation", considers that "our cycle is complete" and posits a line of evolution reproduced here as (178):

(178)   Old Egyptian   sM
          Late Egyptian   Sm
          Coptic   sM,

where sM means "having complex morphology" and Sm "predominantly syntactic". This uncovers phenomena which are, in fact, more complex and specific than vague labels like sM and Sm may lead one to believe. Of the many verb paradigms of Old Egyptian (twenty-three or more, depending on the author), the majority have personal suffixes, some are participial, and two are verbal nouns. In Coptic, on the other hand, the many forms of the conjugation (eight basic tenses plus twenty-six "satellite" constructions, according to Polotsky (1960:400)) have prefixes. Thus, at both ends of this very long history, we have a synthetic stage, while in the middle, we have an analytic stage, as recalled by Erman, who notes (1933:5) that Late Egyptian represents the stage in which "verbs replace their inflection with auxiliaries [...]. Some isolated inflected forms are still extant in the verbs, but they are no more than an adornment". Coptic has proceeded one step further: auxiliaries are spread everywhere, as well as other types of units whose association with verbal roots contributes to renew the conjugational paradigms. All these elements are prefixed to the verb, and there are no traces of the old inflection.

Thus, Old Egyptian contained a particular structure that consisted of a verbonominal basis (the passive perfective participle) followed by the dative preposition *n*, itself followed by, and governing, a suffixed personal index. In other words, the perfect had a possessive structure, represented in Eastern Aramaic, and still extant today in New Syriac. I have illustrated this structure in 2.2.2, with an example that I reproduce here, for ease of reference, as (179):

(179)		*śdm n-f*
		(heard to-him)
		"he has heard".

As early as Middle Egyptian, a new structure appeared, which was to become predominant in Late Egyptian. In this structure, the first element is a personal pronoun, followed by a preposition, which governs an infinitive. Three different prepositions may appear here: *ḥr* "upon" with verbs that do not indicate motion ((180)a), *m* "upon" with motion verbs ((180)b), both giving a progressive meaning, and *r* "towards", which serves to express the future ((180)c):

(180) a.	*ỉwf ḥr śdm*
		(he upon hearing)
		"he hears"

b. *ĭiwf m ĭit*
    (he upon coming)
    "he is coming"
c. *ĭwf r śḏm*
    (he towards hearing)
    "he will hear" (Cohen 1984:124).

This structure is in fact a nominal sentence, in which the predicate is represented by a relator phrase, consisting of a preposition and the infinitive it governs. This predicate, rather than constituting a homogeneous form, is still periphrastic, as is, for example, the future of Tibetan, also expressed by an element, *d-* or *g-*, which indicates a direction towards a goal, but which is a bound verbal prefix (Durr 1950:168). However, in the subsequent stage, represented by Coptic, the structure is frozen into a new verbal paradigm, with prefixed personal indices. Thus, by a spectacular return of old devices, Coptic has reinvented a synthetic conjugation, also using relators, frozen within the complex verbal word. At least in its beginning steps in Middle Egyptian, before this freezing, it was a dynamic and vivid way of expressing events. But in addition, LBs have left precise, if unconscious, traces of their subjectivity. Coptic has a verb form known as *finalis*, and illustrated by such examples as

(181)   *tare-f-sōtəm*
          (*tare*-he-hear)
          "he will certainly hear" (Polotsky 1960:394).

tare comes from **dĭ-ĭ-ĭry* give-I-do = "I do [that I] give", which is used as a future causative. Contrary to Hodge's (1970:5) assertion that "the 'I' is completely lost", what makes this structure interesting is that the speaker guarantees the result of the action he is recommending: the causative, here, is originally a genuine performative verb, meaning that for the speaker, there is no doubt that the event will occur in the future, as if he himself were responsible for its occurring. This is shown by the many examples cited by Polotsky (1944:3-8). (182) below is one of them:

(182)   *sbte pek-šagʸe tar(e)-ou-sotm-ef*
          (prepare your-speech *tar(e)*-they-hear-it).

Rather than "prepare what to say and thus you will be heard", as Hodge (1970:5) translates, (182) means, more exactly, "prepare your speech and if you do, I guarantee that they will listen to it". Polotsky stresses, for that matter, the connexion between the *tare* form and a preceding imperative. Thus, the evolution has resulted here in complex verb forms which represent the morphologization of syntactic structures. These verb forms bring a cycle to completion by restoring a verbal conjugation which had existed millennia earlier.

5.4.3 Two types of cycles in Semitic: verbal paradigms; definite article

The available data on Semitic also reflects a long history, which resembles that of Egyptian. The evolution of Aramaic, studied in Cohen 1984 (the main source used here), is documented uninterruptedly during three millennia. This study will be divided into two sections, each examining a type of cycle:
  a. Verbal paradigms
  b. Definite article.

a. Verbal paradigms

Here again, we see how verbonominal structures come to be used as predicates. In Old Aramaic (9th-4th centuries B.C.), the imperfective conjugation is essentially prefixal, although it sporadically shows some occurrences of an incipient use of participles as predicates. In Biblical Aramaic, i.e., some chapters of Esdras and Daniel (4th-2nd centuries B.C.), as well as in Semitic generally, the suffixal conjugation corresponds to the past and the prefixal conjugation to the future or prospective. For the present, an expressive form is available, namely the participle, which serves to render the simultaneousness between the speaker's time and the event referred to. In the Aramaic of the Palestinian literature (2nd century B.C.-4th century A.D. for the Western dialects, and 2nd century B.C.-9th century A.D. for the Eastern ones), the renewal of the verbal system by the predicativization of nominal (participial) structures is still in progress, but not yet completed. Let us now examine the still living contemporaneous dialect of Western New Aramaic (spoken in the three Syrian villages of Maʕlûla, Ğub-ʕâdîn and Bahʕa), and of Eastern New Aramaic, i.e., New Syriac (still spoken in the villages of Urmia, Tûr ʕabdîn, Thuma and Mangesh in Iraq). In Western New Aramaic we find, along with the prefixal conjugation, a true participial conjugation with personal prefixes on participles, comparable to a famous form found in just the same Semitic family, the Akkadian stative or permansive.

This new participial conjugation has replaced the old prefixal conjugation in most of its non-modal uses, corresponding essentially to the expression of the imperfective. It has thereby reduced the extension of this old paradigm, relegating it to modal uses: interrogative, future, jussive, prohibitive, subordination. Becoming in turn frozen in this grammatical status, the participial conjugation is less and less used for the expression of concomitance, which, as early as Biblical Hebrew, had already begun to be expressed by this very participle. Concomitance is not left unexpressed, though. It is rendered by a compound form, associating a participle with a special morpheme, *fammal*. In Eastern New Aramaic, the active and the passive participles have formed a new paradigm with the whole series of personal suffixes (through a reanalysis in the case of the passive: cf. 2.2.2, where two examples from the Mangesh dialect are cited). This paradigm, having not simply relegated to modal uses, but totally eliminated, the old prefixal conjugation, is itself submitted to the pressure of new forms containing an auxiliary (*hawi* in the dialect spoken by Christians at Urmia). This auxiliary being prefixed, the cycle is going to be completed when the participial paradigm with personal suffixes has been eliminated, in its turn, by the auxiliary paradigm, as schematized in (183):

(183)   Cycle of verbal paradigms in Aramaic:

	Imperfective	Modal
Old Aramaic	prefixal conjugation	prefixal conjugation
Middle Aramaic	participial conjugation	prefixal conjugation
Modern Aramaic	prefixed auxiliary (/vestigial participial conjugation).	participial conjugation

b. *Definite article*

The most common source of the definite article is a deictic adverb or pronoun: Latin *ille* provides the origin of the definite article in Romance languages; Seychellois creole *sa* shows how a deictic element, French *ça*, from Latin *ecce hac*, can become a generic article, and the same is true of the Haitian creole postposed article *-la*, from the French deictic adverb *là*.

This accession of a deictic to a generic article is a frequent phenomenon, illustrating what I propose to call the Linguistic Internalization of the Universe (LIU) law, by which LBs appropriate the universe and "linguisticize" it. There is a transition from deicticity, a *linguisticization of a gesture*, i.e., an operation which concerns someone or something in the outside world, to anaphoricity, i.e., an operation of reference to someone or something already mentioned in the discourse, as though deixis were transported within the limits of the linguistic message. Anaphoricity is thus a double linguisticization, a second degree or abstract gesture. It refers to elements in the same message, as if the message were a concrete space or the mental spatialization of the outside world. Thus the study of anaphoricity sheds light on a crucial cognitive faculty of LBs, namely Speech Memory (SM): the speaker remembers, and assumes that the hearer remembers, the first explicit mention, in the same sentence or the same text, of an entity which is referred to by the linguistic operators of anaphoricity. Many facts of grammaticalization studied in chapter 7 are aspects of the LIU law. As for the steps from deictics to articles, they are, in most cases: ostensive anaphora, ostensive endophora (cf. (103) in 3.2.1), specific endophora, and generic designation. While certain languages simultaneously possess two uses of the same element, representing two stages in this evolution (German *der*, for example, is used either as a stressed deictic/ anaphoric or as an unstressed article; cf. also Hungarian *a(z)*), others, like spoken Finnish, are just in the beginning of the process of article genesis. As for Romance and Germanic languages, they have developed specific from generic articles; hence the definite article of French, Spanish, Dutch, etc.

The following stage is what Greenberg calls "non-generic article", a name he himself finds "not entirely appropriate" (1978:55). The choice here is no more a purely semantic one: it is largely conditioned by the syntactic construction. Thus, in certain Bantu languages such as Kinyarwanda, this stage is represented by a pre-prefix (distinct from the class prefix), which appears before nouns functioning as subjects or complements, but not before adjectives and verbal forms corresponding to relative clauses; it does not appear, either, with nouns and adjectives governed by the locative relators *ku-* and *mu-*, which automatically transfer these nouns and adjectives into locative complements. Complex relators themselves often derive, historically, from the association of a simple relator with the non-pre-prefixed noun it governs: thus, Ovambo *posi* "under" is analyzed as *po* "on" + *si*, a general Bantu root meaning "earth" (Greenberg 1978:70). It is interesting to note that in other languages, any preposition (e.g., Romanian) or certain prepositions (e.g., *ʔà* in Hausa) preclude the use of this second-stage article with the noun, which must appear alone unless it has modifiers with which it constitutes a full noun-phrase; this exclusion is almost total in Western Modern Armenian for nouns in the instrumental (a suffix). The restriction often applies also to negative structures: in Luganda, an object noun does not take the pre-prefix when it follows a negative verb; the noun in this context is therefore treated as generic: generic nouns do not take this second-stage article. The other cases that rule out its uses are those in which there is a nominal which is already inherently specified (proper noun), or an independent personal pronoun, or an old element from which the article itself originates, i.e., a deictic. These cases are illustrated by languages like Tagalog or Nahuatl (cf. Lemaréchal 1989, ch.1).

In view of these considerations, it seems that a possible designation for the second-stage article is *transferrer*. Its use is that of an element that transfers a noun into a participant able to function as subject or complement (Kinyarwanda), unless the noun is either governed by a relator, which already transfers it into an adverbial complement (Kinyarwanda, Romanian), or is the complement of a negative verb, which makes it non-specific (Luganda); adjectives, as well as verbs in relative clauses, since they modify nouns already marked by a *transferrer*, do not need to be so marked themselves. As for Tagalog *aŋ* and Nahuatl *in*, they were natural sources for *transferrers*: both are former deictics, and a deictic or a personal pronoun, being fully specified, does not need a *transferrer* to have access to the sentence.

In the third stage, we have a noun marker, which has lost any connection with the definite article or the *transferrer*. This is, of course, illustrated by the noun class systems of languages such as those of the Niger-Congo stock.

It appears from the above that the three stages, i.e., definite article, *transferrer*, noun marker, are all synchronically represented in distinct languages. LBs appropriate the universe by unconsciously applying the LIU law and thus creating, in a number of languages, generic articles from deictics. The deictics, at a distinct stage, represented in other languages, develop into *transferrers*, whose use is mainly syntactic, making it possible for LBs to build sentences in which the nouns can appear with various functions. This does not mean, however, that there is no language whose history presents the three stages. Such a language does exist: it is Aramaic, already studied above for the cycle of the verbal paradigms. From the 9th to the 2nd century B.C., there is an -ā definite article. In the Eastern literary dialects such as Babylonian Talmudic and Syriac (2nd century B.C.-9th century A.D.), we find a *transferrer*. Eastern Contemporary Aramaic has a general noun marker. But in one of the Eastern dialects, spoken in the village of Tûr ʕabdîn, mentioned above as being among the most innovative ones in terms of renewal of the verb system, a prefixed article with a definite value has developed. LBs have thereby renewed the process which started some 3000 years ago (Greenberg 1978:60).

5.4.4 *Relexicalization of directive markers: Tibeto-Burman*

In Tibeto-Burman, "the relexicalization of morphosyntactic directive marking is a recurrent phenomenon throughout the family", as shown by Delancey in a case study (1985b:370) on "the analysis-synthesis-lexis cycle" in these languages. This cycle is observable not in one particular language, but rather in the comparison of several closely related languages which represent successive stages of the evolution. Thus, in the Naga branch, one language, Lotha, has lexically distinct motion verbs *wò* "to go" and *ró* "to come", which, however, are obligatory with a small set of other motion verbs like *rho* "to enter" and *tshu* "to ascend", and thus behave, in this environment, as *itive* and *ventive* markers respectively (cf. 3.2.1). In Sema, this incipient process by which the lexically distinct motion verbs of Lotha were developing into directives has gone one step further: *-re* is no longer an independent verb; it has been frozen into a directive suffix. Angami represents the following step: the grammaticalized suffix has lost a part of its phonological shape, and we have a proximal suffix *-r*: *vo* "to go", *vor* "to come"; *ke* "to descend", *ker* "to come down". This does not mean that phonological erosion is a prerequisite to the freezing process; but when it occurs, it is a possible signal of this process.

The cycle is not yet completed at this stage; but if we examine a language belonging to the Kuki branch, Lai, we find total relexicalization in a verb of this language, namely *rak* "to come", which reflects *ra-ga*. Thus, we can speak of a cycle in the Kuki-Naga group of Tibeto-Burman. In the Loloish component of another branch of Tibeto-Burman, Lolo-Burmese, Delancey (1985b:374-376) suggests that Lahu *qay* "to go" should be interpreted as *qa + e, in which *qa is a regular reflex of the Proto-TibetoBurman motion verb *ga, and e is cognate to a "particle ye" and to a motion verb i "to go downwards", found in Akha as a member of a four-term basic motion verb set. Thus, considering *ga as the first stage, Akha i (in series whose preceding terms are independent verbs) as the second stage, and the fusion of *qa + e into Lahu qay as the third stage, we are only one stage short of a complete cycle. It so happens that this stage is provided by the Nu-jiang dialect of Lisu. This dialect has a lexically deictic verb ge "to go", in which *ay is absorbed into a new unit.

Thus, there is a recurrent tendency in the Tibeto-Burman stock for lexicalized motion verbs to grammaticalize into directive suffixes, and for the associations of the latter with other units to relexicalize into independent motion verbs. Haiman, for whom "reduction of form is an ECONOMIC-ALLY motivated index of familiarity, not an iconically motivated index", views the opposition between analyzable compound words and simple words – an opposition illustrated here by two successive stages of the cycle – as one between transparent and opaque, corresponding to "the pragmatic opposition UNUSUAL VS. FAMILIAR" (1983:802). To this Delancey objects that the cycle can be seen "as the diachronic manifestation of two competing iconic tendencies", because on the one hand the "bimorphemic encoding of a complex concept" expressed by using "a separate formal unit for each semantic component" is an iconic procedure, but it is no less true, on the other hand, that "in perceptual terms, unitary coding for a perceptually unitary event is more iconic than is periphrasis". Thus there would be competition between two types of iconicity "as applying to two different conceptualizations of the same phenomenon", and "the inability of the TB [Tibeto-Burman.CH] languages to settle on a stable mechanism is the consequence of the insufficiency of the resources of linguistic structure for dealing with the full complexity of cognition" (Delancey 1985b:384). The concept of iconicity sometimes provides clues to the explanation of linguistic phenomena. But here, speaking of a competition between two types of iconicity reveals a kind of inherent contradiction which, although it probably reflects something real, makes the concept less easy to handle. Thus an interpretation in cognitive terms is interesting but does not fully account for the crosslinguistic tendency, in Tibeto-Burman, to combine MOVE and ±HITHER into opaque verbs and then to reanalyze the result, at a subsequent stage, into its semantic components by giving a formal expression to each of them. We should not forget that there is, here as elsewhere, a conflict between two forces always present in the genesis of human language (cf. (49) above): the need for ease of production, by which LBs reduce words and fuse them together, and the search for expressiveness, which results in longer and more easily analyzable words. It may be that this interpretation of cyclical phenomena in languages is not in contradiction with the double iconicity principle. In the framework of the present study, at any rate, it is more appropriate, since it clearly stresses the part taken in the construction of human languages by concrete situations of communication.

PART III

TWO ASPECTS OF

LANGUAGE MORPHOGENESIS

In PART II, we examined the traces left by LBs which testify to their unconscious language building activity. It is time now to study the concrete results of this activity, i.e., the types of new forms by which LBs constantly enrich their languages. Since Meillet's famous 1912 article, generally thought to be the first linguistic work in which the word "grammaticalization" appears (p.133, between inverted commas), grammaticalization is presented as one of the processes by which grammatical tools are constituted. The other process is analogy. It was one of the main topics of the Neogrammarians, whose teaching had been formulated in, among other works, Osthoff & Brugmann 1878. According to them, the laws of sound change, being mechanical processes, should normally admit of no exceptions. The only phenomena able to put into question the effect of these laws are analogical creations. They are of course important in the perspective of this book, since they imply a (not quite unconscious) effort towards regularization and harmonization on the part of LBs. Thus, the ending of the 3PL of the Latin perfect had become -ēre, but, due to the analogy of the present, imperfect and anterior future, it was changed to -ērunt, which, in the prose of the classical period, is the prevailing form:

(184)   dix-ēre → dix-ērunt,

by analogy with dic-unt, dic-e-b-ant, dix-erint. Meillet stressed that grammaticalization had been much less studied than analogy during the forty years preceding 1912. He defined grammaticalization as "the transformation of autonomous words into grammatical elements" and added (ibid.) that "whereas analogy can renew formal details but mostly leaves the whole system unaltered, the 'grammaticalization' of certain words creates new forms, introduces categories which did not have a linguistic expression before and transforms the whole system". In fact, although the term is probably modern, the phenomenon had long been known. Condillac (1746) and Horne Tooke (1786) both indicated that prepositions have a verbal source. Humboldt (1822) was interested in the origin of grammatical forms, as were the founders of the typologies of the Romantic age, i.e., the Schlegels (1808 and 1818), Bopp (1833-1852) among others, and also, much later, von der Gabelentz (1891:251).

Since the beginning of the seventies, with such works as Givón 1971 or Hagège 1975, grammaticalization has started arousing much interest again. A number of studies have taken it as their main topic. However, the process by which autonomous words become grammatical elements is not the only one that deserves to be studied as typical of LBs' building activity.

Another process is lexicalization, by which two elements that, when used in the sentence framework, were in the past or are today free units, or two elements of which one is already frozen into an affix[1], are associated together, through compounding and derivation respectively, and yield a new complex unit. Given that the present book aims at characterizing human beings as language builders, the word morphogenesis, *lumping together both lexicalization and grammaticalization, appears in the title of Part III instead of* grammaticalization *only.* Morphogenesis, *of course, means here "genesis of linguistic forms" in general, not just of morphemes, since the Greek etymon* morphē *simply means "form".* Morphogenesis *includes, besides the genesis of derived words and compounds, the domain traditionally called morphology, which studies the kinds of word structures in the various language types, and was basic in 19th century linguistic typology. Morphology has been flourishing again in contemporary linguistics for some fifteen years, after a period of overemphasis on syntax.*

It thus appears that the freezing of lexical into grammatical units is only a part, albeit essential, of LBs' morphogenetic activity. The other part, for that matter, has some points in common with it: thus, in both lexicalization and grammaticalization, for at least some of the elements involved, there is partial or total loss of the ordinary trappings. The study of grammaticalization and that of lexicalization (keeping in mind that the term as defined above does not refer only, despite its root, to the formation of simple lexical units) jointly contribute to characterize Lb as a fundamental human behavior.

There are important differences between the two processes, however. First of all, although both of them provide an important contribution to the study of LBs' activity, this activity is not defined in the same way in both cases as far as consciousness is concerned. Lexicalization is mostly an unconscious process, but there are some cases of conscious creation (cf. 6.3.3). It is important to note that we can explain the phenomenon of demotivation with reference to the degree of consciousness: in order for a compound not to lose its motivation, the utterance of which it is a reduced form, or which it indirectly reflects, must be very precise; this means that this utterance must clearly define the context in which it is used and the cultural habits which underlie it; if, due to social and cultural changes as time passes, this ceases to be the case, then the compound gets frozen, because it does not correspond any longer to a precise conscious representation in the LBs' minds.

As opposed to that, grammaticalization, except in very rare external cases like writing (cf. 7.2.2 section b.), is not only unconscious, but can even be measured by criteria that are precisely based on this unconscious-ness. Second, the semantic result of lexicalization is often unpredictable, or frozen, whereas grammaticalization often corresponds to semantic broadening. Finally, the products of lexicalization are new units which, although complex, behave like simple lexical units, whereas those of grammaticalization are increasingly subject to grammatical constraints: they themselves become a part of grammar.

PART III will therefore contain two chapters: the first one (chapter 6) will treat lexicalization, and the second one (chapter 7) will treat gram-maticalization[2].

CHAPTER 6

Lexicalization

Using Complex Words (CWs) as the label which refers to both derivatives and compounds (cf. 1.3.3 section b.), I will first stress the links between CW building and LBs' needs (6.1). I will then show that there is no uniform relationship between CWs and syntax (6.2). The following parts of this chapter will examine the way constraints and freedom interact in CW formation (6.3), and as a logical consequence, the extent to which one can speak of LBs' semantic creativeness (6.4).

6.1 CW building and LBs' needs

LBs' creativity, whether conscious or not, is goal-oriented. LBs make the words that fulfil definite needs, even when the formation process seems to be complicated, if looked at from the outside. They seldom build words for purely aesthetical purposes, even when formation processes would be suggested by available models. Hungarian LBs have formed *ajtó+n+áll+ó* (door+on+to~stand+PRES.PARTCP) "usher". They have not formed, although it would make sense, *part+on+áll+ó* (riverbank+on+to~stand+PRES. PARTCP) "one who stands on the riverbank" (cf. Kassai 1974:33): standing on the threshold of a door is a professional activity, while standing on a riverbank is not. Of course, this does not mean that the Hungarian present participle in *+ó/+ő* (cf. 6.4.2) cannot refer to occasional activities; it can and often does. But what LBs' work results in is "to pack a maximum amount of information into a minimum amount of linguistic structure" (Downing 1977:823). *partonálló* is not a simple unanalyzable unit. However, it could well exist; but if it did, it would be irrelevant with regard to *cultural indexing* (cf. 3.2.1), or at least, it would carry less information, since it would give a name to a non-relationship, than *ajtónálló*, which expresses a cultural relationship between a person and a place.

Thus LBs, by *glossogenetic vocation*, label those animate beings, objects, actions, and events that they deem name-worthy. A possible paraphrase or a proposed underlying structure is not the only (or necessary) basis of a

CW, and does not have the same communicative function as the CW does. The forthcoming study will show that the syntactic and semantic relationships between the members of various types of compounds and derivatives do not constitute a list of pre-encoded mechanisms imposed on LBs and yielding fully predictable results. LBs do not start from syntactically defined meaningful components. They start from meanings that meet their communicative needs. These meanings are themselves defined by the various types of relationships LBs have in human societies with others LBs, as well as with objects and notions. From these, due to CP and depending on the type of society, they select one or two features among the many that define the entity to be named. Of course, this does not mean that their choice is not also limited by the constraints on word-structure types that are proper to every language. All we can say is that through the CWs they build, LBs strive to find, for a given meaning, the most convenient expression for the speaker as well as for the hearer.

6.2 CWs and syntax

Many CWs are a faithful transposition of a whole sentence into a single unit. In certain languages, on the other hand, there are CWs in which one of the constitutive elements cannot be defined in terms of the units appearing within the sentence framework. These opposite situations will be studied in the following two parts: sentential and quasi-sentential CWs (6.2.1); incorporation (6.2.2).

6.2.1 Sentential and quasi-sentential CWs

Most languages can use whole sentences as if they were a single unit which functions like a noun. English *forget-me-not*, French *m'as-tu-vu* (lit. "did you see me?") = "one who likes to show off" can be compared in this respect: while *forget-me-not* is asyntactic (the normal prohibitive structure is *do not forget me*) and must, as a consequence, be considered to be a compound, nothing distinguishes *m'as-tu-vu* from an ordinary interrogative sentence, except for the intonational curve and the fact that this word is, when used within a sentence as a CW, generally preceded by an article and functions like a simple noun. Thus, if *m'as-tu-vu* is also a compound, it is not for the same reason as *forget-me-not*.

Compounds of this type are well represented in polysynthetic languages such as those of the Iroquoian stock. But they are also very frequent in various languages as vulgar designations of living species. Many African languages have CWs such as Mbum *sòì+hé+yá* (snake+climb+NEG) "*Vitex doniana* Sweet" (because this shrub has a smooth bark, so that snakes cannot climb over it when it is used as a fence around houses). One can also mention other sentential CWs of Mbum which do not refer to living species but also show how complex the results of LBs' language building activity can be when they reflect precise cultural representations: *pélé+mì+á+nzì+mbáp* (to-morrow+I+IMM.FUT+grow+too) "ring finger" (because this finger, although not the biggest one, is seen as aspiring to become so, hence the sentence "tomorrow I will be big too"); *zì+ndôk+ mòkón* (fail+finger+three) "seven" (because in the old numeral system based on hand gestures, seven was seen as three fingers short with respect to ten = two hands) (Hagège 1970, I: 162 and 166 respectively).

Another process by which LBs convert a whole sentence into a single noun is possessivization, as in (185), from spoken (dialectal-like) Hungarian:

(185)   *játsz+hat+nék+ja van*
          (to~play+POT+1SG.COND+3SG.POSS is),

literally "there is his 'I could play' ", i.e., "he feels like playing".

In other cases, the CW does not reproduce a complete sentence: one or more elements are lacking. I propose to speak, then, of quasi-sentential CWs. The absence of an element which, in a given language, is necessary for the sentence to be complete must be considered a privative mark of compounding (cf. *forget-me-not* above, in which the specific sequence and the absence of *do* were so considered). This applies to the element which, if the CW were a sentential CW, would be the subject of a complete sentence formally identical with the CW. This element is lacking in the crosslinguistically widespread type of quasi-sentential CWs made of two elements corresponding to what, in a complete sentence, would be

– a verb and its nominal object, e.g., French *protège-tympan* or *garde-meuble*, respectively, "ear-protector" and "furniture-repository", which, by the way, do not contain verbal elements as in French;
– a verb and its adverbial complement, e.g., Mbum *ŋbá+ðáká* (take+care-fully) "brittle" (Hagège 1970, I: 164); the result here is not a noun, but an adjective.

In this Mbum example, not only the subject but also the object are lacking. However, the concept of quasi-sentential CW may be extended to this type of association, because the relationship between its members is a faithful reflection of that between free units in the sentence framework. CWs in other languages also retain the indication of the relationship between elements corresponding to verb and adverbial complement in the sentence. A typical illustration is Hungarian, in which we find such CWs as *nagy+ra+vágy+ás* (big+towards+to~aspire+NMN.SUFF) "ambition". In this CW, which is both a compound and a derivative, the association of a relator *ra(/re)* and its complement *nagy* – as well as that between this whole relator phrase and the verb – are kept unchanged, even though the framework is not the sentence, but a CW whose nominal status is marked by the suffix *+ás*. However, the indication of the syntactic relationship is not always maintained. Thus, in *dolg+a+végez+etlen* (affair+POSS+settle+ PRIV.SUFF) "without having settled his/her affairs", there is a possessive marker *-a* which remains unchanged in the CW, but no *-t* marker of the definite object, although in the complete sentence corresponding to this CW, such a marker is obligatory in Hungarian.

Thus, sentential and quasi-sentential CWs, as total or partial copies of the material form of a complete sentence, represent one of the possible transpositions of the structures belonging to one level into those of another level. LBs' work, here, does not consist in building an entirely new form, but in treating a complex association in the same way as if it were a single unit.

6.2.2 Incorporation

Besides that examined in 6.2.1, there exists a quite different type of relationship between CWs and syntax. It is illustrated by a phenomenon called *incorporation*. Here the CW, far from totally or partially reproducing a sentence, contains an element whose relationship with the rest of the CW is marked in a way that would be asyntactic if used in the framework of a sentence. In many languages, LBs have built verb-noun or noun-verb compounds whose noun can no more be considered as a full-fledged noun since a mark of its dependency is the absence of the usual trappings that define its nominal status when used in the sentence framework. Incorporation is a well-studied phenomenon (cf., in particular, Sapir 1911, Hagège 1978, 1980b, Mithun 1984, 1986, Sadock 1986). Not only does the incorporated noun lose, in most cases, the markers associated with it in its independent use: articles, deictics, possessive morphemes, etc., but the incorporating verb sometimes undergoes various kinds of alterations: phoneme changes, syllabic reductions, prosodic (tone, stress) modifications. As an example of phoneme change, added to those given in (170)a-b, consider (186), also from Iaai, and also showing two kinds of alterations of the verb: spirantization of the first consonant and vowel raising; moreover, there is a palatalization of the last consonant (*kot* becomes *xuc*):

(186)   *a-me   xuc+bwəə*
          (3SG-PROGR   beat+leaf)
          "he spits medicinal leaves" (Ozanne-Rivierre & Moyse 1978).

As can be noted from this example, not only does the incorporated noun lose its usual trappings, not only does the verb undergo phoneme changes, but in addition, the noun, which means "leaf" when used freely, takes, when incorporated, a meaning which is both generic and idiomatic: "any medicinal leaf in general".

Thus, both materially and semantically, there may be a relative independence between an incorporated nominal and the corresponding noun that appears in the sentence framework. It is interesting, in this connection, to recall Salishan lexical suffixes, which would represent the following stage. As studied in 2.1.2 section b. (cf. example (31)), lexical suffixes are not even reduced forms of nouns, hence not a case of incorporation. Most of them are original forms constituting a limited set of units that cannot be derived from free nouns.

An important observation may be deduced from a comparison between the various devices studied above, sentential and quasi-sentential CWs, incorporation and lexical suffixation: between CWs and syntax, there are various types of dependency relationships. It is therefore useful to examine the interaction of constraints and freedom as a characteristic feature of LBs' work in CW formation. This will be done in 6.3 below.

6.3 The interaction of constraints and freedom in CW formation

I will try to show here that although CWs are morphological units whose constitutive members are linked together by various constraints, it may happen that some languages are freer than others with respect to these constraints. LBs often build expressive CWs, even though the latter are constantly exposed to freezing. The present study will contain three parts: violations in CW formation (6.3.1); peninsular phenomena (6.3.2); from motivation to freezing (6.3.3).

6.3.1 Violations in CW formation

Within a compound, the order of succession of the constitutive members is not random. It is either the same as that between the syntactic units of which the compound is the morphological reflection, or different from it. If it is different, it may be because it represents an archaic type of sequence that belongs to the history of the language. But it may also be because it has been borrowed. As seen in 4.1.1, sequential borrowing may accompany contact-induced borrowing of the material form of words. This is especially the case when there is massive borrowing. Massive borrowing from Chinese in the form of Sino-Japanese and Sino-Korean V + N compounds is an important feature of Japanese and Korean. In both languages, the object noun precedes the verb in the sentence, whereas in Chinese, it follows it. Therefore the Sino-Japanese and Sino-Korean V + N compounds, in which the Chinese sequence is borrowed along with the words themselves, represent violations of Japanese and Korean word order. Due to the deep impregnation of Japanese and Korean by Chinese during many centuries, this sequential habit soon ceased to be perceived as a violation and became one among other automatisms. However, LBs have exploited it in an original way, since it is possible in Japanese to specify the general meaning of the nominal element in these compounds by adding in the sentence, this time according to the Japanese word order, i.e., before the predicate, a nominal complement with a specific meaning, as in (187):

(187)   *imôto wa Yokohama no kôkô ni tû+gaku+site+iru*
           (sister TOP.M Y. CONN high~school in go+school+doing+is)
           "my sister attends a high school in Yokohama"
                                                    (Kageyama 1982:232).

tû "to attend" + *gaku* "school" is one among the enormous number of disyllabic V + N compounds which are the Japanese treatment (Sino-Japanese) of Chinese binomials. In association with the verb *suru* "to do" (here in its habitual form, with the *iru* "be" auxiliary), these binomials behave as incorporated nominals, i.e., they are compounds entering other more complex compounds. Thus, the relationship between *gaku* and *kôkô* in (187) is comparable with that found between *hnek* and *o+ɛ:tá:+ki+?* in (188), from Onondaga (comparable but not identical, of course, since *hnek* is not a V + N compound but a classifying noun root meaning "liquid", and *o+ɛ:tá:+ki+?* is a sentential CW, as the literal translation shows); both (187) and (188) are cases of classificatory incorporation:

(188)   *hati-hnek+aét-s   o+ɛ:tá:+ki+?*
        (they/it-liquid+gather-ASP   it+tree+be~soup+ASP)
        "they gather maple syrup" (Woodbury 1975:11).

Here again, as in (187), the relationship between the incorporated element and the unit located outside the CW is an original one. It is not possible to derive *hati-hnek+aét-s* from a sentence containing a verb and its object, since this analysis would leave unexplained the fact that the verb also has another object that specifies the meaning of *hnek*. Thus, *hati-hnek+aét-s* cannot be explained away by a transformational procedure or accounted for in terms of parts of speech as defined by sentential syntax.

6.3.2 Peninsular phenomena

Peninsular phenomena are another instance of the relative freedom with which LBs often break the constraints linking together the constitutive members of CWs. In various languages, an element belonging to a CW, i.e., to an island which it cannot leave, behaves as if it were an independent unit, i.e., as if the CW were, in fact, a peninsula: the element in question bridges a gap between the CW and the rest of the sentence, by building a syntactic relationship with another element located outside the CW. Among various types of peninsular phenomena (cf. Corum 1973, Hagège 1988b), I will recall that mentioned by Sadock (1980) as a case of noun incorporation – which it is, provided that we do not lose sight of its complexity, the noun being both incorporated and peninsular. The example is taken from Greenlandic Eskimo. Here, the bound verb *+sivoq* "he bought" may be preceded by the bound generic noun *pi+* "thing", yielding *pi+sivoq* "he bought something". So far, we have a case of noun incorporation, since the relationship between *pi+* and *+sivoq* cannot be interpreted in terms of the syntactic relationships between units in the sentence, and, moreover, the result is an intransitive compound verb: if we want to mention the specific object that was bound, we must put the noun designating it in the instrumental, marked by -*mik*; hence, with *sapangaq* "bead" (whose *q* is dropped and *ng* is geminated in this combination), we obtain the sentence *sapannga-mik pi+sivoq* "he bought a bead"; if an adjective is added, we get (189), where there is case agreement between the adjective and the noun:

> (189)   *sapannga-mik kusanartu-mik pi+sivoq*
>   (bead-INSTR beautiful-INSTR thing+bought(INDIC.3SG))
>   "he bought a beautiful bead".

However, it is also possible, with the same meaning as in (189), to incorporate *sapangaq*. The striking phenomenon in that case is that *kusanartu-mik* remains unchanged; it keeps its case agreement with the noun, even though the latter, being incorporated, has of course lost its case suffix:

> (190)   *kusanartu-mik sapangar+sivoq*
>   (beautiful-INSTR bead+bought(INDIC.3SG))
>   (before *s*, the *q* of *sapangaq* becomes *r*).

The adjective may even take the plural instrumental suffix -*nik*, meaning that there are several beads; thus we have both case and number agreement, even though the agreement-triggering noun is a bound member of a CW:

> (191)   *kusanartu-nik sapangar-sivoq*
>   "he bought beautiful beads".

And if the incorporated noun is formally plural, as is, for example, *qamutit* "carriage", plural agreement is obligatory, even on the numeral *ataaseq* "one", as in (192), where *qamutit* is incorporated into the bound verb -*qarpoq* "he has", and the numeral (here *ataatsi-*), despite its typically singular meaning, takes plural (as well as case) agreement, marked by the already mentioned suffix -*nik*:

> (192)   *ataatsi-nik qamute+qarpoq*
>   "he has one car".

The CWs behaving like peninsulas in the Eskimo examples (190)-(192) are compounds. But derivatives themselves may also behave like peninsulas, despite the even stronger constraints characteristic of a CW of which one member is frozen into an affix. Certain languages allow syntactic relationships between a member of a derivative and an external word. It may be, for example, a noun-modifier (adjective) or a verb-object relationship. The first case is illustrated by Hungarian, the second one by Japanese.

In Hungarian, *-u/-ü* is a very frequent adjectival suffix appearing in nominal structures with successions of modifiers. In

(193)   *magyar nyelv-ü újság*
          (Hungarian language-ADJ.SUFF newspaper)
          "a Hungarian newspaper",

-ü makes it possible for *magyar nyelvü* to modify *újság*. But *nyelv* ("language") itself, although it is locked up within an *-ü* adjective, behaves as if it were a free noun, since it is modified by *magyar*. We know it by the fact that if we delete *magyar*, we are left with a meaningless association **nyelvü újság*. Thus, Hungarian LBs, by treating *nyelv*, the root of the adjective *nyelvü*, as if it were a free unit, extract it from its morphological framework and "resyntacticize" it (cf. also English *computer scientist, moral philosopher*, etc.).

Now consider (194), from Japanese:

(194)   *Yooroppa o kenbutu+si+ta+sa ni*
          (Europe OBJ.M sightseeing+do+DESID+NMN.SUFF out~of)
          "out of a desire to go sightseeing in Europe".

Here, the nominalizing suffix *+sa* does not prevent *kenbutu si-* (an allomorph, when before the desiderative suffix *ta(i)*, of *kenbutu suru*, i.e., of a V+N+*suru* compound, with twofold incorporation (cf. 6.3.1)) from governing an object NP *Yooroppa*, followed by the object marker *o*. This is not true of any nominalizing suffix, however. Thus, *-kata*, "method to, manner of" and *-te* "-er (agent)" do not allow this peninsular government:

(195)   *opera no utai+te*
          (opera CONN sing+NMN.SUFF)
          "an opera singer".

In (195), *opera* is the modifier, related by the connective *no* to the modified noun *utai+te,* where *utai+* is an allomorph of the verb *utau* "to sing". (195) is grammatical, but **opera o utai+te,* in which *opera* would be the object of *utai+,* is not. Kageyama, who cites these examples, describes them in the framework of Transformational Grammar: according to him (1982:253-254), in examples such as (194), "the object NPs of the underlying predicates show up as such in the surface structures", whereas expressions like (195) are "derived as NPs in deep structure".

Of course, the term "peninsula" must be taken as metaphoric. It should not imply that CWs must necessarily be islands in any language, as they are in English, where we cannot say, for example, **totally destruction,* **small intestinally,* or **to shiny new bicycle around the block* (Sadock 1980:316). Structures of this kind, on the other hand, are perfectly normal in Eskimo, Hungarian, or Japanese, as recalled above. While incorporated nominals, such as illustrated by Iaai (6.2.2), Sino-Japanese or Sino-Korean Ns in V + N compounds (6.3.1), etc., are defined as members of compounds by the asyntactic character of their association with a verb, peninsular phenomena cannot be defined without reference to syntax if we are to account for the fact that bound elements follow case and number agreement rules. Thus, peninsular phenomena provide arguments in such a debate as the relationship between syntax and word formation, or between the advocates of prelexical syntax or the precyclical character of incorporation rules on the one hand, and the advocates of presyntactic lexical insertion on the other hand (Sadock 1980: 300). But more importantly for the perspective proposed in this book, peninsular phenomena testify to the relative freedom of LBs with respect to the constraints of morphology, as LBs are able to bridge the gap between bound elements functioning within CWs where they do not have the status of free lexemes, and other elements located outside these CWs.

6.3.3 From motivation to freezing

We have seen (2.3.1) that linguistic forms resulting from the efforts made by LBs to remotivate their expressive means tend, as time passes, to lose their motivation and to become opaque: various parts of these forms are finally reduced or eliminated, pending a new stage of ER, since, as recalled in 5.2, the process is cyclic. This applies to CWs, of course. In most known languages (if we disregard the ones whose monosyllabic stage started very long ago, the preceding stages being scarcely documented), there are many monosyllabic words that were CWs at a remote stage; but no average user would think of analyzing them, today, into original constituent parts. Only specialists of etymological research know that English *lord* comes from Anglo-Saxon *hlaf+weard* "bread-guard", which yielded itself Old English *hlaford* and later, by apheresis and syncope, *lord*. The same is true of *world*, from Anglo-Saxon *weor+old* "man-age", an association which is clearer in Dutch *wereld*. Even when the word is polysyllabic and the structure more transparent, this does not suffice to make the analysis easier for LBs – especially if the building device has become unproductive: given that it is not possible, in Modern French, to form a CW from the association of a verb with a preceding noun referring to an instrument, a word like *maintenir* "to maintain", literally "to keep" (+*tenir*) + "hand" (*main*+), appears as a fossil (of course, this applies even more to its English equivalent, since *maintain* was borrowed as such, and neither *main* (in this meaning) nor *tain* are English words); other such associations in French are *culbuter* "to knock down", literally "to throw (on)" (+*buter*) + "buttocks" (*cul*+), or *saupoudrer* "to powder (with salt)", literally "to powder" (+*poudrer*) + "salt" (*sau*+, unstressed dialectal variant (14th century) of *sel*) (Benveniste 1974:106).

In another case (universally represented in human languages), i.e., CWs derived from proper names, the degree of transparency depends on when the CW was formed. CWs formed on proper names at a very recent date remain transparent for most LBs, of course. But few native speakers of English know the source (if they use this word at all!) of *serendipity*, coined by Horace Walpole (*ca.* 1754) after *The Three Princes of Serendip*, a Persian fairy tale in which the prince makes fortunate discoveries accidentally, hence the meaning of this word: an aptitude for making such discoveries. It is not sure that all of the Russian speakers who use *oblomovščina* "flabbiness" are still aware of the fact that it comes from *Oblomov*, a character in Goncharov's novel of the same title (1859). Haitian Creole speakers born after 1971 do not necessarily refer *bospent* "to make away with (s.o.)" to the profession (*bos pent* = "boss painter") of a police officer known, during the period of the dictatorship in Haiti (1957-1971) for his habit of treating his enemies rather expeditiously. Words of this type, depending on whether their origin is more or less recent, are identified and analyzed or not. When they no longer are, the covert nature of their history contributes to make them conventional, hence efficient, tools for communication. But at the time of their birth, they are original inventions, and they can be dated, as in the case of these three examples.

We may also suppose that there was a high degree of original motivation in CWs formed by the association of a metalinguistic generic verb "to say" with another element involving the core meaning of "sound". But in languages possessing this device, the verb "to say" does not keep its full value in all its uses. In Amharic, it tends to become a tool for the formation of CWs: if the semantic relationship between alä "to say" and the notion of saying is direct in (196)a, it is indirect or absent in (196)b. In Papuan languages like Asmat, Enga, Kalam or Hua, the association of a metalinguistic verb functioning as an auxiliary with an adjunct verb or noun is a widespread phenomenon, but in Enga, for example, not all the complex verbs so formed are directly related to the notion of saying ((197)a; cf. also the last examples given for Kalam in (29)); many of these verbs refer to states, feelings or actions ((197)b):

(196)

a.	sitạṭṭ+alä	(rubbing+say)	"to make a rubbing noise"
	zəmm+alä	(hush+say)	"to shut up"
b.	mar~mar+alä	(honey~honey+say)	"to be as sweet as honey"
	əlləm+alä	(disappearance+say)	"to disappear"
			(Cohen 1970:263-266)

(197)

a.	aé+lengé	(squeal+say)	"to squeal"
	kosée+lengé	(cough+say)	"to cough"
b.	lyaka+lengé	(drought+say)	"to be dry"
	auú+lengé	(liking+say)	"to like"
	yoó+lengé	(pull+say)	"to pull" (Foley 1986:120).

In both (196)b and (197)b, the semantic analysis does not yield convincing results: the semantic "weakening" of the second element is a sign of freezing.

This is less true of CWs originally formed, in languages with a lexicon resorting to many types of combinations of simple elements, by polysynthetic and easily reanalyzable devices, such as description or metaphor. The descriptive device may be illustrated by the word for "milk" in Galibi:

manātlll+aiku+po (breast+liquid+PRIV), literally "liquid of the breast, (but) which is no longer there", or by the word for "man" in Dieguño: *ʔiskwi+č* (big+that~who), literally "the one who is big" (Hagège 1982:63 fn. 24). The word for "blue" in Cahuilla provides an example of the metaphoric device: *túk+va+s+nek+is*, which, according to Dressler (1987:100), means, literally, "having accomplished the process of becoming like the thing where something curved is fastened". It is worth noting that "milk", "blue" and "man" are notions which, in most Indo-European languages, are expressed by simple and synchronically unanalyzable words, often mono-syllabic, or bisyllabic.

The motivation of CWs is even higher when they are created by a conscious collective or individual will. As far as the former is concerned, I have studied in 1.3.1 section g. the neological activity by which, in literate societies, new units are created. I have cited examples taken from Hungarian (portmanteau words, various suffixations) and Hebrew (revival of old syllabic schemes filled with borrowed material). But experts in neological creations, in order to meet new requirements in communication, often introduce devices that were rare or unknown in the language they deal with. Thus, Semitic languages are characterized by a dearth of compound formations. In order to compensate for it, various types of CWs have been introduced in Israeli Hebrew, making it thereby very different, in that respect, from Biblical Hebrew, and enriching the nominal and adjectival lexicon: *bahuvrîhi* compounds such as *kxol+ʃeynayim* (blue+eyes) "blue-eyed", viewpoint compounds like *ʃiver+cvaʃim* (blind+colors) "color-blind", possessive compounds such as *ben+xayil* (possessor (lit. "son") +success (*xayil* "success"= obsolete word)) "smart fellow"; to a large extent, these adjectives are calques of English adjectival structures, but they keep the Hebrew word order; the same is true of nouns, such as *kadur+sal* (ball+basket) "basket-ball" (Rosén 1966). The reformers of another Semitic language, Arabic, have also introduced compound adjectives; they have borrowed, among others, the following structure: prepositional element+ noun+adjectival suffix, illustrated in English *super+son+ic* or French *pré+logique*, whose equivalents in Modern Written Arabic are *faw+ sawt+iyy* and *qab+manṭiq+iyy*, respectively, where the prepositional element presents an interesting morphological mark of its new status, i.e., the loss of the third consonant of the all-pervasive three-consonantal stem characteristic of Classical Arabic, since the full forms of the prepositions meaning "over" and "before" are *fawqa* and *qabla*, respectively; Israeli

Hebrew also possesses adjectives with the same structure: *tat+hakarat+iy* (under+con-sciousness+ADJ.SUFF) "subconscious", *anti+dat+iy* (anti+religion+ADJ.SUFF) "antireligious".

An individual's will may also result in the creation of fairly motivated CWs. If they are well accepted, they become less and less motivated as time passes, which is both the ordinary fate of motivated CWs and a sign of their wide acceptance (cf. 1.3.1 section f.). Instead of creating new CWs, it is also possible to remotivate an old one by trying to replace one of its parts with another element. Thus, in the United States, the feminist campaign against *chair+man*, whose structure is transparent, has proposed *chair+person*, which, according to the situation, can refer either to a chairman or to a chairwoman. The success of *wo+person*, proposed instead of *woman*, is less clear: *wo+*, from Old English *wif+* "female", is opaque in this context. Finally, it is well-known that, just as there are cases of morphological analysis, by LBs, of CWs into their elements (cf. 1.3.3 section b.), there are many cases of creations: the CWs thus created are easily understandable, although nonexistent. Examples are German *Zu+r+ verfügung+stellung* (to+the(=(de)r)+disposal+putting) "the fact that something is made available" (Stolz 1987a:17), or Chinese *bù+kĕ+nì+xing* (NEG+can+to~reverse+quality) "irreversibility": I have heard this word used by a Chinese colleague during a conversation; although it does not seem to be mentioned in dictionaries, it is perfectly clear, because both *bù+kĕ* "not+can", added as prefixes to the stem, and the adjunction of the suffix -*xing* "character, quality" to form abstract nouns, are quite common devices in Modern Chinese.

6.4 CWs and LBs' semantic creativeness

We have seen that there is no uniform relationship between CWs and sentential syntax (6.2), and that the search for expressiveness, characteristic of LBs, often results in violations of constraints on CW structure, or remotivation of frozen formations (6.3). We are thus led to the following question: what is the role of LBs' semantic creativeness, conscious or not, in CW formation? The following two parts will try to answer this question: the variety of internal relationships in CWs (6.4.1); the difficulty of predicting the semantic result of CW formation (6.4.2).

6.4.1 The variety of internal relationships in CWs

Consider (198), from Japanese[1]:

(198)	a.	*gaman+zuyoi*	(patience+strong)	"patient"
	b.	*hara+guroi*	(stomach+black)	"black-hearted"
	c.	*kokoti+yoi*	(feeling+good)	"comfortable"
	d.	*kyômi+bukai*	(interest+deep)	"very interesting"
	e.	*darasi+nai*	(tidiness+nonexistent)	"slovenly".

It is not easy to say what exact relationship links together the two members of these nominalization-compounds. The reason for this is that in a language with case-marking on nouns such as Japanese, nominal elements which make part of such compounds lose their case-marker in that context. Compare, however, (199) and (200):

(199)   *aitu   wa   hara-ga   kuroi*
         (guy TOP.M stomach-SUBJ.M black)
         "This guy has a black heart"

(200)   *aitu   wa   hara+guroi*
         (guy TOP.M stomach+black)
         "This guy is black-hearted".

These two sentences have almost the same meaning. Moreover, it is possible to replace *hara-ga kuroi* of (199) and *hara+guroi* of (200) by *darasi-ga nai* and *darasi+nai*, respectively, with more or less the same meaning of "this guy is slovenly"; this proves that *darasi* itself, although almost out of use today as a free noun, can also appear as a subject if we substitute a full sentence for the CW. However, we immediately note that *rendaku* (cf. 5.2.1) is applied when the structural conditions for its application are met, hence the voicing of initial *t-, k-* and *f-* of *tuyoi, kuroi* and *fukai* into *z-, g-* and *b-* in *zuyoi, guroi* and *bukai* respectively ((198)). Thus, there is no doubt as to the status of these CWs as compounds. Since the framework is no longer that of a sentence, and therefore the nominal elements in these CWs are no longer subjects, why not interpret their relationship to the following component in terms other than subject to predicate? The first component could be assigned the status of an adverbial complement, referring to the viewpoint. The words in (198), then, would mean "strong", "black", "good", "deep", and "nonexistent", respectively, "as far as patience, stomach, feeling, interest, and tidiness are concerned". There is no reason for accepting only one type of analysis (cf. Hagège 1991).

The same applies to another kind of CWs also observed in Japanese: *ame+huri* (rain+fall) "rainfall" could be analyzed either as a N+V or as a N+N compound, and *otoko+zuki* (man+love) is ambiguous "between the readings 'x likes men' and 'men like x' " (Kageyama 1982:222). Furthermore, Japanese has N+V compounds of which the first member refers to the instrument of the action referred to by the second member, e.g., *te+gaki* "hand+writing", *mizu+arai* (cold~water+washing) "washing with cold water", *bas+tû+gaku* (bus+go+school; here, *tû+gaku* itself is a Sino-Japanese compound: cf. (187)) "going to school by bus", *suna+asobi* (sand+playing) "playing with sand"; the structure of these compounds is the same as that of other compounds in which the first member may refer to a location: e.g., *Doitu+umare* "German+born"; a source: e.g., *Amerika+ gaeri* (America+returning) "one who has returned from America"; a goal: e.g., *gaikoku+yuki* (foreign~country+going) "going to foreign countries"; a cause: e.g., *ryokô+zukare* (travel+being~tired) "being tired from travelling"; or a manner: e.g., *hitori+aruki* (one~man+walking) "walking alone" (Kageyama 1982: 222-223 and Hagège 1991).

In other languages also, the internal structure of compounds is far from uniform. In English, German and Hungarian compound adjectives with the form N+Adj (or participle, or N), it is hard to assign a single specific status to the first member. It may refer to an instrument like the first member of the Japanese instrumental compounds mentioned above: Hungarian *ember+ csinált-a* (man+made+3SG.POSS) and its English equivalent *man+made* are examples of a very productive formation also illustrated by *awe+struck* and many others. But the first member corresponds to the comparison standard in *grass+green*, and to the viewpoint in *fire+proof* = *feuerfest* in German, which, besides +*fest*, also uses, with the same meaning, +*frei* or +*sicher* as second members, e.g., *kugelsicher* "bullet-proof" (French does not seem to resort to CWs to express this meaning: the French equivalent of these two German adjectives are *à l'épreuve du feu* and *à l'épreuve des balles*: Lipka 1968).

To sum up, we may say that as an effect of the absence of case markers, which is characteristic of associations within the limits of a single CW, the compounds studied above are very uniform: in human languages, word order alone does not provide many distinctive possibilities. But within these sequential constraints, LBs have given free play to their semantic creativeness. The examples proposed here to illustrate it are just a few among many others, which could be multiplied in a crosslinguistic survey.

6.4.2 The difficulty of predicting the semantic result of CW formation

As a consequence of LBs' semantic creativeness, it is not always possible to predict the meaning of CWs. This does not apply only to compounds, examined in 6.4.1 above. Derivatives themselves, even though the affixes they contain normally belong to closed sets of well-known elements, may have various meanings, depending on the meaning of the stem and the type of relationship between the stem and the affix. Thus, the Hungarian present participle in +ó/+ő mostly refers to the agent (not always a homogeneous concept itself, for that matter), but it can indicate, in certain combinations, the place where something occurs: néz+ő, from néz (leaving off the infinitive marker -ni) "to look at", means "the one who looks at" or "beholder"; fut+ó, from fut "to run", means "runner" (professional or occasional); kiad+ó, from kiad "to publish", means "publisher" but sometimes also "publishing firm"[2]; altat+ó, from altat "to put (s.o.) to sleep", means either "lullaby" or "narcotic"; boroz+ó, from boroz "to drink wine", means "wine shop".

Similarly, the French suffix -eur, allegedly used to form nouns of agents, is far from always referring to a person whose activity consists of doing the thing indicated by the stem, as a transformational analysis could lead us to believe: min+eur "miner" does not refer only to "celui qui fait des mines" (the one that makes mines), as is remarked in Benveniste 1969a (= 1974:115-116), but also and more commonly to the one who works in a mine. Corbin criticizes (1986:2-3,413) the practice which (going much further than Swadesh (1939) when he spoke of "internal syntax" with reference to Nootka) consists of applying to the analysis of CWs the same procedures as to sentence structure. But nonetheless she remains convinced that the stem must necessarily belong to a syntactic category; therefore she posits, for aviat+eur and électrique, respectively, a verb *avier and a noun *électre, which are both nonexistent. Such a procedure ignores LBs' creativeness in word-building and the construction of meaning from elements that do not necessarily coincide with pre-existent syntactic categories. As for the French suffix +*ier*, Guilbert (1977:XXXII) writes that the noun X, derived from a stem Y and ending in this suffix, refers to the human who "makes Y come into existence". This is scarcely true of *chapel+ier*, from *chapeau*, and *jardin+ier*, from *jardin*; a *chapel+ier* sells hats much more commonly than he makes them, and a *jardin+ier* tends gardens at least as often as he makes them. As for *encr+ier* "inkpot", from *encre* "ink", the author, somewhat embarrassed, considers that the function of +*ier* here is to promote the inkpot to the dignity of an animate! An inadequate method produces monsters. By assigning a very rigid status to the constitutive parts of a derivative as a strictly rule-defined product, one runs the risk of forgetting that LBs, given the insufficiency of the resources provided by languages, adopt, even if unconsciously, the most straightforward method: they build synthetic associations, defined simply by the general semantic relationship they have with the thing referred to; hence the variety of the semantic results when this is applied to specific cases: what a *batel+ier* does to a ship (*bateau*) is to drive it, while an *écol+ier* does not drive, but attends, a school (*école*), a *fermier* does not attend, but exploits, a farm (*ferme*), a *prisonnier* does not exploit, but is shut up in, a prison (*prison*) and a *geôlier* is not shut up in, but watches, a jail (*geôle*) (cf. Serbat 1988:70).

Thus, there is no ready-made and unalterable meaning for the affix; neither is the stem assigned to a precise syntactic category. An original new unit is built by human morphogenetic activity. This does not imply, of course, that the affix is a meaningless element or an "empty morph". Even when the meaning of the stem does not change if an affix is added, the affix has a certain role to play. Russian possesses derivatives made of a preposition + a nominal element + the suffix -*nja*, which are interesting in this respect. Before seeing why, it is useful to note that, as in the cases studied above, the meaning of these derivatives has something to do with, but is by no means the necessary addition of, the exact meanings of elements assigned to a unique grammatical category in the sentence framework, i.e., a preposition and the noun it governs: *na+topor-nja* (on+axe-*nja*) "ring for hanging an axe"; *po+dorož-nja* (along+way-*nja*) "prayer said on the way (full form = *doroga*) to somewhere". It is the cohesive force of the suffix -*nja* which is responsible for the semantic originality of these CWs. But the most interesting fact here is that there are CWs which, although the presence of -*nja* does not change their meaning, coexist with the non-suffixed word: thus, *škol'-nja* means "school" just like *škola*, and *kuzov-nja* means "basket" just like *kuzov*; but *-nja* makes the CW belong to a paradigm which is characteristic of the Russian nominal lexicon (cf. Ferrand 1985:18-28), and which contains, among others, names of buildings and tools. This Paradigmatic Assignment (PAS) reflects the constructive work done by LBs when they build the lexicon according to various morphosemantic groupings.

Thus, the difficulty of systematically predicting the semantic result of CW formation is one more proof of LBs' creativity and of the vanity of algebraic models which expel the human dimension of language.

CHAPTER 7

Grammaticalization

Having studied lexicalization in chapter 6 after recalling in the introduction of PART III the features that distinguish it from the other important aspect of language morphogenesis, i.e., grammaticalization, I will now examine the latter. Grammaticalization is, as stated above, a much-studied process in modern typological work, but, given the purpose of the present book, I will concern myself here with those, among its aspects, that are related to LBs. After a brief introduction opposing it to reanalysis (7.1), I will study the main criteria on which we can rely to say that LBs have grammaticalized a linguistic element (7.2). In a third part, I will propose characterizing grammaticalization as a process reflecting an uninterrupted morphogenetic activity (7.3), and in the fourth part, I will try to show what semantic operations LBs perform in this process (7.4). A conclusion (7.5) will sum up the results of PART III of the present book.

7.1 Grammaticalization and reanalysis

Grammaticalization should not be confused with, nor reduced to, reanalysis. Heine & Reh (1984:95 ff.) are right when they criticize this frequent confusion. But their criterion, according to which grammaticalization is unidirectional while reanalysis is not necessarily so, will not be retained here. There are cases which, although not being the reverse of grammaticalization, consist of the lexematic use of a morpheme which is itself the product of grammaticalization (cf. 7.3.3). Reanalysis has been defined (2.2.1) as the operation by which LBs replace a certain analysis of syntactic units by a new one, with various markers of new relationships. As for grammaticalization, it is a dynamic process, which results in the appearance of new morphemes or classes of morphemes. Of course, a reanalysis may lead to a grammaticalization. Thus, in serial languages, depending on the environment, V1 or V2 within a V1 + V2 series may either remain a verb or be reanalyzed as a relator. As is shown by this very example, one of the main differences between reanalysis and grammaticalization is that the framework of the former is the succession of units that constitute the sentence (syntagmatic axis), whereas the latter creates or enriches the sets of relators, auxiliaries, etc. (paradigmatic sets) that make part of the morphosyntactic system of a given language. The relationship between the two axes is of course important: syntagmatic phenomena are the speech-chain manifestation of a specific paradigmatic status. Conversely, a reanalysis may be considered to be a case of grammaticalization when the new distribution of functions within a certain syntactic framework affects all occurrences of the units defined by these functions, thereby creating a new type of unit.

7.2 The main criteria of grammaticalization

Besides the classical ones, there are further criteria and a particular principle, which I would like to introduce here because they are interestingly related to LBs' activity. This study will therefore contain three parts: the classical criteria (7.2.1); further criteria (7.2.2); the Proof by Anachrony principle (7.2.3).

7.2.1 The classical criteria

Several authors, including Lehmann (1982b:125-179), Heine & Reh (1984:17-66), Hagège (1989c:661-666), have studied the various processes which can provide parameters of grammaticalization. It may be useful, in the perspective adopted here, to recall the main ones. LBs need tools in order to limit the semantic scope of verbal and nominal lexemes, hence the formation of *verbants* and *nominants* (cf. 2.3.3). They also need tools that are able to mark the relationships between lexemes, hence the formation of relators. The grammaticalization of lexematic units makes it possible to specialize these units in order to mark distinctions that have a more systematic character than those between the many terms of lexical sets. On the other hand, LBs need to make the new units identifiable as distinct from the lexemes which represent their historical origin. This double need explains both the nature of the word-classes which, in the languages of the world, are the result of a grammaticalization process, and the phenomena on which the classical criteria are based. I will now expound these two topics in some detail.

If we do not take into account particular situations like the derivation of personal pronouns from nouns (cf. 1.3.3 section a.), the main types of units which are crosslinguistically produced by grammaticalization are
– *verbants*: tense, aspect, mood markers, often negation markers;
– *nominants*: articles, quantifiers (including number markers).

For certain *nominants* it is hard, in fact, to find a lexematic source in the available material. In most known cases, definite articles are derived from deictics (cf. 5.4.3), which are themselves very old – and quite probably "primitive" – units (Hagège 1984b:17). Quantifiers are sometimes derived from numerals (e.g., in Melanesian languages), but may also come from 3PL personal morphemes, as in Ewe and creoles such as Jamaican, or Papiamentu (cf. 4.3.2). Other *nominants*, such as possessives, are, often enough, personal pronouns; also, they are often very old morphemes. Therefore, I will not treat these *nominants* here, but will rather treat others (cf. (212) and (213)).

– *relators*: I propose to retain this label as a cover-term for prepositions, postpositions, circumpositions, case markers, conjunctions of subordination and coordination. It seems preferable to speak of *relators* rather than of adpositions, even though some linguists would object that *relator* makes reference to a semantic, not to a formal, property. Speaking of adpositions, thereby lumping prepositions and postpositions together, does not suffice if one chooses to retain a sequential designation: it does not make it clear that while postpositions are attached to the preceding element and sometimes have variable forms conditioned by its structure, prepositions are not attached, in general, to the first part of the unit they govern.

Of course, not all *verbants* and *relators* are everywhere the demonstrable results of a grammaticalization process. This is only a general framework, as is the following set of criteria:

1) formal reduction, by
   a) attrition and loss of (a) relevant sound feature(s) (subphonemic) or phoneme(s) or syllable(s), either without a conditioning factor in the neighborhood, or by elision at a boundary (phonic reduction), or by
   b) loss of marker(s) that so far contributed to the identification of the lexeme as such (morphological reduction);
2) formal fusion: in many cases, no element can be inserted between the new unit (NU) resulting from grammaticalization and the imme-

diately contiguous element with which it acquires a new relationship;
3) sequential fixation: the NU cannot be permuted with the contiguous
element with which it comes into relationship;
4) combinatory limitedness: the NU does not have the same combinatory latitudes as its source (S);
5) syntactic specialization: the NU does not have the same functions
in sentences as its S, or it appears in only one of the possible functions of S, and there with much higher frequency than S;
6) semantic modification: the NU does not have, in the context where
it appears, the same meaning(s) as S.

To these criteria, which characterize the NU in syntagmatic terms, others
must be added, that characterize it as a paradigmatic event. The NU, when
its S is a V or an N, cannot, contrary to this S, be replaced by any V, or
any N, as the case may be, but only by members of a set. This set, although it is not so closed as is often believed (cf. 7.3.1), is more restricted
than the class to which S belongs. It is sometimes, at a given (provisory)
historical stage, made of numerically countable units. Moreover, the members of this restricted set are often (but not always: cf. 7.4.2 section b.)
obligatory in the context where they appear, as opposed to S.
The above criteria will now be illustrated by some examples:

(201)   ≠nùl̩ (≠n: nasal   ≠nuè
        alveolar click; ᵛ: rising   one of the present tenses indicating
        tone)   that one does something sitting
        "to be seated"   (Kxoe (Köhler 1981:530))

(202)   vá "to come"   →   á future tense marker (Ewe)

(203)a. le beet-ik k-u y-uuch-ul t-ech le he'l-o'
         (DET make-TRANS IMPERF-3SG it-happen-INTRANS to-2SG DET
         DEM-2DX)
         "This is why that happens to you" (Yucatec (Lehmann
                                                     1987b:5))
      b. uuch-ts' iib-nak-en-e'
          (FAR~PAST-write-SUBJ-ABS.1SG-DECL)
          "I wrote long ago" (Yucatec (ibid.))

(204)a. *mo fi àdé gé igi*
(I took machete cut tree)
"I cut the tree with a machete"

b. *mo fi ogbon gé igi*
(I took cleverness cut tree)
"I cut the tree cleverly" (Yoruba (Heine & Reh 1984:37))

(205) *mo ń-š'išę̀ Òjó sì ń-ję+un*
(I PROGR-work O. "join" PROGR-eat+thing)
"I am working and Ojo is eating" (Yoruba (Welmers
1973:377))

(206) *é súsú bé yē á-vá*
(he think that LOG FUT-come)
"he thinks that he will come" (Ewe (Hagège 1989c:665)).

In (201), the NU results from loss or modification of subphonemic features: nasality and tone. In (202), it results from the loss of a phoneme. In (203)b, we see that the subject and the intransitive marker, which characterize the S as a verb "to happen", have disappeared in the NU, a tense marker; moreover, the criteria of formal fusion and sequential fixation mentioned above apply here. In (204)a, there might be some hesitation as to whether *fi* should be treated as a verb or a relator; but in (204)b, treating *fi* as a verb would imply that an abstract quality such as cleverness can be taken in hand like a concrete object. Other African languages, like Igbo or Nupe (cf. Hagège 1975:364 fn.8), have also grammaticalized a verb "to take" into an instrument marker. In Chinese, the use of *bǎ* "to take" as a relator referring to an instrument began as early as the Wei dynasty (3rd century A.D.) and was generalized during the Tang dynasty (7th-9th centuries); then, by a new semantic leap, *bǎ* became a patient marker; at any rate, there is no longer any *bǎ* verb in Modern Chinese (cf. Hagège 1975:360-361). As opposed to this, when the verb is still in common use as such, which is the case in Yoruba, the semantic argument resorted to here to distinguish two uses of *fi* in (204)a-b could appear to be insufficient. The same could be said of (205), in which we treat *sì* as the coordinating morpheme "and" rather than the verb "to join" because the sentence does not mean "I am working, Ojo, joining (me), is eating". However, there is an additional criterion here; this is a non-segmental indication: the intonation curve remains at the same level between -šišé and Òjó, which shows that we do not have two independent sentences, but two clauses within one and the same sentence. In other cases, a semantic criterion is reinforced not only by prosodic, but also by morphological arguments. Thus, in (206), bé is not the verb "to say", as it is in the other contexts, but the complementizer "that"; we could, by resorting to a semantic argument, consider that when one thinks, one does not speak; but this is not always true, and there is another argument: if bé were a verb "to say", it would be followed by direct discourse, i.e., by mē "I"; in fact, what we have is a special form yē, which I have called (Hagège 1974) logophoric pronoun (cf. (103)-(105) in 3.2.1), i.e., a pronoun referring to the subject of the main verb when this verb governs a subordinate clause which reports the subject's speech, thought, desire, etc.

7.2.2 Further criteria

Two further criteria must also be taken into account and combined with those recalled in 7.2.1.
   a. Occurrence rate,
   b. Degree of consciousness.

a. *Occurrence rate*
If a given word remains formally identical in two distinct environments (a) and (b) despite a change in meaning, we must examine its occurrence rate in each environment. If, for a text of a certain length (novel, narration, myth, conversation, etc.), it appears much more often in (a) than in (b), this difference in occurrence rate points to a difference in status. We will say, combining semantic and occurrence rate arguments, that in (a) the word in question is becoming an NU.

b. *Degree of consciousness*
As stated in 1.4, there is no concerted Lb plan for the whole set of structures that define human languages. LBs need grammatical tools, which they can use in an automatic manner, in order to specify the scope, and mark the mutual relationships, of lexematic units. But this does not imply, in most cases, that LBs lucidly decide in public meetings to generate these tools as the best way to reach definite goals. There are some exceptions,

however. Two of them were studied in 1.3.3 sections c. and d. Another one
is provided by an institution which is related to language and known for
having resulted from a generally conscious, often originally private, activity
(cf. Hagège 1983b:25-28). This institution is writing. In certain cases, it has
produced a set of norms that reveal a difference in treatment between
lexemes on the one hand and, on the other hand, morphemes as grammaticalized stages of the latter. In Japanese, for example, *koto* is usually
written in *kanji* (Chinese characters) when it means "thing, affair, matter",
but in *hiragana* (Japanese syllabary) when it is used as a complementizer
meaning "(the fact) that". Similarly, *miru, oku, shimau, kureru, morau* are
normally written in *kanji* when used as full-fledged verbs meaning, respectively, "to see", "to lay", "to finish", "to give", "to receive", but in *hiragana* when used as auxiliary verbs after a main verb in *-te*, in which case
they correspond, respectively, to the following meanings in English: "to try
to", "to do... in advance", "finally", "for, on behalf of (the speaker or s.o.
belonging to the speaker's personal sphere)" (cf. 3.2.2) and "to get s.o. to
do for oneself".

   Starting from the last decades of the 19th century, after the beginning of
the Meiji era in 1868, the Japanese system of writing has been, during
almost one hundred years, the target of numberless debates and polemics:
was it good to abandon the Chinese characters, was it better than that to
only diminish their number, was it preferable to both solutions just to sim-
plify the *kanas*? The normalization just recalled is one among many uses
which became more or less established habits. But it shows that the reformers were aware of the difference between the lexematic and morphematic
uses of the same unit, since they assigned them to one or another of the
graphic devices whose number (three) is a unique characteristic of the
Japanese system of writing. However, this criterion, interesting though it
is, remains marginal for two reasons. First, writing is an institution, and
therefore the arguments it provides are not, whatever its link with language,
internal arguments. Second, this case, as just recalled, is far from frequent:
the metalinguistic consciousness of Japanese writing reformers is a fairly
rare phenomenon, as are those mentioned in 1.3.3, if compared with word-
coining (1.3.1). Is there, then, still another more reliable criterion of grammaticalization?

7.2.3 The Proof by Anachrony principle (PA)

In almost all cases of grammaticalization, the degree of consciousness is not only lower than that exhibited by the particular aspect of Japanese writing mentioned in 7.2.2 section b. It is zero. This is because LBs use languages as systems adapted to the fulfilment of their communicative and expressive needs. Therefore, they are mostly unconscious of morphosyntactic changes, especially when NUs become increasingly frozen. Of course, the degree of freezing is quite variable; but when it is high, an interesting result is that two stages of the same word, one representing the S, the other, chronologically later, representing the NU, may appear in the same sentence, sometimes in contiguity. This co-occurrence of two chronologically different stages is no obstacle for the speakers-listeners, who insert the two units in the same sentence as if they belonged to the same synchronic plane. Their identity of origin is ignored, since they can co-occur without pleonasm and are therefore treated as totally different. We may then consider this a proof that one of them is the product of a grammaticalization process, and posit a PA. The following are some illustrations, taken from Finnish ((207)), Israeli Hebrew ((208)), Japanese ((209)) and ((210)), Hindi ((211)), Burmese ((212)) and Iaai ((213)):

(207)   *lentokone-et suris-i-vat pää-mme päällä*
        (plane-PL hum-PAST-PL head-1PL.POSS above)
        "the planes were humming above our heads"

(208)   *lixvod kvod ha-rektor*
        (to honor ART-rector)
        "to His Honor the Rector"

(209)   *kono eiga-o issho~ni mi-ni itte-mi-mas-en ka*
        (this film-ACC together see-to go(-*te* form)-CON.AUX-POL-NEG
        INTERR)
        "wouldn't you come with me to see this film?"

(210)   *kami-o hikidasi-ni simatte-simatta*
        (paper-ACC drawer-in put~away-TERM.AUX(PAST))
        "he finally put away the paper in the drawer"

(211)   *Râm-se le-lo ɪr Shyam-ko de-do*
        (R-from take-AV.AUX(IMP) and S-to give-BEN.AUX(IMP))
        "take (it) from Ram and give (it) to Shyam"

(212)   *ʔèyn tə-ʔèyn*
        (house NUM.one-CLSF(of~houses))
        "one house" (Hagège 1982:78)

(213)   *umwə-k uma*
        (CLSF(of~houses)-1SG.POSS house)
        "my house" (Ozanne-Rivierre 1976: 191).

In (207) the postposition *päällä*, analyzable as *pää* "head"+-*llä* suffix of
the adessive, governs the very noun *pää*, on which it was itself built; but,
for any Finnish speaker, *pää-mme päällä* means "above (and not "on the
head of") our head". In (208), *lixvod* is a complex preposition resulting
from the association of the old Hebrew preposition *l(i)* "to, for" with
k(a)vod "honor", i.e., the very same noun governed by this complex preposition; but there is a sign of the insertion of *kvod* within a CW: its initial
k- becomes *x-* after a vowel. Thus, a literal translation of (208) would be
"to-honor (of) honor the-rector". Israeli Hebrew exhibits other illustrations
of the same phenomenon, like *biršut ršut ha-pituax*, literally "in power (of)
power the-development", i.e., "under the Development Authority". In the
following three examples, the NU that appears in contiguity or near contiguity with its S is no longer a relator, but a *verbant*, and more specifically,
an auxiliary. In (209), the *mi* in *itte-mi-mas-en* is a conative auxiliary,
adding the meaning "try to V" or "why not V?" to the preceding V in the
-*te* form, i.e., *itte* "going", which itself has a directional-final complement
mi-ni "in order to see", containing the very same verb *mi(ru)* "to see",
from which the conative auxiliary is derived. As for (210), it contains two
occurrences of *shimau*, one as a verbal lexeme meaning "to put away", the
other one as an auxiliary meaning "finally". (211) shows that Hindi, in the
same way, uses in contiguity a verb (*le(nâ)* "to take", *de(nâ)* "to give") and
the auxiliary which is derived from it, i.e., an aversive and a benefactive
verbant, respectively. The last two examples are illustrations of the PA as
applied to classifiers used in near contiguity with the nouns from which
they are derived. This derivation is obvious in (213), because the classifier
umwə is a reduplicated form of the N *uma*. In both (212) and (213), the

nominant is generic, like most classifiers, and the N has a specific meaning within the same semantic field. Thus, in Burmese and in Iaai, the position of the classifier (Burmese) or possessive classifier (Iaai) may not remain empty; it is filled by these generic units.

A noticeable fact in the examples above is that the NUs, when they are auxiliaries (*verbants*), as in (209)-(211), or noun classifiers (*nominants*), as in (212)-(213), bear the various markers normally attached to verbs or nouns, i.e., POL and NEG in (209), PAST in (210), IMP (Hindi suffix -*o*) in (211), NUM in (212), POSS in (213). Thus, although they are no longer full-fledged verbs or nouns used as *verbants* or *nominants*, they keep the trappings of a full lexeme, just like *va* in (214), from French, and *is going* in (215), its English translation: these auxiliaries, which express the IMM.FUT, illustrate the contradiction between morphosyntactic primacy and semantic centrality (cf. 2.1.2), since they are both inflected like ordinary verbs, while the semantically main verb is reduced to a nominal form (infinitive):

(214)   *il va y aller*

(215)   *he is going to go there.*

Of course, the PA applies only when the S and the NU derived from it appear in the same sentence. When the PA applies, we often have additional signs of grammaticalization: thus, in (202), a phoneme is lost, and in (209), if Japanese writing is used, the first occurrence of *mi* is noted in Chinese characters and the second one in Japanese syllabary (cf. 7.2.2 section b. above). Finally, the application of the PA is not limited to cases of grammaticalization. The PA is also applicable when a constituent member of a CW (cf. chapter 6) happens to be in contiguity with the lexeme which is its historical source. For instance, in Israeli Hebrew, *ben* "son" may appear just before *ben-*, a prefix diachronically related to it and meaning "possessor of":

(216)   *ben ben+xameš*
          (son possessor~of+five)
          "a five-year old son".

7.3 Grammaticalization as a continuous process

Three logically related characteristics show that grammaticalization is a continuous process. First, certain categories, such as relators, are constantly fed by new elements which are starting their transformation into grammatical tools. Second, the grammatical status of a word considered to be the product of grammaticalization is not always definitively established. Finally, in the case of NUs whose grammatical status is not questionable, we often observe a process by which these units yield, in turn, even more grammaticalized NUs. The study will therefore contain three parts: constantly renewed feeding (7.3.1); completed and uncompleted grammaticalization (7.3.2); from grammaticalized to even more grammaticalized (7.3.3).

7.3.1 Constantly renewed feeding

A morpheme whose grammatical status is long-established can be used again as a basis to form a new morpheme. This is a fairly natural way of enriching the set of grammatical tools human languages need. Very often, old relators are associated with lexemes to yield, by a process of endocentric compounding, new relators. I have mentioned Hebrew examples (cf. (208) and the comment thereupon) and others, taken from German (cf. 2.3.1). In contemporary Hungarian, a number of abstract nouns, followed by a possessive suffix, itself followed by the marker of the inessive, *-ben/-ban*, or the superessive, *-n*, are becoming postpositions (cf. also Finnish or Turkish, as well as Latin postpositions coming from old ablatives: *causā, gratiā*). Thus, we have in Hungarian *alap+já+n* "on the basis of" (literally "on its basis"), *ter+é+n* "in the domain of", *tekintet+é+ben* "with respect to", *ok+á+n* "because of", etc. Although these relators belong to officialese rather than to ordinary speech, they testify to the vitality of an old process characteristic of many Uralic languages: nouns have long provided, and go on providing, the source of postpositions. The same is true of many other languages. This alone would suffice to discard, unless we consider a very narrow synchronic stage, the alleged criterion according to which grammatical elements constitute closed sets. Such a criterion is in contradiction with the very notion of grammaticalization, in which the suffix *-ization* refers to a dynamic and constantly active process.

7.3.2 Completed and uncompleted grammaticalization

It is not always easy to demonstrate that the grammaticalization of a lexeme is completed. Thus, relators of verbal or nominal origin are often considered to be defective verbs or nouns, respectively, rather than relators, particularly when criteria of formal reduction and formal fusion (7.2.1) are lacking or scanty. I will consider here that if the semantic modification criterion (*ibid.*) is supported by another one, such as the occurrence rate criterion (7.2.2 section a.), we have sufficient evidence to posit a relator. In serializing languages, for instance (cf. 2.1.2 section b.), this applies to the element occupying position V1 or V2 (depending on the type of word order that is characteristic of the language in question) within a series V1+N1+V2+N2 or N1+V1+N2+V2. Such a structure is well-known for being, in this type of language, an important framework for relator genesis. In Chinese, an isolating language with a very low rate of morphological variation, *gēn*, *wàng* and *tì* mean "with", "towards" and "instead of", respectively, in a certain environment (position (a)), and "to follow", "to move forwards", "to replace", respectively, in another environment (position (b)). Furthermore, out of the total number of occurrences, we find 92%, 81% and 80% in (a), but 8%, 19% and 20% in (b), respectively. This suggests treating these units as prepositions in position (a) (Hagège 1975: 87). The change in meaning and the difference in occurrence rate reflect a change of syntactic status. In (b), these units are the syntactic centers of complete independent sentences, which is not the case in position (a). In position (a), moreover, a further criterion applies: there is no intonational fall between N1 and V2; this indicates that, here as in example (205) above, we do not have two independent sentences; what we have instead is, according to the Chinese word order rules, a relator followed by the noun it governs, itself followed by the verbal predicate, formerly the V2 in a V1+N1+V2+N2 series.

As far as relators with a nominal source are concerned, some authors (e.g., Welmers 1973:452-459) insist on calling them "relational nouns", due to the alleged lack, at least in Niger-Congo languages, of convincing arguments pointing to a more precisely grammatical status. But consider the Mbum words *fôl* "front" and "in front of", and *Bîl* "belly" and "within" (Hagège 1970, II: 267-269). They meet at least two of the classical criteria (7.2.1):

– syntactic specialization, since their use as subjects or objects with the first of the two meanings indicated here for each of them is extremely rare: in 98% of their occurrences, they function as adverbial complements;
– combinatory limitedness: they cannot take plural markers, or be associated with demonstratives, quantifiers, adjectives or relative clauses; nor is it possible to link them with a noun or pronoun through the use of the connective à, whereas ordinary nouns require à in this case, and are not submitted to any of these combinatory restrictions.

This difference appears if we compare (217) and (218):

(217)   *fôl ké*
        (in~front~of 3SG)
        "in front of him"

(218)   *pàk à ké*
        (house CONN 3SG)
        "his house".

We can therefore say that in Mbum, *fôl* and *Bîl* can no longer be considered as ordinary nouns, not even as a subpart of the nominal category, but must be viewed as relators.

This does not mean, of course, that NUs lose in every language all the features of their S. LBs leave marks of the previous stages of elements which their unconscious linguistic behavior has transformed. Thus, the criterion of formal fusion (7.2.1) is met in many cases, but by no means in all; in (219), from French, and (220), its English translation, the auxiliaries remain contiguous to the adverbs that modified the verbs which are the historical source of these auxiliaries:

(219)   *il avait souvent chanté*

(220)   *he had often sung.*

In Portuguese, a personal index remains inserted between the verb and the auxiliary (itself in final position), thus reflecting the old word order pattern, even though the auxiliary has undergone syllabic attrition and become a suffix:

(221)   *cantá-la-ei*
          (to sing(*canta*(*r*))-3SG.FEM-1SG.FUT((*h*)*ei*))
          "I will sing it (= *a cantiga*(FEM) "the song")".

In French, by contrast, the old word order pattern (unstressed personal index + unstressed verb + stressed auxiliary (also reduced, however, to a suffix) (cf. example (168) in 5.1) being what it is, there is no such insertion: *je la chanterai*.

With respect to relators, whatever their origin, nominal or verbal (cf. 7.4.1 section a.), it is, at least to some extent, possible to predict what morphemes are likely to be retained as vestigial constituent parts of the lexemes from which these relators are formed as a result of the process of grammaticalization. As far as relators with a nominal source are concerned, they often retain the definite article as one of their constituent parts when it has an important function within the NP. This is typically the case in Western Modern Armenian, where the definite article is central to the syntax of the NP: the postpositions *etew* "behind", *mēǰ* "within", *šurǰ* "around", *tak* "under" *verǰ* "after", *vray* "upon" keep the definite article even in the environments where they can be shown, on the basis of various criteria, not to be nouns any longer. It is true, however, that the loss of the article in this language may also be a sign of grammaticalization, or, interestingly enough, a criterion of semantic distinction: *teł* is a noun "place" when it takes the article, and a postposition "instead of" when it does not; *dēm* means "against, towards" with the article, and "in front of" without it (Donabédian 1991:77,174-175).

With regard to relators with a verbal source, the tendency is for them to keep the inner *verbants* rather than those whose semantic scope is the whole sentence and not just the verb to which they are attached by affixation or cliticization. In other words, aspect markers are more often kept than tense markers, and tense markers themselves more often than case markers, which indicate a syntactic relationship of the verb with its arguments. Moreover, among the relators that retain aspect markers, those whose verbal source has a dynamic meaning, in particular those that refer to a movement, outnumber those which do not have this feature. This can explain why the Kwakiutl relator *lá* "towards", which, like its verbal source, is followed by an accusative marker, remains a rarity (cf. Hagège 1989c:680). It also explains why, in Chinese, the aspect marker *zhe* is optionally retained after *yóu* "from", *gēn* "following", *suí* "along", *cháo* "towards", while other prepositions, such as *gěi* "for", *zài* "in", *gēnjù* "according to", *tóng* "together with", generally do not take aspect markers. It is fair to add that *zhe* is partly frozen here and that to some extent, it has a rhythmical function which is very important in Chinese speech (cf. Hagège 1975:61, where the notion of *phonic thickening* is proposed). But LBs have not completely got rid of its aspectual value, since it indicates concomitance, a meaning compatible with that of the units in which it has survived, whereas another aspectual marker, *le*, which indicates the perfective, is retained rather than *zhe* in relators whose verbal source implied the completion of a process, e.g., *chúle* "except, in addition to", from an old verb *chú* "to remove, do away with", or *wèile* "for, on behalf of", from a verb *wèi* "to aim at", which is very rare today (Hagège 1975:61, 71-72).

7.3.3 From grammaticalized to even more grammaticalized

An element which several criteria concord to assign to an NU does not necessarily represent the ultimate stage of the grammaticalization process. It may in turn yield a new, even more grammaticalized, element; or, while still belonging to the same grammatical category, it may take on a more abstract use. This occurs both within the same language and in the transition from one language to its offshoots. The evolution of Latin *ad* illustrates the process by which a morpheme becomes abstract. *Ad*, already a preposition, but less often with an abstract meaning than with the concrete spatial meaning "to, towards", yielded Spanish *a*, which is, when in the vicinity of a transitive verb, the marker of a human, or strongly individualized, object, corresponding to a patient in terms of the three viewpoints theory (cf. 3.1). This passage from the directional to the accusative is also illustrated, within Spanish, by the original situation of the dialect of Ortes Calemar, which, according to Escobar (1960), has specialized the morpheme *onde*, meaning "where" in Old Spanish, into a beneficiary and patient marker. Two further examples of the same process may be mentioned: Latin *de* meant "down from", but its reflexes in Romance languages – French *de*, Italian *di*, Portuguese *de*, Spanish *de* – are mainly used as connectives (cf. Hagège 1990a); another case of a relator yielding a connective by increasing specialization is Bulgarian and Macedonian *na*, which, after the decay of the declension system in these Slavic languages (as opposed to the other members in the same family), added to its locative use a new use, by which it marks a genitive-dative relationship (cf. Qvonje 1980).

As regards the process by which an NU yields, in turn, an even more grammaticalized element, it is illustrated by the further grammaticalization of relators into verbal morphemes. Examples of this widespread morphogenetic phenomenon are provided not only by Latin (*exire e vita*), but also by Hungarian (Boiron 1985), Nadeb, Rama, Winnebago (Craig & Hale 1988), and Kxoe, in which the causative, comitative and directional verbal suffixes are derived from postpositions (Köhler 1981:503 ff.).

In certain cases, we cannot arguably decide which of two NUs is the source of a further grammaticalization process, but we can nevertheless observe an interesting semantic connection between the original lexeme and two, sometimes three, grammatical uses of this lexeme. Thus, Newari *tọl*, when not used as a verb "to keep", serves, depending on the context, as a marker of a benefactive relationship, or perfective tense-aspect, or evidential mood. According to Genetti 1986, these connections can be explained by saying that the speaker keeps, as a witness, the traces of a past event, and this meets his needs. We have seen in 3.2.2 other illustrations of the functional and semantic versatility of certain morphemes in Quechua (ex. (120)) and in Yuman languages (comments on Diegueño -*k* and -*m* in the same paragraph).

As seen in 7.3.2 above, when the grammaticalization of one of the members of a V + V or N + N association is completed (first or second member depending on the dominant word order in the language considered), we can no longer say that this member still belongs to the class of (secondary) verbs or (relational) nouns. In languages that make use of the VS (cf. 2.1.2 section b.), the sentence becomes monocentric, since one of the Vs has yielded a relator. In languages that form relators from one of the members of an N + N association, it is worth mentioning that a pragmatic factor contributes to trigger the change from relational noun to relator: the generic value of the modified noun. It becomes more and more generic, more and more topical, while the other N, the modifying member, is rhematic, since it specifies the meaning of the modified N. The modified N, although it is syntactically central, will yield a relator, while the modifying N, although syntactically dependent, is pragmatically dominant and will remain an N – becoming, in the framework of the full sentence, an adverbial complement whose function is indicated by the former center, now a relator. Thus, in Kru we have (Givón 1975:73):

(222)   *sra   de*
         (house back)
         "behind the house" (in this language, the word order is modifying N + modified N).

Being a process, grammaticalization is generally held to be irreversible. According to Lehmann, who cites (1982b:16,20) several works sharing this view, there are "no cogent examples of degrammaticalization". This is probably true to the extent that we cannot predict the types of formal and semantic phenomena that might lead to the relexematization, if any, of a grammatical unit through a process allegedly appearing as the exact reverse of the one described above (7.2.1) in terms of a set of criteria. This does not mean, however, that a language cannot lexematize a morpheme. Examples of this process are more numerous than is often believed. It is not the reverse of grammaticalization. It simply shows how flexibly LBs adapt their language to their needs. Classical and Modern Greek *phílos* "friend" is held to come from the dative singular *sphi* of an old third person enclitic pronoun which was often used with a reflexive meaning before it was eliminated, towards the end of the 5th century B.C., by *h(e)autôi* (Bailly 1950:1880). In Uralic languages, locative postpositions have been used as bases for derived nouns: Finnish *sisällä* "within, inside" yields *sisäll+ys* "content" (e.g., of a book); *päällä* "above" (itself from *pää* "head" + *-llä* suffix of the adessive, as illustrated in example (207)) yields *pääll+ys*[1] "upper part, cover"; the same process is observed for Mari (Cheremis) and Mordvinian postpositions (Alhoniemi 1988). The Japanese suffix *-nagara*, which, after the conjunctive form of the verb, means that the action expressed by this verb (V1) is concomitant with that expressed by the following verb (V2): "while doing V1, do V2", appears in the colloquial expression *nagara+zoku* "the -ing crowd", applied to the people who do their job while watching TV, listening to the radio, etc. In this expression, *nagara* behaves as a lexematic (nominal) root which itself modifies another nominal element, *zoku*, meaning "tribe, race". In Hungarian the suffix *+féle*, meaning "a kind of", may itself receive the nominalizing suffix *+ség*, yielding *féleség*, also meaning "a kind of"; although *féleség* must be preceded by a noun and may not be used independently, it has the morphological aspect of a noun.

Besides these cases of lexematic CWs, formed in Uralic languages, in Greek, Japanese and Hungarian, on the basis of morphemes, and therefore belonging to morphology, another possibility remains open: in various languages, one can use a morpheme, this time in the syntagmatic framework of an NP or a VP, by associating this morpheme with *verbants*, *nominants* or numerals. Certain (rare) variants of spoken American English use the suffix *+ade* of *orangeade* or *lemonade* with an article, or a plural marker, or a numeral, etc., as a generic noun referring to drinks of this kind; similarly, spoken Mexican Spanish uses the suffix *+ate* of such words as *guayabate* "guava jelly" as a generic noun: *ates* refers to jellies of the same kind as *guayabate*. In the political phraseology of modern continental China, it is frequent to speak of *sān tóng* "the three withs", using a numeral *sān* "three" with the comitative preverb *tóng*, and thus nominalizing this preverb, to refer to the three duties imposed on intellectuals during the Cultural Revolution: *tóng+zhù* "live with", *tóng+lào* "work with" and *tóng+chī* "eat with (the peasants)". Other morphemes such as the prefix *fǎn+* "anti-" or the suffix *+huà* "-ize" are also used as nouns, e.g., *sì huà* "the four -izations" (= modernization in four domains).

7.4 Grammaticalization and semantic operations

Meaning is a basic factor in the grammaticalization process. This is why various semantic facts have already been mentioned above (7.2.1, 7.3.2, 7.3.3). The semantic aspects of grammaticalization will be studied here in a more systematic way. First, there are certain semantic prerequisites to this process. Second, the treatment of meaning here is far from uniform. These points will be studied in the following two parts: semantic prerequisites to the grammaticalization process (7.4.1); the fate of meaning in grammaticalization (7.4.2).

7.4.1 Semantic prerequisites to the grammaticalization process

Not just any lexematic unit may yield a grammaticalized unit. This will be illustrated here by studying two important fields of linguistic morphogenesis. This study will thus contain two sections:

a. Relator genesis
b. Tense-aspect-mood *verbant* genesis

a. *Relator genesis (RG)*
– Relators with a verbal source
The following table is based on the examination of many languages. The meanings in A are those of the verbs most frequently gammaticalized into relators; the meanings in B are those of the relators derived from the verbs whose meanings are given in A:

(223)

	A		B
a.	"to be (located) in"	→	"in, at"
	"to front"	→	"in front of"
b.	"to go to"	→	"to, towards"
	"to move towards, head for"	→	"towards"
	"to accompany"	→	"with; behind"
	"to follow"	→	"with; along"
	"to get out from"	→	"from"
	"to proceed, arise, result from"	→	"from, because of, due to"
	"to go through, cross"	→	"through; by means of"
c.	"to refer to"	→	"as for"
	"to look like"	→	"like, (same) as"
	"to conform to, to measure"	→	"according to, after"
	"to compare"	→	"with respect to, in comparison with"
d.	"to use"	→	"by means of, with, by"
	"to take"	→	*id.*
	"to exclude, eliminate"	→	"without; except"
	"to replace"	→	"instead of"
	"to lean on, rely on"	→	"on the basis of"
	"to take"	→	"along with"
	"to oppose"	→	"against"
	"to give"	→	"to, for, on behalf of"
	"to aim at"	→	"for, for the sake of"
	"to surround"	→	"around; about, concerning"
e.	"to take; "to treat or consider as"	→	patient marker

Table (223) does not aim at being exhaustive; it only presents the most frequent types of situations. The syntactic framework for relator genesis on a verbal source with the semantic relationships shown in (223) is a verbal series which can be represented (leaving aside the subject and retaining only the predicates and complements) by the following formula (in SVO languages): V(P)1 + N(P)1 + V(P)2 + N(P)2, already illustrated by Creole and African examples in 4.3.3 section b. and 7.2.1:(162)-(163) and (204)a-b ("take" → "with (concrete or abstract means)"), (164)-(165) ("give" → "to"), (166)-(167) ("take" → "(along) with").

LBs apply here a principle that may be characterized as the More General More Frequent (MGMF) principle: due to the needs of human intercourse, LBs tend to use on a large scale the words that express general notions corresponding to everyday life. Some of these notions are expressed by verbs which constitute a part of the semantic primitives of human language (cf. Wierzbicka 1972); but the notion of semantic primitives is taken here in the literal acceptation of an unanalyzable meaning that constitutes a part, as a component, of other meanings, whereas for Wierzbicka, whose list does not contain any of the items in (223), the notion does not exactly refer to this, but to the ultimate components of thought, in terms of which meanings can be compared and described. Most of the verbs that have, so to say, a vocation for grammaticalization have broad and general meanings. This makes them fairly versatile, and therefore particularly frequent. We find among them verbs with a static meaning ((223)a), verbs indicating various types of concrete or abstract movement ((223)b), verbs denoting reference or comparison ((223)c), or verbs with a dynamic meaning, that are related to some of the main kinds of concrete or abstract actions of one entity upon another ((223)d). It is noteworthy that certain verbs are particularly versatile: depending on the language, "take" may yield an instrument marker, a comitative marker (cf. the Creole and African examples just recalled above), or a patient marker ((223)e); this case is illustrated by the Chinese preposition *bǎ* (cf. comment in the end of 7.2.1), or the Nitinaht preposition *ʔōyoqw*.

Chinese, with its very long history, provides good examples of the MGMF principle. Such elements as *wéi* "to be, do or make", *zài* "to be (located) in", *yǐ* "to take, use", *bǎ* "to grasp, take", *zì* "to start from", *yǔ* "to give to", *yú* "to refer to" (as well as *qù* "to go to") are constantly utilized throughout the history of Chinese (cf. Li 1980). What is even more striking is that some of them, *yǔ*, *yǐ*, *wéi*, *zì*, *zài* and *yú*, go back to very remote times and are still in use today: *yú* is already present as far back as the *Jiǎgǔwén* (tortoise bone inscriptions: 14th century B.C.); *yǐ* appears as soon as the beginning of the Early Archaic period (9th century B.C.); *wéi* is found in texts dating back to Late Archaic (= Classical) Chinese (5th-3rd centuries B.C.), *zì*, *zài* and *yǔ* in texts from the Early Han period (206 B.C.-25 A.D.) (Peyraube 1988, Hagège 1990d).

The MGMF principle does not apply only to a few particularly useful verbs having a general meaning, as opposed to the rest of the verbal lexicon, but also to that one, among several verbs with an analogous meaning, that eventually imposes itself over its rivals. Chinese, again, provides an illustration here: *yǔ*, being the most general of the verbs meaning "to give", eliminated, during the Late Han period (25-220 A.D.), the other verbs with a more precise meaning. Then, in the Late Medieval period (*ca.* 500-1250), another principle applied, the More Frequent More Grammaticalizable (MFMG) principle; according to this principle, *yǔ*, having imposed itself as more and more frequent and finally as the only verb "to give", underwent an uncreasing specialization when it appeared in the particular context of the attributive structure V1 (attributive verb) + N(P)1 (given object) + *yǔ* + N(P)2 (receiver)[2]. Interestingly enough, at about the same time (second part (8th-9th centuries) of the Tang dynasty (618-907)), a comparable process produced one of the main verbants in Modern and Contemporary Chinese: the verb *liǎo* "to finish", having become (after the elimination of *bì*, *qì*, *yǐ* and *jìng*, roughly synonymous with it) the only verb indicating the end of a process, finally yielded – by formal reduction and semantic specialization – the perfective marker *le* (Peyraube 1988:214).

Despite the semantic modification of the verb when it becomes a relator by a change in the semantic structure of the sentence, the meanings in (223)B are mostly deducible from those in (223)A. However, there are some less obvious cases. Thus, in spoken Mandarin Chinese, the relator corresponding to *gěi* "to give " has three different meanings, depending on the context. While one of these, "to, for", is quite expected and abundantly illustrated in languages where a verb "to give" has yielded a dative marker (cf. again (223)d A-B and examples (164)-(165) in 4.3.3 section b.), the other two are less straightforward: *gěi* is used with two opposite values, as agent marker, or as patient marker. The use as an agent marker may be explained by interpreting the structure "give s.o. do sth." as "give s.o. the possibility of doing sth.", i.e., by an intermediate causative stage (cf. English *I got him to go* and French *il me l'a donné à réparer* (Paris 1989:77)). As for the use as a patient marker, it might be explained by proposing to interpret the structure "give s.o. do sth." as "inflict on s.o. an act consisting in doing sth.". Besides, another language, Manchu, also uses as dative or factitive or passive the same morpheme, i.e., *bu*.

– Relators with a nominal source

Based on many languages, table (224) presents, in A, the meanings of the nouns whose grammaticalization into relators yields the meanings in B (the meanings between brackets are the relatively rare ones):

(224)

A		B
a. body parts		
"head"	→	"on"
"foot", ("anus")	→	"under"; ("because of")
"face", "eye", "mouth", "forehead"	→	"in front of"; "according to"; "instead of"
"back", ("nape")	→	"behind"
"ear", "side", "flank"	→	"beside"
"stomach", "belly", ("heart"),		
("palm")	→	"in, within"
("body")	→	("at …'s house")
("hand")	→	("by"),("for"),("at …'s house")
b. portions of space		
"top, upper part", "sky",		
("surface")	→	"above"
"bottom, lower part", "base",		
("earth"), ("world")	→	"below"
"front part", ("field")	→	"in front of"
"back part"	→	"behind"
"inside", ("hole")	→	"in, within"
"outside", "end", "extremity"	→	"out(side) of"
"side"	→	"near"
"middle"	→	"amid, among"
"intermediate space"	→	"between"
"river-bank"	→	"across, beyond"
c. abstract notions		
"thing", "affair", ("word")	→	"because of"

The syntactic framework for relator genesis on a nominal source is, depending on the language and the dominant word order type, either

modified   N + modifying N(P)   →   preposition + governed N(P), as in
"foot"   "man"   →   "below (the) man"

or

modifying N(P) + modified N   →   governed N(P) + postposition, as in
"man"   "foot"   →   "man   below".

The former modified N is no longer a relational noun. As shown in 7.3.2, although it does not always lose its *nominants* (cf. Armenian examples), it has become a relator: it exhibits formal reduction and formal fusion, as well as combinatory limitedness and syntactic specialization (cf. 7.2.1). With respect to the last of these criteria, we may note that in Japanese, spatial postpositions meaning "above", "below", "in front of", "behind", "inside", "outside", "near", "between", are in fact complex associations in which the elements with these meanings are followed by the old relator *ni* "in" and preceded by the governed N(P), to which they are linked by the connector *no*, e.g., *X no naka ni* "inside X"; the same structure is found in Bantu languages such as Bemba; in other African languages, the complex relator is also formed by means of an old relator which either replaces the class affix, as in Gola, or is added to the noun when there is no class affix, as in Krongo. In addition to the pragmatic factor mentioned in 7.3.3 as one of those that trigger the grammaticalization process (cf. example (222) and its explanation), there is an important semantic factor: the former modified N belongs to the semantic fields of body parts and spatial location (as well as, in a few cases, abstract notions); therefore, it has a static meaning, which gives it a vocation to express, by specialization, various types of situations, of persons and objects.

This study of relator genesis from a nominal source confirms the central position of ego and ego's body in the *anthropophoric system* (cf. 3.2.1). But there are other possible reference centers which, although they belong to ego's ecology, do not coincide with ego. It is useful to note, in this connection, that in certain pastoral societies, the designation of portions of space, though based on body parts, does not refer to man, but to cattle; this is especially true of the Cushitic and Nilotic languages; the head being not necessarily the upper part of these bodies, but their most anterior part, "head" (*εn-dukúya*) yields "in front of" (*dukúya*, with loss of the class prefix) in Masai; it yields "in front of", in addition to "on", in Dinka (*nhom*); the back of a four-legged animal is horizontal, hence in Somali *dul-* "back" yields "on", and in Shilluk "on" is expressed by both a relator coming from "back" (*kwom*) and one coming from "head" (*wic*); Western Nilotic **tha(a)r* "buttock, anus" often yields "under", but in Shilluk (*tha*) and Achooli (*tɛ*), it also yields "behind" (Heine 1989:91-92).

These semantic relationships, rare though they may be, are just as easy to understand as those shown in table (224)a-b. With respect to abstract notions ((224)c), the semantic relationships are somewhat less transparent, but not totally opaque: various languages build a causal relator on the basis of a noun meaning "thing, affair", or, less often, "word", as in Mbum (*Bè*), or "care, worry", as in Latvian (the N *bēda* yields, in the ACC.SG, the postposition *bēdu* "for, because of"); Latvian also grammaticalizes an N meaning "impression" (*iespaida*) into a postposition meaning "under the influence of" (*iespaidā*, LOC.SG of *iespaida*). One also finds fairly rare phenomena, among which the following one is especially worth mentioning: in Drehu, *hnene* "place" yields an agent marker.

Some theories, taking over an idea present in Lakoff & Johnson 1980, claim that a metaphorical operation underlies the process of grammaticalization. Thus, according to Claudi & Heine (1986), metaphors, as expressive ways of designating space as an object (e.g., what lies behind is viewed as the posterior part) and an object as a person (e.g., its front part is viewed as its face, or mouth, or forehead), are based on a resemblance between elements which, however, are not identical. This metaphorical operation is held to be responsible for the desemanticization which, according to these authors, leads to grammaticalization. In fact, if there is general agreement that the extension of spatial to temporal meanings in the relators of many languages is based on a metaphorical process, the relationship between nouns and relators as presented in (224) is rather metonymic than metaphorical: there is a metonymic shift from the literal spatial meaning to a meaning that refers to the human (or animal) body and natural (or man-made) objects, both being, in LBs' everyday life, specific and anthropologically significant parts of space. The metonymic transfer from objects of space to human persons is also evidenced by languages which use spatial adverbs with the meaning of personal pronouns: Japanese *kotira* "here" often refers to the speaker, Vietnamese *đây* "here" and *đấy* (or *đó*) "there" are used with the meanings "I" and "you" respectively when one wants to avoid the hierarchical or affective connotations linked to the use of personal pronouns (Nguyen Phu-Phong 1992). Finally, Claudi and Heine's metaphoric interpretation, if it may be applied – with the qualifications made here – to relators with a nominal source, is less easy to apply to those with a verbal source, many of which do not have a static meaning like relators indicating spatial locations, but a dynamic meaning (cf. (223)b and d).

b. *Tense-Aspect-Mood Verbant Genesis (TAMVG)*

The most common sources for *verbants* indicating tense or aspect are verbs, and less often, adverbs (and relators). They will be studied successively here, leaving aside the development of tense markers from aspect markers, a relatively well-studied process (cf., e.g., Binnick 1976), which is a case of continuous grammaticalization (cf. 7.3), not of evolution of a lexeme into an aspect marker.

– TAMVG from a verbal source

Summing up the observations made on a number of languages, table (225) presents, in A, the meanings of the verbs whose grammaticalization into *verbants* yields the elements whose meanings are indicated in B (the meanings between brackets are those which are less often represented):

(225)

A		B
"start", "begin", "enter", ("go")	→	ingressive; inchoative; (future)
"become", ("come"), ("go")	→	resultative; passive; (future)
"get out", "finish", "abandon",	→	egressive, completive;
"stop, cease"; ("go"); ("give")		terminative,
		perfective; past
"be in", "remain", "continue";	→	continuative, progressive
"be sitting"		
"be used to", "get used to"	→	static or dynamic habitual
"go beyond, exceed"	→	exhaustive, excessive
"return, go back"	→	reiterative, regressive

From the morphosyntactic point of view, the elements in B, depending on the language and the stage reached in the grammaticalization process (cf. 7.3.2), may be auxiliaries, semi-auxiliaries (generally modals), or full lexical verbs. In many cases, the auxiliaries have undergone formal reduction, formal fusion, and sequential fixation, thus becoming pure aspect morphemes. Such is the case, for instance, in creoles: Papiamentu *ta* = progressive, Saramaccan and Sranan *kabá* = egressive, Krio, Jamaican, Gullah, Guyanese *don* = completive, Chad Arabic Pidgin *ḫlas* = completive, Hawaiian Creole English and Cameroonian Pidgin English *bin* = past, Caribbean French Creole *te* = past, come, respectively, from Spanish *estar*, Spanish *acabar*, English *done*, Arabic *ḫlas*, English *been*, French *était*. But when the elements in B have remained full lexical verbs, the criteria that establish their aspectual status are the occurrence rate criterion on the one hand (cf. beginning of 7.2.2 section a.), and, on the other hand, the semantic difference with respect to their use as independent verbs. However, in purely morphological terms, aspectual finite verbs are not distinct from ordinary verbs, as is evidenced by Spanish examples such as (32) above. It remains nevertheless true that verbs of this kind, even though they are inflected like any other verb, are defective, or at least marginal in some way as far as their construction is concerned: Spanish *acabar*, depending on whether it is a terminative or an immediate past marker, governs a gerund or an infinitive (cf. example (34)a-b). Japanese auxiliaries whose verbal source may still be used today as a main verb are divided into two groups; the members of the first group require the coordination form (-*te* form) of the preceding (= semantically main) verb, while the members of the second group require the conjunctive form of the preceding verb; moreover, for some of those belonging to the second group, the transitive form of the verbal source (when there is an opposition between a transitive and an intransitive form) is obligatory, even if the preceding verb is intransitive. Thus, corresponding to English *begin*, which, depending on the context, is either transitive or intransitive, Japanese has *hazimeru* transitive and *hazimaru* intransitive, but the aspect marker is always *hazimeru*, whatever the orientation of the main verb: this is illustrated by (226), in which *huri* is the conjunctive form of the intransitive verb *huru* "to fall":

(226)   *ame ga huri-hazime-ta*
        (rain SUBJ.M fall-INGR-PAST)
        "it began to rain" (Shibatani 1990:247).

The coordination structure illustrated by the Japanese -*te* form has other manifestations, among which a frequent one is the *hendiadys*, a coordination of two finite verbs, one aspectual, the other semantically central. Thus, to express a progressive meaning associated with a reference to body position, Dutch links a verb in the infinitive (semantically central) with a finite auxiliary verb ((227)), while Afrikaans, a Dutch-based creole, coordinates two finite verbs ((228)):

(227)   *wij zitten te eten*
        (we sit at eat)
        "we are eating while sitting"

(228)   *ons sit en eet*
        (we sit and eat)
        same meaning (Stolz 1990:462).

The semantic relationship between A and B in (225) seems easy to account for if we consider, as in the case of relators with a nominal source, that there is a metonymic shift from the literal meaning (body position, body moves, concrete or abstract activities, whether conscious or semiconscious) to the aspectual meaning. This is illustrated by African languages such as Achooli, Logbara and Shilluk (cf. Boretzky 1988:79-80) or certain creoles (those just mentioned above and others, especially Portuguese- and Dutch-derived creoles such as those of the Cape Verde and Gulf of Guinea Islands, Sri-Lanka Portuguese Creole, Negerhollands, etc.). In all these languages, verbs meaning "get out", "finish", "abandon", and "stop" yield an egressive, completive, terminative and perfective marker, respectively.

This process is also illustrated by Chinese, in which an old verb *liǎo* "finish" yielded the perfective marker *le*, distinct, despite synchronic homophony, from the resultative marker *le*, which is a reflex of the verb "come" (Chao 1968:246 fn.31), and indicates, at the end of a sentence, that as a result of a given event, a new situation has occurred. Another illustration is Old English: the verbs *cunnan* "know, understand", *magan* "avail, prevail, cause", *sculan* "owe" and *willan* "wish, want" produced, in the course of history, *can, may, shall* and *will* respectively, i.e., modal auxiliaries of Modern English (Collins 1986:135). We may also witness the birth of a grammatical category of perfective *verbants* based on verbs that express a change in location or posture, or an action that entails such a change, in Indo-Aryan languages: "go", "give", "take", "strike", "fall", "come", "sit", etc.; cf. "go" and "give" in Hindi-Urdu (Hook 1989).

Thus, table (225) confirms that the grammaticalization of a verb into a tense, aspect, or mood *verbant* does not apply to all verbs; this process implies certain specific meanings, and (225) shows what verbs are preferably grammaticalized into *verbants*. But, despite the conclusions one could be tempted to draw from an examination of the semantic kinships between A and B items in (225), it is not easy to explain or predict all the phenomena observed in human languages, and in particular to tell what verb will, in a given language, yield a TAM verbant, or what will be the meaning of a TAM verbant coming from a certain verb. Some evolutions are understandable, others are less so. We can understand why Tamil and Telugu have a grammaticalized use of a verb "beat" as a factitive marker, since the verbs with which this marker combines denote an action or event which is inimical to the causee (Fedson 1985:19). We also can understand (cf. 3.2.1 on *itive* and *ventive* morphemes) why, besides the copula *essere*, Italian, depending on whether the event is viewed as directed towards, or originating from, the speaker, uses as a passive marker either the ventive *venire* "come", generally implying an action or its result (same use for *ğâ* "come" in an Arabic dialect, Maltese, under Italian influence), or the itive *andare* "go", implying that the patient has reached a certain stage under the pressure of an agent (same use for *jānā* "go" in Hindi-Urdu), with an element of obligation in some contexts. All these cases, like those studied in 3.2.1 (recall, especially, Catalan (ex.(110)) and Kiksht), are illustrations of an important process in Lb, which I propose calling Deictic Erosion (DE) and considering as typical of LBs' morphogenetic behavior: in the course of grammaticalization, elements with a precise deictic meaning lose a part (but not all) of this meaning as they become markers of tense (cf. table (111)), aspect, or mood. Finally, we can explain why Western Arabic dialects use a morpheme *râ-h*, originally the imperative of a verb "see", with a suffixed 3SG personal index, to express a modal meaning. This morpheme establishes a link between the speaker and the hearer: it can be translated by "see it!", "here we are!" or "such is the situation (despite your expectations or as opposed to what you said)" (Caubet 1992).

Other semantic shifts, if equally understandable, are less frequent, or less straightforward. In Ait Seghrouchen Berber, *Tux* "I forgot" has yielded a past tense marker (Bentolila 1987:87). After the *-te* form of a verb, Japanese uses certain auxiliaries whose meanings are not immediately deducible from those of the verbs in independent use: we know (cf.7.2.2 section b., and 7.2.3) that *miru* "see" takes on a conative meaning ("try to"), *oku* "put, lay" an anticipative meaning ("do in advance"), and *morau* "receive" means that the subject gets someone to do something on his behalf. It is not totally unexpected that Japanese verbs such as *nokosu* "leave" and *siburu* "show some reluctance to" may, when associated with another verb, mean, respectively, non-exhaustion and reluctance with respect to the action denoted by this verb. But this grammaticalization is not an unescapable necessity, nor is it obvious why these elements should have, as they do, the status of auxiliaries, requiring the conjunctive form of the preceding verb. Similarly, it is not obvious why in Burmese "know" yields a habitual ("usually"), as is also the case in two Iberian- and Iberian-Dutch-derived creoles, Palenquero and Papiamentu respectively, as well as in Moore, where, in addition, "ignore", "run" and "get tired" yield, respectively, "never", "already" and "finally" (Hagège 1982:83). Likewise, while we can understand why languages such as those of the Polynesian and Yuman stocks have specialized into a negation a verb "fail" (cf. English *I fail to see why...*), we can just as well understand why languages whose negation building strategy is not verbal have reinforced the original negative morpheme by a noun referring to a *scalar minimum* (on this notion, cf. Hagège 1982:85): French *ne... pas* (literally "not (even a) step"), Italian *non.. mica* (literally "not (even a) crumb"), Western Arabic dialects *ma...š(i)* (literally "not (even a) thing"); these strategies themselves, for that matter, are far from representing the only possible solution.

In view of these facts, it seems difficult to always maintain with Givón that "it is possible to infer, from the specific presuppositions and implications of an M[modality]-verb, the type of sentence modality likely to evolve from it. The tense-aspect system in language thus represents a natural outgrowth of our verb system." (1973:924). All we can infer from the facts examined above is that LBs avail themselves of the possibilities offered by productive structural models to unconsciously give a grammatical status to certain lexemes whose meaning has a cultural importance in a given social context. The same could be said of another kind of grammaticalization not studied in detail here, i.e., that of intransitive verbs of motion into directional markers, abundantly illustrated in Mayan languages, for instance. LBs need special morphemes for special purposes, and these purposes are common to many situations in all human societies.

Thus, on the one hand, there are some unexpected facts and some cross-linguistic diversity in the sources LBs use and the semantic results of grammaticalization; but on the other hand, there is a homology as far as the general scheme is concerned: it is the vocation of LBs to make tools corresponding to particular needs and TAMVG from verbal origin is, like RG, a fundamental human activity. The same may be said of TAMVG from an adverbial source, which will be briefly examined now.

– TAMVG from an adverbial source

We have just seen that the semantic shift illustrated by TAMVG from a verbal source is often transparent, but may at times be less easy to interpret. TAMVG from an adverbial source is less widespread but more transparent. Various stages of the association of adverbs to the VP as *verbants* are represented in languages whose descriptions are available. Central African languages such as Aka, Baka, and Sango possess a structured system of tense adverbs that remain formally and semantically independent of the verb, so that in these languages, there are no real tense morphemes, i.e., morphemes which are part and parcel of the VP (Diki-Kidiri 1988:118-119, Thomas 1988:59-60). But tense, and aspect, adverbs may also be used when translating from a language in which tense and aspect specifications are not expressed by verbal inflection into a language where they are, as was shown for Hungarian, as opposed to English and French, in examples (35)-(37) above. In other cases, we can see the birth of TAM *verbants*. In Kru languages of the Grebo complex, there is phonological and distributional evidence that shortened forms of time adverbs have become tense markers; to these material. criteria, a semantic one may be added: the tense markers do not carry specific time reference any longer, i.e., the *verbant* whose source means "yesterday", for example, has been generalized to cover all past actions, as is evidenced by the application of the PA in Grebo as well as other Kru languages of the same area, Neyo and two dialects of Bassa (Marchese 1984). The grammaticalization of adverbs (and, less often, relators) into TAM *verbants* is even clearer in creoles, since the sources in this case do not belong to the creoles themselves but to the languages from which they are historically derived: to take examples only from tense-aspect *verbants* referring to the future or aspects related to it, I will recall Papiamentu *lo*, from Portuguese *logo* "soon, right away", Bichelamar *bambae*, from English *by and by*, Mauritian *pu*, future, desiderative, final, from the French preposition *pour*, and

Caribbean creoles *ap*, progressive, immediate future, from the French preposition or adverb *après*.

7.4.2 The fate of meaning in grammaticalization

Given that one of the effects of the grammaticalization process is to freeze and demotivate linguistic units, one could believe that a valid criterion here is the loss of the original meaning of S. In fact, things turn out to be less simple than one might surmise. It will be shown below that although there are many cases of semantic freezing, linguistic units resulting from grammaticalization are far from being empty words; they often keep traces of the meaning of the S. The study will therefore contain the following sections:

a. Semantic freezing
b. Semantic "weakening"
c. Semantic pressures.

a. *Semantic freezing*

In 7.2.3 I introduced the PA, according to which the contiguity or near contiguity of two elements (often formally identical if no reduction has occurred), one being the source from which the other is historically derived, may be taken as a proof of grammaticalization. If LBs were totally conscious of the historical sameness of these two elements, they might hesitate to combine them in one sentence, even taking into account that their meanings are not identical. But they do not hesitate. Neither are they disturbed by certain cases of semantic incompatibility, as revealed by a historical analysis. Thus, in Iaai, not only may the noun in a possessive classifier NP be the very noun from which the possessive classifier is derived (a phenomenon illustrated by example (213) above, but which I illustrate again by (229) for ease of comparison), but it may also be a noun whose meaning is in contradiction with that of the nominal source of the classifier (ex.(230)):

(229)   *nuu-k nu*
        (CLSF(of~planted~things)-1SG.POSS   coconut~tree
        "my coconut tree"

(230)   *nuu-k iwat*
(CLSF(of~planted~things)-1SG.POSS pandanus)
"my pandanus tree" (Ozanne-Rivierre 1976:191).

nuu- is the possessive classifier derived from *nu* "coconut tree" and referring, generically, to any planted thing. In (229), it functions as a *nominant* in near contiguity with its own historical source; therefore this example, like (213), is an illustration of the PA. In (230), given that a coconut tree is not a pandanus tree, there is a contradiction. But this contradiction passes unheeded. This shows that *nuu-* is, to some extent, semantically frozen: it is, essentially, a possessive classifier. Thus, we may posit an Unheeded Contradiction (UC) principle, which is a subclass of the PA. The (near) contiguous units to which the UC applies are not always derived from each other. For example, according to Askedal (1984:22), it is possible in German to use the auxiliaries *bekommen* or *kriegen*, whose connotation is favorable or neutral[3], in passive structures which, given the meaning of the verb (in the past participle), imply that the patient is adversely affected:

(231)   *der Bub bekommt/kriegt das Spielzeug weggenommen*
(the kid gets the toy taken~away)
"the kid has his toy taken away from him".

Other illustrations of the UC are to be found in the field of aspect. Thus, in Egyptian Arabic, we have a verb *ʔâm* "to get up", corresponding to Classical Arabic *qâma*. *ʔâm* is also used in the past (with gender, number and person inflection) as an auxiliary to express an inchoative meaning. Now, nothing prevents this auxiliary from appearing in association with a verb whose meaning is contrary to the notion of getting up, as in (232):

(232)   *ʔom-t nim-t*
(INCH.1SG-PAST sleep~1SG-PAST)
"I fell asleep".

In the Mouroum dialect of Ngambay-Moundou, the progressive auxiliary *áo* comes from a verb meaning "to go", whatever the meaning of the main verb (ex. (233)); but when the main verb is *áo* itself, the progressive auxiliary, in this case only, is *ísí*, from a verb meaning "to sit", despite the semantic contradiction (ex. (234)):

(233) m-áo m-úsā né
       (I-PROGR I-eat something)
       "I am eating"

(234) d'-ísī d'-áo
       (they-PROGR they-go)
       "they are leaving" (Vandame 1963:95-96).

b. *Semantic "weakening"*
   Despite the number of linguistic facts such as those mentioned in section a. above, grammaticalization is far from systematically resulting in frozen or empty words. Besides the cases where the PA or the UC apply, what occurs in many other cases is not a freezing process, but a specialization. Specialization, contrary to a commonly shared assumption, does not mean weakening in the sense of an impoverishment of semantic content. For instance, a relator resulting from the grammaticalization of a verb, just because it is a tool apt to mark a syntactic relationship, may have a variety of meanings, depending on the context constituted by the noun it governs and the verb with respect to which it marks this noun as an adverbial complement. Grammaticalization does not make a word lose in semantic substance, as is often claimed. Rather, the word in question undergoes a process that could be called *resemanticization*. Moreover, it may appear in the same sentence as a lexeme whose meaning is close to that of the S, without this coexistence resulting in mere repetition.

   Specialization and generalization, far from being mutually exclusive, are logically related. Grammatical units such as relators are specialized to the extent that they function as tools; they are the products of a generalization process to the extent that their meaning is partly determined by the context. This is why they are often polysemic. Thus, the Chinese preposition *yú*, historically derived from a verb which already had a fairly broad meaning, "to refer to" (cf. 7.4.1 section a. above), may, depending on the context, correspond to such various English relators as "to", "in", "on behalf of", "towards", "from", "against", "with", "in comparison with" (Hagège 1975:152). As for *r*, which is the only relator in Palauan (Hagège 1986:112-114), it has of course even more context-dependent meanings. The polysemy of many relators in human languages meets the need for economy which characterizes a certain stage of language change. Thus, it appears that relators are two quite different things for logicians and for linguists. For logicians, relators, linking unsaturated variables, provide the basis from which to read the relation, whereas the linguists need to consider the meaning of the saturated variables in order to specify the asserted relation (cf. Tamba-Mecz 1988:57). And what the variables refer to are living beings, objects, notions which belong to LBs' physical, psychological, and social life.

Just because they are often context-dependent, certain relators may in some circumstances be omitted. This does not in the least imply that they are empty, but only that the lexemes between which they would establish a syntactic relationship unambiguously refer to well-known situations. This may be illustrated by cases of *cultural indexing*, in which place names referring to traditional activities or routine professional business do not require the use of a spatial relator (cf. 3.2.1). In addition to this, LBs are even free, in certain contexts, to use or to omit a relator, depending on the meaning they want to convey. This applies, for instance, to the famous preposition which introduces definite (often animate) patients in several Romance languages. In Béarnais for example, according to Joly (1971:304), the speaker may say either (235) with *a* if he wants to refer to his hurry or eagerness to see John, or (236) if no such meaning is intended:

(235)   *abest bist a Yan ?*
          (you~have seen at John)
          "have you seen John?"

(236)   *abest bist Yan ?*
          "have you seen John?"

This relative liberty to choose one among two possibilities gives support to the concept of *semantics of syntax* (Hagège 1990b:171-172); the phenomenon studied here provides a new illustration thereof.

c. *Semantic pressures*
   Not only are the NUs resulting from grammaticalization original types of *resemanticization*, but in many cases they also preserve semantic features (in addition to formal trappings: cf. (209)-(215) and the comment thereupon). It often happens that the meaning of the S imposes some restrictions on the combinatory latitudes of the grammaticalized unit, even though the latter has acquired a new content. This occurs, for example, in

some of the many formulas used by various languages to express the progressive. Of course, it does not occur everywhere; the formula is often frozen, as it is in Dutch, where *bezig te*, originally "busy to", corresponds to the English *-ing* form, whether or not the subject is really busy and even if it refers to a concrete thing or to a concept, e.g.,

(237) *dit effect is nu bezig te verdwijnen*
       (this effect is now "busy to"(=PROGR) disappear)

means

       "this effect is now disappearing"

and not

       "? this effect is now busy disappearing" (literal translation of (237)).

As opposed to this, Japanese *totyuu da*, literally "be halfway", one of the formulas expressing the progressive, can be used only with verbs that refer to a movement from one point to another. In a number of languages, the progressive is expressed by postural auxiliaries that retain at least a part of the lexical meaning. Thus, in Ngambay-Moundou (but not in the Mouroum dialect illustrated above by (233)-(234)), the same event may be expressed by the auxiliary *-ár*, from a verb *ár* "to stand", or the auxiliary *-ísī*, from a verb *ísī* "to sit" (also used with *áo* "to go" in Mouroum: cf. ex. (234)), depending on the position of the participant represented by the subject of the VP:

(238) *m-ár m-úsā dā*
       (I-PROGR("stand")   I-eat meat)
       "I am eating meat"

(239) *m-ísī m-úsā dā*
       (I-PROGR("sit")   I-eat meat)
       "I am eating meat" (Vandame 1963:93).

As shown by Raztorgeva (1952,I:166-178), Tajik *istodan* "to stand", when it appears in position V2, makes up a part – contrary to the verb that occupies position V1 (main verb from the semantic viewpoint, but in the gerundive) – of a countable set of units (a criterion of grammaticalization: cf. 7.2.1), and expresses the progressive; but it does not completely lose, at least in the durative perfect, its original meaning: it implies that V1 is done in a motionless or continuous fashion. Even the most desemanticized of the units undergoing a grammaticalization process in position V2, i.e. *raftan*, still keeps something of the lexical meaning of the S: as a full verb, it means "to go", and as an aspectual auxiliary, it marks the completive (cf. table (225)); thus, Tajik expresses the completion of an action as the ultimate point reached by someone going somewhere.

The same is true of words that refer to sensory events, whose importance in everyday life is obvious in all human societies. French has a static passive built on the pronominal form of the verb *voir* "to see". This structure is used to indicate that the undergoer is either a victim of the event or not responsible (or active), even if the event is favorable:

(240)   *il s'est vu mettre en prison*
         "he was put in jail" (with an implication that he was not prepa-
         red to what happened to him: cf. another translation such as
         "he found himself (put) in jail").

This structure is also used to topicalize the beneficiary while expressing the patient (i.e., the given object in (241) below). French has no other structure to do it, since it cannot, here, passivize the verb, as in the English translation of (241):

(241)   *il s'est vu offrir un livre*
         "he was offered a book".

Now, experiments made with native speakers of French (cf. Bearth 1984:33-34) reveal that the original meaning is not forgotten, since infor-mants reject, or frown upon, such sentences as (242):

(242)   *l'aveugle, hésitant à traverser la rue, s'est vu soudain prendre*
         par la main
         "the blindman, hesitating to cross the street, suddenly had his
         hands taken by someone".

Even in (240) and (241), the original meaning is not completely deleted, as the use of *s'est vu* implies that the participant is the inactive ocular witness of an event happening to him. The reluctance of many informants to accept sentence (242) shows that in this sentence, there is a strong pressure of the original meaning of *se voir*: a blindman does not see things. Moreover, from an inquiry I recently made on a sample of fifty-two native speakers of French, it appears that such a sentence as

(243)   *il s'est vu dire la vérité*
         "he was told the truth (which he did not expect)",

is not quite acceptable: the truth is heard, not seen, so that most informants prefer, instead of (243), another formulation, such as

(244)   *il s'est entendu dire la vérité*
         "he heard the truth told to him",

in which *entendre* "to hear", contrary to *voir*, is not a passive auxiliary, but a full verb[4].

Since many speakers avoid using a verb "to see" when referring to a blindman (ex. (242)) or to things heard (ex. (243)), some might simply conclude that *se voir* is not really an auxiliary but a verbal lexeme. This objection must be rejected. The frequency of *se voir* in sentences expressing the passive or topicalizing the experiencer, as well as the fact that *se voir* is commonly used – odd though this may appear from a "logical" viewpoint – in the administrative and scientific styles when the referent of the patient is an abstract notion, are two important arguments. They lead us to consider *se voir* as something other than an ordinary lexeme in this context, to say the least.

Thus, the treatment of meaning is an essential aspect of grammaticalization. The semantic shift, which is not radical enough for the NUs to lose every trace of the original meanings, and the conservation of features, which is not important enough for the NUs to still be considered as only a particular use of lexemes, are fundamental processes.

7.5 Conclusion to chapters 6 and 7

By studying lexicalization and grammaticalization as two aspects of language morphogenesis, we have seen how LBs, unconsciously in most, but not in all, cases,

- build complex lexical units, i.e., derivatives and compounds, which establish a relationship between morphology and syntax;
- convert certain lexical units into grammatical tools, thus providing not only *nominants* and *verbants* as part and parcel of NPs and VPs respectively, but also relators, as function words associating together the syntactic units that constitute a sentence.

Throughout this study, we have seen how constraints and freedom constantly interact during the uninterrupted morphogenetic activity reflected by the operations which LBs perform in order to meet their communicative needs. Thus, lexicalization and grammaticalization play a significant role in the present book, whose main purpose is to characterize humans' linguistic behavior, i.e., that of speakers-listeners as language architects.

Conclusion

The framework proposed here can serve for a much wider study. It is important to add, however, that just as it is not the purpose of this book to be an exhaustive study of linguistic morphogenesis, the model adopted does not lay claim to being the only possible way of conceiving language. It nevertheless seems reasonable to assume that if we take the notion of social science at face value, we have every reason to expect a linguistic study to teach us something about human beings as social entities. "Social" here refers both to the individual and inter-individual dimensions of human behavior. As regards the former, especially in its psychological aspect, the study of linguistic morphogenesis shows how mankind has progressively got away from the sensorial universe. The process of demotivation, a stage in a cyclical evolution, results in the organization of a consistent system of grammatical categories, with only some parts – such as the classes in certain types of languages with noun-classes – being closely related to perception. We can now understand why languages are coherent sets of abstract entities. If they remained wholly rooted in the universe of experience, as we may presume they were in their most archaic stages, they could not have developed parts of speech nor syntactic functions. Parts of speech and syntactic functions are systematic sets, and they are so to the extent that they belong to the universe of representation, not to the universe of experience. Experience does not contain such things as nouns and verbs, nor does it exhibit processes by which prepositions and auxiliaries, for instance, are derived from nouns and verbs, respectively. In that sense, language behaves like a theoretical interpretation of the universe, and as such, it is the precondition to the possibility of science – although, of course, it does not in itself constitute scientific knowledge.

The other dimension, the inter-individual one, is the factor that gives an impulse to the organization of languages. Human beings do not make grammatical tools from lexemes for art's sake. Human beings need to emit and receive meaningful messages. Therefore glossogenesis is a goal-directed activity. It is not surprising that theories such as those of Hjelmslev or

Chomsky, who view languages as autonomous systems, disregard both its dynamic nature and its social function.

This book has tried to show that it is not entirely true that Lb is a totally unconscious activity. But the fact that it contains some partly conscious aspects does not imply that human languages are the products of plans explicitly drawn up by LBs. Many changes, in syntax as well as in phonology, are local, even though they may trigger reorganizations that reveal the systematic character of languages. A change often provokes another change, and if in the long run a balance seems to be reached, it results from a series of interconnected changes rather than from a general project. It is precisely because linguistic evolution does not correspond to a preconceived global scheme that languages present, at any stage of their history, a number of gaps and leaks. Studying linguistic morphogenesis as a basic human activity provides one more reason for qualifying the opposition between synchrony and diachrony. No strictly synchronic study of a human language is conceivable, given the constant reshaping work done by LBs even when a language seems to have reached a state of equilibrium.

LBs, it is recalled, is the name proposed here to designate all human beings, not just some language architects. Thus, humans are characterized here as LBs. LBs leave many traces of their activity, as we have seen in chapters 3 and 7, among others. But humans are not only the makers of languages: they are also made by them. There are many manifestations of this reciprocal relationship (cf. Hagège 1990b: 103-107). However, we may assume that glossogenesis has logical and chronological priority: the dialogic species, even before the organization of a social life, must have possessed the faculty of language in its genetic code as an inborn property (cf. Hagège 1990b: chapter 1); this, of course, does not imply that any principle of so-called "universal grammar", such as advocated in recent works of the Chomskyan school, is inborn. Thus it appears that glossogenesis is an activity coeternal with human beings. This alone suffices to justify its choice as a specific object of research. Such research deserves to be enlarged, for all it can teach us about the place of humans in nature.

Notes

Notes to chapter 1

1. On the difference between the use of a participle in Slovenian and an infinitive in Russian, cf. 2.2.2.

2. In particular, *ʕal Ha-Mišmar* of 5 November-12 November 1953; *Davar* of 4 February 1964. My thanks go to the Maxon Limorešet Ben Gurion (Ben Gurion's Heritage Institute) for kindly communicating them to me, and to Mrs L. Yariv-Lahor, Professor of linguistics at the Hebrew University of Jerusalem, for sending me the newspaper clippings.

Notes to chapter 2

1. In particular, the Nahuatl absolutive suffix whose variants are -*tl* and -*li* is equally applied to most nominal roots, including "adjectives", as it appears in (18) b, d, e, f and (19) (Launey 1988:544-546).

2. Despite the suggestions of the title of the first section below, the division of the present passage into these two sections does not coincide with the distinction between the language-internal and the crosslinguistic distribution of tasks.

3. The notion of adverbial strategy appears in an article (Lehmann 1990) which I happened to come across while completing the drafting of this chapter. The author also speaks of verbal strategy and applies this notion, as I do here, to Spanish verbs specialized as aspect markers. He does not insert the notion of verbal strategy within a theoretical framework centered on the morphogenetic activity of LBs. His perspective is interesting, however: he views verbs and adverbs as "two alternative primary categorizations of a class of concepts" (Lehmann 1990:177).

4. This is not unrelated to the problem of the cultural patterns which determine, with respect to communication, certain social values reflected in linguistic theorizing (cf. Harris 1981).

Notes to chapter 3

1. According to Buddhist teaching, it is better to reincarnate as a human than as a god in order to reach the state of Buddha.

2. Anaphorics and cataphorics are terms belonging to tradition. Exophorics and endo-
    phorics are taken from Halliday & Hasan (1976). All other terms have been intro-
    duced in various works by Hagège (1974, 1982, 1990b).

3. One may recall, in this connection, Goethe's sentence: "und wenn du mich liebst,
    was geht mich das an?" (Kassai 1974:27 fn.8).

4. Number agreement of the ergative agent may also be found in Modern Colloquial
    Georgian. But just as the dative is retained in (127) the ergative agent remains
    ergative even though it is treated like a subject; and the nominative also remains
    unchanged, e.g.,

    > *student-eb-ma dac' er-es c' eril-i*
    > (student-PL-ERG write-3PL letter-NOMIN)
    > "the students write a letter" (Danielsen 1980:22).

Note to chapter 4

1. It is interesting to note in this connection that the youngest generation, at the time
    of the inquiry, was made of native speakers of other African languages spoken in
    Zaire. Therefore the situation of Kituba is typically that of a pidgin from this point
    of view, despite the differences between the sociocultural and economical conditions
    of its birth and those of Caribbean pidgins. Kituba is also interesting from another
    viewpoint: it is a welcome antidote to the view that there are universal pidgin and
    creole features, and to the related view that pidgins and creoles constitute a typolog-
    ical group with such properties as lack of inflection; Kituba has preserved some
    inflections characteristic of Bantu languages. In a comparable way, Plantation Pidgin
    Fijian, Plantation Pidgin Hindustani and Fiji Hindustani, rarely or never mentioned
    in the works of linguists who hold a universalist-nativist-antisubstratist view, have
    preserved much of the form of their lexifier language (cf. Siegel 1987).

Notes to the Introduction of part III

1. The affix is not always a segmental morpheme. In tone languages (e.g., Bantu), it
    often takes the form of a tone variation.

2. The manuscript of the present book was already completed when my attention was
    drawn to the existence of Traugott & Heine 1991, which is devoted to grammaticali-
    zation. As far as I can see, the theoretical framework in which grammaticalization
    is treated here, i.e., the relationship between grammaticalization and the morpho-
    genetic activity characterizing human beings as LBs, is quite different from the
    perspectives adopted by most contributors to Traugott & Heine. Thus the two
    directions of research should complement each other.

Notes to chapter 6

1. Data taken from Shibatani & Kageyama (1988:454), except for 198d, which has been obtained by the present writer.

2. *Kiadó* also means "(house) to be rented out".

Notes to chapter 7

1. One may note that the *Suomen kielen etymologinen sanakirja* (Etymological Dictionary of the Finnish language), 1962: 689-691, does not consider this noun as derived from the postposition *päällä*, but from an inflected form of the stem *pää*. In fact, the postposition itself being, originally, an inflected form of the stem *pää*, there is no fundamental difference between these two interpretations.

2. *yǔ* was itself superseded by *gěi*, the dative marker of contemporary Chinese, in the 18th-19th centuries (it was, as often, a slow evolution).

3. In fact, this remains open to discussion. Some would suggest that *bekommen* and *kriegen* have long lost their favorable meaning.

4. Due to the fact that, for both ACC and DAT, French has the same form *se/s'* (unstressed personal clitic), (244) is, in fact, ambiguous between two meanings: besides the one given here (*s'* = DAT), another one is "he heard himself telling the truth" (*s'* = ACC).

References

AKUP = Arbeiten des Kölner Universalien-Projekts (Köln)
BSLP = Bulletin de la Société de Linguistique de Paris (Paris)
BSOAS = Bulletin of the School for Oriental and African Studies (London)
CLS = Chicago Linguistic Society (Chicago)
CNRS = Centre National de la Recherche Scientifique (Paris)
ForLing = Forum Linguisticum (Lake Bluff, Ill.)
GLECS = Groupe Linguistique d'Études Chamito-Sémitiques (Paris)
IJAL = International Journal of American Linguistics (Chicago)
JALL = Journal of African Languages and Linguistics (Leiden)
LACITO = Laboratoire de Langues et Civilisations à Tradition Orale, CNRS (Paris)
LACUS = Linguistic Association of Canada and the United States Lake Bluff, Ill.)
SAES = Société des Anglicistes de l'Enseignement supérieur (Paris)
SELAF = Société d'Études Linguistiques et Anthropologiques de France (Paris)
UCPL = Univ. of California Publications in Linguistics (Berkeley & Los Angeles)
ZPSK = Zeitschrift für Phonetik, Sprachwissenschaft und Kommunikationsforschung (Berlin)

ABBOUD, Peter F. & Ernst McCARUS, eds. 1983. *Elementary Modern Standard Arabic.* Cambridge: Cambridge Univ. Press.
ADAM, Lucien. 1873. *Grammaire de la langue mandchoue.* Paris: Maisonneuve.
ADELUNG, Johann Christoph. 1806-1817. *Mithridates; oder allgemeine Sprachenkunde mit dem Vater Unser als Sprachprobe in bey nahe fünfhundert Sprachen und Mundarten.* Ed. by Johann Severin Vater. 4 vols. in 6. Berlin: Voss.
ALHONIEMI, Alho. 1988. "Postpositiorakenteiden synkroniaa ja diakroniaa". *Sananjalka* (Turku) 30.27-44.

ALLEYNE, Mervyn C. 1980. *Comparative Afro-American*. (Linguistica Extranea; Studia, 11) Ann Arbor, Mich.: Karoma.

ALLSOPP, Richard. 1977. "Africanisms in the Idioms of Caribbean English". Kotey & Der-Houssikian 1977.429-441.

AL-ZAĞĞÂĞÎ (d.933). 1962. *Maǧâlis al-ulamâ?*. Ed. by A. M. Hârûn. Kuwait-City.

AL-ZAMAḪŠARÎ (d.1160). 1981. *Al-?unmûḏaǧ fî l-naḥw*. Beirut: Dâr Al ?Afâq Al-ǧadîda.

ANDERSON, Stephen R. 1976. "On the Notion of Subject in Ergative Languages". Li 1976.1-23.

— 1985. "Typological Distinctions in Word Formation". Shopen 1985 III, 3-56.

— 1989. Review article on P. N. Johnson-Laird, *The Computer and the Mind: An introduction to cognitive science* (Cambridge, Mass.: Harvard Univ. Press, 1988). *Language* 65.800-811.

ASKEDAL, John Ole. 1984. "Grammatikalisierung und Auxiliarisierung im sogenannten 'bekommen/kriegen/erhalten-Passiv' des Deutschen". *Kopenhagener Beiträge zur Germanistischen Linguistik* 22.5-47.

BACHIR, Attouman M. 1978. "Propos sur le hausa". *Études sur l'aspect*, ed. by Catherine Fuchs, 107-132. Paris: Département de Recherches Linguistiques, Univ. de Paris VII.

BAILEY, Beryl L. 1966. *Jamaican Creole Syntax: A transformational approach*. Cambridge: Cambridge Univ. Press.

BAILLY, Alexandre. 1950. *Dictionnaire grec-français*. 6th ed. Paris: Hachette.

BAKER, Philip. 1982. "On the origins of the first Mauritians and of the Creole language of their descendants: A refutation of Chaudenson's 'Bourbonnais' theory". *Isle de France Creole, Affinities and origins*, ed. by Philip Baker & Chris Corne, 131-259. Ann Arbor, Mich.: Karoma.

BALLY, Charles. 1926. "L'expression des idées de sphère personnelle et de solidarité dans les langues indo-européennes". *Festschrift Louis Gauchat*, 68-78. Aarau: Sauerländer.

— 1952. *Le langage et la vie*. 3rd ed. Genève & Lille: Droz.

BAMGBOSE, Ayo. 1966. *A Grammar of Yoruba*. Cambridge: Cambridge Univ. Press.

BARATIN, Marc. 1989. *La naissance de la syntaxe à Rome*. Paris: Éditions de Minuit.

BEARTH, Thomas. 1984. "Périphrases du passif français et la notion de contrôle". *Bulletin de la Section de Linguistique de la Faculté des Lettres de Lausanne*, 6 (Rencontres Régionales de Linguistique, Lausanne 7-9 juin 1984), 27-40. Lausanne.

BENTOLILA, Fernand. 1987. "La transitivité et ses corrélats en berbère". *La transitivité et ses corrélats*, ed. by D. François-Geiger (U.E.R. de Linguistique Générale et Appliquée, Centre de Linguistique; Travaux, 1), 83-93. Paris: Univ. René Descartes.

BENVENISTE, Émile. 1952. "La construction passive du parfait transitif". *BSLP* 48:1.52-62. (Repr. in Benveniste 1966.176-186).

— 1958. "Les verbes délocutifs". *Studia philologica et litteraria in honorem Leo Spitzer*, ed. by Anna Granville Hatcher & K. L. Selig, 57-63. Berne: A. Francke. (Repr. in Benveniste 1966.277-285).

— 1960. " 'Être' et 'avoir' dans leurs fonctions linguistiques". *BSLP* 55:1.113-134. (Repr. in Benveniste 1966.187-207).

— 1966. *Problèmes de linguistique générale*. [Vol.I]. Paris: Gallimard.

— 1967. "Fondements syntaxiques de la composition nominale". *BSLP* 62:1.15-31. (Repr. in Benveniste 1974.145-162).

— 1968. "Mutations of Linguistic Categories". *Directions for Historical Linguistics*, ed. by Winfred P. Lehmann & Yakov Malkiel, 85-94. Austin & London: Univ. of Texas Press.

— 1969a. "Mécanismes de transposition". *Cahiers Ferdinand de Saussure* 25 (*Mélanges Henri Frei*), 47-59. (Repr. in Benveniste 1974.113-125).

— 1969b. *Le vocabulaire des institutions indo-européennes*. Paris: Éditions de Minuit.

— 1974. *Problèmes de linguistique générale II*. Paris: Gallimard.

BICKERTON, Derek. 1975. "Creolization, Linguistic Universals, Natural Semantax and the Brain". *Working Papers in Linguistics* 6.3:124-141. Hawaii: Univ. of Hawaii.

— 1981. *Roots of Language*. Ann Arbor, Mich.: Karoma.

— 1985. "Substrata vs. Universals". Lecture delivered at the Workshop 'Universals vs. Substrata in Creole Genesis'. Amsterdam: Amsterdam Univ.

BINNICK, Robert I. 1976. "How Aspect Languages Get Tense". Steever, Walker & Mufwene 1976.40-49.

BOAS, Franz. 1911. "Introduction". *Handbook of American Indian Languages* (Smithsonian Institution, Bureau of American Ethnology; Bulletin 40, Part I), 5-83. Washington, D.C.: Government Printing Office.

BOCK, J. Kathryn & Anthony S. KROCH. 1989. "The Isolability of

Syntactic Processing". *Linguistic Structure in Language Processing*, ed. by Greg N. Carlson & Michael K. Tannenbaum, 157-186. Dordrecht: Kluwer.

BOIRON, Bernard. 1985. "Situation, valeurs et genèse de la catégorie du préverbe en hongrois". *BSLP* 80:1.265-295.

BOISSON, Claude. 1984. "Analogues de l'auxiliaire DO anglais en Nouvelle-Guinée et ailleurs". *Congrès de la SAES*, 1-5. Pau (France).

BOPP, Franz. 1816. *Über das Conjugationssystem der Sanskritsprache in Vergleichung mit jenem der Griechischen, Lateinischen, Persischen und Germanischen Sprachen.* Frankfurt am Main: Andreäische Buchhandlung. (Repr., Hildesheim: Georg Olms, 1975).

—— 1833-1852. *Vergleichende Grammatik des Sanskrit, Zend, Armenischen, Griechischen, Lateinischen, Lithauischen, Altslawischen, Gothischen und Deutschen.* 6 fasc. Berlin: Ferdinand Dümmler.

BORETZKY, Norbert. 1988. "Zur grammatischen Struktur des Nubi". Boretzky, Enninger & Stolz 1988.45-88.

——, Werner ENNINGER & Thomas STOLZ, eds. 1986. *Akten des 2. Essener Kolloquiums über "Kreolsprachen und Sprachkontakte".* Bochum: Norbert Brockmeyer.

——, — & —, eds. 1988. *Beiträge zum 4. Essener Kolloquium über "Sprachkontakt, Sprachwandel, Sprachwechsel, Sprachtod".* Bochum: Norbert Brockmeyer.

BOULLE, Jacques. 1987. "Aspect et diathèse en basque". *Actances* (Paris: CNRS) 3.85-121.

BOURDIN, Philippe. 1992. "L'andatif et le vénitif en linguistique générale: Pérégrinations notionnelles et grammaticales". Danon-Boileau & Morel 1992.287-300.

BRÉAL, Michel. 1921. *Essai de sémantique.* 7th ed. Paris: Hachette. (1st ed., 1897).

BREIVIK, Leiv E. & Ernst Håkon JAHR, eds. 1989. *Language Change: Contributions to the study of its causes.* (Trends in Linguistics; Studies and Monographs, 43) Berlin & New York: Mouton de Gruyter.

BRETTSCHNEIDER, Gunter & Christian LEHMANN, eds. 1980. *Wege zur Universalienforschung.* (Tübinger Beiträge zur Linguistik, 145) Tübingen: Gunter Narr.

BREUILLARD, Jean, ed. 1989. *Études de linguistique à partir du domaine russe: Traduction, énonciation, aspect.* (La Licorne, 15) Poitiers: Publications de l'UFR de Langues et Littératures de l'Univ. de Poitiers.

BROSCHART, Jürgen. 1988. *On the Sequence of the Techniques on the Dimension of Participation*. (AKUP, 76) Cologne: Institut für Sprachwissenschaft, Univ. zu Köln.

BROWN, Roger W. & Albert GILMAN. 1960. "The Pronouns of Power and Solidarity". *Style in Language*, ed. by Thomas A. Sebeok, 253-276. Cambridge, Mass.: MIT Press.

BUSE, J. E. 1963. "The Structure of the Rarotongan Verbal Piece". *BSOAS* 26.152-169.

BUYSSENS, Eric. 1965. *Linguistique historique*. Bruxelles: Presses Universitaires de Bruxelles.

CANU, Gaston. 1976. *La langue mo:re, dialecte de Ouagadougou (Haute-Volta)*. (Langues et Civilisations à Tradition Orale, 16) Paris: SELAF.

CAUBET, Dominique. 1992. "Deixis, aspect et modalité: les particules *hā-* et *rā-* en arabe marocain". Danon-Boileau & Morel 1992.139-149.

CAVE, George. 1976. *Sociolinguistics and Child Play in Guyana*. Washington, D.C.: Georgetown Univ. Mimeo.

CÉROL, Marie-Josée. 1991. *Une introduction au créole guadeloupéen*. [Pointe-à-Pitre]: Éditions Jasor.

CHAFE, Wallace L. 1968. "Idiomaticity as an Anomaly in the Chomskyan paradigm". *Foundations of Language* 4.109-127.

CHAMBON, Jean-Pierre. 1986. "Les noms propres délocutifs". *Nouvelle Revue d'Onomastique* 7/8.159-166.

CHAO, Yuen-Ren. 1968. *A Grammar of Spoken Chinese*. Berkeley & Los Angeles: Univ. of California Press.

CHARACHIDZÉ, Georges. 1981. *Grammaire de la langue avar*. (Documents de Linguistique Quantitative, 38) Paris: Jean-Favard.

CHARPENTIER, Jean-Michel. 1979. *Le pidgin bislama(n) et le multilinguisme aux Nouvelles-Hébrides*. (Langues et Civilisations à Tradition Orale, 35) Paris: SELAF.

CHOMSKY, Noam. 1981. *Lectures on Government and Binding*. Dordrecht: Foris.

CLAUDI, Ulrike & Bernd HEINE. 1986. "On the Metaphorical Base of Grammar". *Studies in Language* 10:2.297-335.

CLEMENTS, George N. 1975. "The Logophoric Pronoun in Ewe: Its role in discourse". *Journal of West African Languages* 102.141-177.

COHEN, David. 1984. *La phrase nominale et l'évolution du système verbal en sémitique*. (Collection Linguistique publiée par la Société de Linguistique de Paris, 72) Leuven & Paris: Peeters.

COHEN, Marcel 1970. *Traité de langue amharique (Abyssinie)*. (Travaux et Mémoires, 24) Paris: Institut d'Ethnologie.

COLE, Peter, W. HARBERT, Gabriella HERMON & S. N. SRIDHAR. 1980. "The Acquisition of Subjecthood". *Language* 56.719-743.

COLLINS, Janet D. 1986. "The Rise of the Periphrastic Verb Form in Old English". *The Twelfth LACUS Forum 1985*, ed. by Mary C. Marino & L.A. Pérez, 132-138. Lake Bluff, Ill.: LACUS.

COMRIE, Bernard. 1980. "Agreement, animacy and voice". Brettschneider & Lehmann 1980: 229-234.

— 1981. *Language Universals and Linguistic Typology*. Oxford: Basil Blackwell.

COMTET, Maurice. 1989. "La prolepse en russe contemporain". Breuillard 1989.379-394.

CONDILLAC, Étienne Bonnot de. 1746. *Essai sur l'origine des connais sances humaines*. Amsterdam.

COOPER, William E. & John Robert ROSS. 1975. "World order". *Papers from the Parasession on Functionalism*, ed. by Robin E. Grossman, L. James San, Timothy J. Vance, 63-111. Chicago: Chicago Linguistic Society.

COOREMAN, Ann M. 1987. *Transitivity and Discourse Continuity in Chamorro Narratives*. (Empirical Approaches to Language Typology, 4) Berlin-New York-Amsterdam: Mouton de Gruyter.

CORBIN, Danielle. 1986. *La morphologie dérivationnelle et la structuration du lexique*. Lille: Atelier de reproduction des thèses.

CORNE, Chris. 1987. "Verb Fronting in Creole: Transmission or bioprogram?". *Pidgin and Creole languages: Essays in memory of John E. Reinecke*, ed. by Glenn G. Gilbert, 93-112. Honolulu: Univ. of Hawaii Press.

CORRIENTE, Federico. 1977. *A Grammatical Sketch of the Spanish Arabic Dialect Bundle*. Madrid: no publisher supplied.

CORUM, Claudia. 1973. "Anaphoric Peninsulas". *Papers from the Ninth Regional Meeting*, ed. by Claudia Corum, T. Cedric Smith-Stark & Anne Weiser, 89-97. Chicago: Chicago Linguistic Society.

COSERIU, Eugenio. 1983. "Linguistic Change Does Not Exist". *Linguistica nuova ed antica* 1.51-63.

COULMAS, Florian. 1986. "Reported Speech: Some general issues". Coulmas 1986.1-28.

—, ed. 1986. *Direct and Indirect Speech*. (Trends in Linguistics; Studies and Monographs, 31) Berlin-New York-Amsterdam: Mouton de Gruyter.

CRAIG, Colette, ed. 1986. *Noun Classes and Categorization*. (Typological Studies in Language, 7) Amsterdam & Philadelphia: John Benjamins.

— & Kenneth HALE. 1988. "Relational Preverbs in Some Languages of the Americas: Typological and historical perspectives". *Language* 64.312-344.

CRAZZOLARA, J. P. 1960. *A Study of the Logbara (Madi) Language: Grammar and Vocabulary*. London-New York-Toronto: Oxford Univ. Press.

DAHL, Östen. 1979. "Typology of Sentence Negation". *Linguistics* 17.79-106.

DANIELSEN, Niels. 1980. *Linguistic Studies*. Heidelberg: Carl Winter.

DANON-BOILEAU, Laurent & Marie-Annick MOREL, eds. 1992. *La deixis. Colloque en Sorbonne, 8-9 juin 1990*. Paris: Presses Universitaires de France.

DeCAMP, David. 1971. "Introduction: The study of pidgin and creole languages". *Pidginization and Creolization of Languages*, ed. by Dell Hymes, 13-39. Cambridge: Cambridge Univ. Press.

DELANCEY, Scott. 1985a. "Agentivity and Syntax". Eilfort, Kroeber & Peterson 1985.1-12.

— 1985b. "The Analysis-Synthesis-Lexis Cycle in Tibeto-Burman: A case study in motivated change". Haiman 1985.367-389.

— 1986. "Towards a History of the Tai Classifier System". Craig 1986.437-452.

DEMUTH, Katherine, Nicholas G. FARACLAS & Lynell MARCHESE. 1986. "Niger-Congo Noun Class and Agreement Systems in Language Acquisition and Historical Change". Craig 1986.453-471.

DENNY, J. Peter. 1978. "Locating the Universals in Lexical Systems for Spatial Deixis". *Papers from the Parasession on the Lexicon*, ed. by Donka Farkas, Wesley M. Jacobsen & Karol W. Todrys, 71-84. Chicago: Chicago Linguistic Society.

— & Chet A. CREIDER. 1986. "The Semantics of Noun Classes in Proto-Bantu". Craig 1986.217-239.

DERBYSHIRE, Desmond C. 1986. "Comparative Survey of Morphology and Syntax in Brazilian Arawakan". *Handbook of Amazonian Languages*, ed. by D. C. Derbyshire & Geoffrey K. Pullum, Vol.I, 459-566. Berlin-New York-Amsterdam: Mouton de Gruyter.

DE REUSE, Willem J. 1989. "Morphological Change and Internal Syntax in Eskimo". Wiltshire, Graczyk & Music 1989.56-67.

DIFFLOTH, Gérard. 1972. "Notes on Expressive Meaning". *Papers from the Eighth Regional Meeting*, ed. by Paul M. Peranteau, Judith N. Levi & G. C. Phares, 440-447. Chicago: Chicago Linguistic Society.

— 1979. "Expressive Phonology and Prosaic Phonology in Mon-Khmer". *Studies in Tai and Mon-Khmer Phonetics and Phonology in honour of Eugénie J. A. Henderson*, ed. by T. L. Thongkum, P. Kullavanijaya, V. Panupong, M. R. Kalaya Tingsabadh, 49-59. Bangkok: Chulalongkorn Univ. Press.

DIKI-KIDIRI, Marcel. 1988. "Aspects, modes et temps en sango". Tersis & Kihm 1988.117-124.

DIXON, Robert M. W. 1969. "Relative Clauses and Possessive Phrases in two Australian Languages". *Language* 45.35-44.

— 1979. "Ergativity". *Language* 55.59-138.

DONABÉDIAN, Anaïd. 1991. *L'article dans l'économie des catégories nominales en arménien moderne occidental*. Doctoral dissertation. Paris: Université de la Sorbonne Nouvelle-Paris III.

DOWNING, Pamela. 1977. "On the Creation and Use of English Compound Nouns". *Language* 53.810-842.

DRESSLER, Wolfgang U. 1987. "Word Formation as Part of Natural Morphology". *Leitmotifs in Natural Morphology*, ed. by W. U. Dressler, Willi Mayerthaler, Oswald Panagl & Wolfgang U. Wurzel, 99-126. Amsterdam & Philadelphia: John Benjamins.

DURR, Jacques A. 1950. *Morphologie du verbe tibétain*. Heidelberg: Carl Winter.

EILFORT, William H., Paul D. KROEBER & K. L. PETERSON, eds. 1985. *Papers from the Parasession on Causatives and Agentivity*. (CLS 21:2) Chicago: Chicago Linguistic Society.

ENGLAND, Nora C. 1983. *A Grammar of Mam, a Mayan Language*. Austin: Univ. of Texas Press.

ERMAN, Adolf. 1933. *Neuägyptische Grammatik*. 2nd ed. Leipzig: Wilhelm Engelmann.

ESCOBAR, Alberto. 1960. " 'Onde', 'donde' con valor flexivo de acusativo personal". *Sphinx: Anuario del Instituto de Filología de Lima* 13.94-99.

FEDSON, Vijayarani J. 1985. "A Note on Periphrastic Serial or Compound Verb Causative Constructions in Tamil". Eilfort, Kroeber & Peterson

1985.13-20.

FEHDERAU, Harold Werner. 1966. *The Origin and Development of Kituba*. Ann Arbor, Mich.: Univ. Microfilms.

FERRAND, Marcel. 1985. *Le suffixe -nja en russe moderne*. (Bibliothèque russe de l'Institut d'Études Slaves, 74) Paris: Institut d'Études Slaves.

FODOR, István. 1959. "The Origin of Grammatical Gender". *Lingua* 8:1.1-41, 8:2.186-214.

—— 1983. "Hungarian: Evolution – stagnation – reform – further development". Fodor & Hagège 1983-1984 II, 49-84.

—— & Claude HAGÈGE, eds. 1983-1984 (Vols.I–III), 1989 (Vol.IV), 1990 (Vol. V). *Language Reform: History and future*. 4 vols. Hamburg: Helmut Buske.

FOLEY, William A. 1986. *The Papuan Languages of New Guinea*. Cambridge: Cambridge Univ. Press.

—— & Robert D. VAN VALIN Jr. 1977. "On the Viability of the Notion of 'subject' in Universal Grammar". *Proceedings of the Third Annual Meeting of the Berkeley Linguistic Society*, 293-320. Berkeley: Univ. of California.

FÓNAGY, Ivan. 1986. "Reported speech in French and Hungarian". Coulmas 1986.255-309.

FÖRSTEMANN, Emil. 1852. "Über deutsche Volksetymologie". *Zeitschrift für vergleichende Sprachforschung* 1.

FRAJZYNGIER, Zygmunt. 1985. "Logophoric Systems in Chadic". *JALL* 7.23-37.

FRUYT, Michèle. 1987. "Interprétation sémantico-référentielle du réfléchi latin". *Glotta* 65:3/4.204-221.

GABELENTZ, Georg von der. 1891. *Die Sprachwissenschaft: Ihre Aufgaben, Methoden und bisherigen Ergebnisse*. Leipzig: T. O. Weigel.

GENETTI, Carol. 1986. "The Grammaticalization of the Newari verb *tol*". *Linguistics of the Tibeto-Burman Area* 9:2.53-70.

GENIUŠIENĖ, Emma. 1987. *The Typology of Reflexives*. (Empirical Approaches to Language Typology, 2) Berlin-New York-Amsterdam: Mouton de Gruyter.

GERAGHTY, Paul A. 1989. "Language Reform: History and future of Fijian". Fodor & Hagège 1989 IV, 376-396.

GIVÓN, Talmy. 1971. "Historical Syntax and Synchronic Morphology: An archaeologist's field trip". *Papers from the Seventh Regional Meeting*, 394-415. Chicago: Chicago Linguistic Society.

— 1973. "The Time-Axis Phenomenon". *Language* 49.890-925.

— 1975. "Serial Verbs and Syntactic Change: Niger-Congo". *Word Order and Word Order Change*, ed. by Charles N. Li, 47-112. Austin & London: Univ. of Texas Press.

— 1979. *On Understanding Grammar*. New York: Academic Press.

GORBET, Larry P. 1979. "The Case-Marking of Diegueño Complement Clauses". *IJAL* 45.251-266.

GOUGENHEIM, Georges. 1972. "L'action de l'homonymie sur le lexique". *BSLP* 66:1.299-302.

GREENBERG, Joseph H. 1963. *The Languages of Africa*. The Hague: Mouton & Co. (for Indiana Univ. Research Center in Anthropology, Folklore, and Linguistics).

— 1978. "How Does a Language Acquire Gender Markers?". *Universals of Human Language*, ed. by J. H. Greenberg, Vol.III, 47-82. Stanford, Calif.: Stanford Univ. Press.

GRÉGOIRE, Claire. 1984. "Le syntagme déterminatif en mandé nord". *JALL* 6.173-193.

GRONDÍN, Marcelo N. 1971. *Método de quechua*. Oruro (Bolivia): Quelco.

GROSS, Maurice. 1979. "On the Failure of Generative Grammar". *Language* 55.859-885.

GUILBERT, Louis. 1977. "De la formation des unités lexicales", *Grand Larousse de la Langue Française*, IX-LXXXVI.

GUILLAUME, Gustave. 1971. *Leçons de linguistique, 1948-1949*. Ed. by Roch Valin. (Série B: Psycho-systématique du langage; Principes, méthodes et applications I, tome 2) Québec: Presses de l'Univ. Laval; Paris: Klincksieck.

HAGÈGE, Claude. 1969. *Esquisse linguistique du tikar*. (Bibliothèque de la SELAF, 11) Paris: SELAF.

— 1970. *La langue mbum de Nganha (Cameroun): Phonologie-grammaire*. 2 vols. (Bibliothèque de la SELAF, 18) Paris: SELAF.

— 1973. *Profil d'un parler arabe du Tchad*. (Comptes rendus du GLECS; Supplément 2: Atlas linguistique du monde arabe, Matériaux, 1) Paris: Paul Geuthner.

— 1974. "Les pronoms logophoriques". *BSLP* 69:1.287-310.

— 1975. *Le problème linguistique des prépositions et la solution chinoise (avec un essai de typologie à travers plusieurs groupes de langues)*. (Collection Linguistique publiée par la Société de Linguistique de Paris,

71) Paris & Louvain: Peeters.

— 1978. "Lexical Suffixes and Incorporation in Mainland Comox". *ForLing* 3:1.57-71.

— 1979. Foreword to Charpentier 1979, 13-21.

— 1980a. "Three Viewpoints on the Organization of Linguistic Utterances". *The Sixth LACUS Forum 1979*, ed. by William C. McCormack & Herbert J. Izzo, 68-77. Columbia, S.C.: Hornbeam Press.

— 1980b. "On Noun Incorporation in Universal Grammar (further comments on a previous article)". *ForLing* 4:3.241-245.

— 1981a. *Critical Reflections on Generative Grammar*. Transl. by Robert A. Hall, Jr. (Edward Sapir Monograph Series in Language, Culture and Cognition, 10) Lake Bluff Ill.: Jupiter Press.

— 1981b. "The Concept of Function in Phonology". *Phonologica 1980*, ed. by Wolfgang U. Dressler, Oskar E. Pfeiffer, John R. Rennison (Innsbrucker Beiträge zur Sprachwissenschaft, 36), 187-194. Innsbruck: Institut für Sprachwissenschaft der Univ.

— 1981c. *Le comox lhaamen de Colombie britannique: Présentation d'une langue amérindienne*. (Amérindia, numéro spécial 2) Paris: Association d'Ethnolinguistique Amérindienne.

— 1982. *La structure des langues*. (Que sais-je?, 2006) Paris: Presses Universitaires de France. (2nd ed., 1986).

— 1983a. "Pour un retour d'exil des périphériques". *Modèles Linguistiques* 5:1.107-116.

— 1983b. "Voies et destins de l'action humaine sur les langues". Fodor & Hagège 1983-84 I, 11-68.

— 1984a. "Sur les trois structurations de l'énoncé dans les langues humaines". *Lingua e Stile* 19:3.349-379.

— 1984b. "Du concept à la fonction en linguistique, ou la polarité verbo-nominale". *La Linguistique* 20:2.15-28.

— 1986. *La langue palau: Une curiosité typologique*. (Forms of Language Structure, 1) Munich: Wilhelm Fink.

— 1988a. "Contribution des recherches typologiques à l'étude diachronique des langues". *La Linguistique diachronique: Histoire et théories*, ed. by André Joly, 271-278. Lille: Presses Universitaires de Lille III.

— 1988b. "Les péninsules syntaxiques, la liberté de l'énonceur et la nostalgie des îles". *BSLP* 83:1.1-20.

— 1989a. Review of Cooreman 1987. *BSLP* 84:2.473-481.

— 1989b. Review of Siegel 1987. *BSLP* 84:2.481-484.

— 1989c. "La morphogenèse linguistique comme activité humaine de construction". *Annuaire du Collège de France 1988-1989*, 657-683. Paris: Collège de France.

— 1990a. "Morphogenèse des conjonctifs, des connectifs et du genre grammatical". *Annuaire du Collège de France 1989-1990*, 687-697. Paris: Collège de France.

— 1990b. *The Dialogic Species: A linguistic contribution to the social sciences.* Transl. by Sharon L. Shelby. New York: Columbia Univ. Press.

— 1990c. "Do the Classical Morphological Types Have Clear-Cut Limits?". *Contemporary Morphology*, ed. by Wolfgang U. Dressler, H. C. Luschützky, Oskar E. Pfeiffer, John R. Rennison, 297-308. (Trends in Linguistics; Studies and Monographs, 49) Berlin & New York: Mouton de Gruyter.

— 1990d. "Sur l'évolution des constructions datives dans l'histoire du chinois. A propos d'un ouvrage d'A. Peyraube". *T'oung Pao* LXXVI:4-5.311-321.

— 1991. "Keitai-tôgoron ni okeru ningen no ichi [Man's place in morphosyntax]". *Gengo* 20:n°8. 78-83; n°9.76-82. Tokyo.

— 1992. *Le souffle de la langue. Voies et destins des parlers d'Europe.* Paris: Éditions Odile Jacob.

— Forthcoming. *Mbum-English dictionary.*

— & André HAUDRICOURT. 1978. *La phonologie panchronique.* Paris: Presses Universitaires de France.

HAIMAN, John. 1978. "Conditionals Are Topics". *Language* 54.564-589.

— 1980. "The Iconicity of Grammar: Isomorphism and motivation". *Language* 56.515-540.

— 1983. "Iconic and Economic Motivation". *Language* 59.781-819.

—, ed. 1985. *Iconicity in Syntax.* (Typological Studies in Language, 6) Amsterdam & Philadelphia: John Benjamins.

— & Pamela MUNRO, eds. 1983. *Switch-Reference and Universal Grammar.* (Typological Studies in Language, 2) Amsterdam & Philadelphia: John Benjamins.

HALE, Kenneth N. 1966. "Kinship Reflections in Syntax: Some Australian Languages". *Word* 22:1-3.318-324.

HALL, Robert A., Jr. 1966. *Pidgin and Creole Languages.* Ithaca & London: Cornell Univ. Press.

HALLIDAY, Michael A.K. & Ruqaiya HASAN, 1976. *Cohesion in English.* London: Longman.

HAO RAN. 1972. *Jinguang dadao* [The bright way]. 2 vols. Peking: Renmin Wenxue Chubanshe.

HARBSMEIER, Christoph. 1981. *Aspects of Classical Chinese Syntax*. (Scandinavian Institute of Asian Studies; Monograph Series, 45) London & Malmö: Curzon Press.

HARNING, Kerstin E. 1980. *The Analytic Genitive in the Modern Arabic Dialects*. Göteborg: Acta Universitatis Gothoburgensis.

HARRIS, Roy. 1981. *The Language Myth*. London: Duckworth.

HARRISON, Sheldon P. 1973. "Reduplication in Micronesian". *Oceanic Linguistics* 12.407-454.

HAYEK, Friedrich A. 1978. *The Three Sources of Human Values*. London: The London School of Economics and Political Science.

HEATH, Jeffrey. 1985. "Discourse in the Field: Clause structure in Ngandi". Nichols & Woodbury 1985.89-110.

HEINE, Bernd. 1989. "Adpositions in African Languages". *Linguistique Africaine* 2.77-127.

— & M. REH. 1984. *Grammaticalization and Reanalysis in African Languages*. Hamburg: Helmut Buske.

HENNING, Rudolf. 1895. "Über die Entwicklung des grammatischen Geschlechts". *Zeitschrift für vergleichende Sprachforschung* 33.1-36.

HERMAN, József. 1983. "The History of Language and the History of Society: On some theoretical issues and their implications in historical linguistics". *Acta Linguistica Academiae Scientiarum Hungaricae* 33.3-12.

HEWITT, Steve. 1988. "A reply to H.L.C. Tristram's Criticism". Unpubl. paper.

HILL, Jane H. 1987. "Women's Speech in Modern Mexicano". *Language, Gender and Sex in Comparative Perspective*, ed. by Susan U. Philips, Susan Steele & C. Tanz, 121-160. (Studies in the Social and Cultural Foundations of Language, 4) Cambridge: Cambridge Univ. Press.

HODGE, Carleton T. 1970. "The linguistic cycle". *Language Sciences* 13. 1-7.

HOFFMANN, Carl. 1963. *A Grammar of the Margi Language*. London: Oxford Univ. Press.

HOLM, John A. 1987. "African Substratal Influence on the Atlantic Creole Language". Maurer & Stolz 1987.11-26.

HOOK, Peter E. 1989. "Determining Thresholds for the Emergence of Perfective Aspects in Indo-Aryan Languages". Wiltshire, Graczyk &

Music 1989.203-212.

HOPPER, Paul J. 1986. "Discourse Function and Word Order Shift: A typological study of the VS/SV alternation". Lehmann 1986.123-140.

HORNE TOOKE, John. 1786. *Epea pteroenta or The diversions of Purley*. London: J. Johnson.

HUDSON, Joyce. 1978. *The Core of Walmatjari Grammar*. Canberra: Australian Institute for Aboriginal Studies; Atlantic Heights, N.J.: Humanities Press.

HUMBOLDT, Wilhelm von. 1822. *Über das Entstehen der grammatischen Formen und ihren Einfluss auf die Ideenentwicklung*. Berlin: Verlag der Akademie der Wissenschaften.

HUTTAR, George L. 1975. "Some Kwa-like Features of Djuka Syntax". Paper presented to the International Conference on Pidgins and Creoles, Honolulu.

HYMAN, Larry M. & Bernard COMRIE. 1981. "Logophoric Reference in Gokana". *JALL* 3.19-37.

HYMES, Dell. 1975. "From Space to Time in Tenses in Kiksht". *IJAL* 41:4.313-329.

IBN YAʕÎŠ (d.1265). 1882. *Šarḥ al-mufaṣṣal*. Leipzig: no publisher supplied.

JACOBI, Heidi. 1973. *Grammatik des thumischen Neuaramäisch (Nord ostsyrien)*. Wiesbaden: Otto Harrassowitz.

JACOBSEN, William H., Jr. 1967. "Switch Reference in Hokan-Coahuil tecan". *Studies in Southwestern Ethnolinguistics*, ed. by D. Hymes, 238-263. The Hague: Mouton.

— 1983. "Typological and Genetic Notes on Switch Reference Systems in North-American Indian Languages". Haiman & Munro 1983.151-183.

JAHR, Ernst Håkon. 1989. "Language Planning and Language Change". Breivik & Jahr 1989.99-113.

JAKOBSON, Roman. 1968. "Poetry of Grammar and Grammar of Poetry". *Lingua* 21.597-609.

JAXONTOV, Serguei E. 1965. *Drevnekitajskij jazyk*. (Jazyki Narodov Azii i Afriki) Moscow: Nauka.

JESPERSEN, Otto. 1917. *Negation in English and Other Languages*. Copenhagen: Videnskabernes Selskab.

— 1941. *Efficiency in Linguistic Change*. Copenhagen: Einar Munksgaard.

— 1955. *Growth and Structure of the English Language*. 9th edition. New York: Doubleday. (1st ed., 1905).

JOLY, André. 1971. "Le complément verbal et le morphème *a* en béarnais". *Zeitschrift für Romanische Philologie* 5/6. 286-305.

JOSEPH, John E. 1989. Review of Koerner 1988. *Language* 65.595-602.

KABORÉ, Raphaël. 1980. *Essai d'analyse de la langue mòoré (parler de Waògàgò: Ouagadougou)*. Doctoral dissertation. 2 vols. Paris: Univ. de Paris VII.

KAGEYAMA, Taro. 1982. "Word Formation in Japanese". *Lingua* 57. 215-258.

KARLGREN, Bernhard. 1920. "Le proto-chinois, langue flexionnelle". *Journal Asiatique*, avril-juin 1920, 205-232.

KASSAI, György. 1974. "Syntagmes figés et attirance entre lexèmes". *Studia Romanica* (Debrecen), Series Linguistica 3.23-37.

KEENAN, Edward L. 1976. "Towards a Universal Definition of 'Subject'". Li 1976.303-333.

KELEMEN, Yolan. 1988. *De la langue au style: Éléments de linguistique contrastive français-hongrois*. Budapest: Akadémiai Kiadó.

KENDALL, Martha B. 1975. "The /-k/, /-m/ Problem in Yavapai Syntax". *IJAL* 41:1.1-9.

KIRTCHUK, Pablo 1987. "Structures actancielles en quechua". *Actances* (Paris: CNRS) 3.159-177.

KOERNER, Konrad. 1988. *Saussurean Studies/Études saussuriennes*. Geneva: Slatkine.

KÖHLER, Oswin. 1981. "La langue kxoe". Perrot 1981.483-555.

KOHNEN, B. 1933. *Shilluk Grammar with a Little English-Shilluk Dictionary*. Verona: Missioni Africane.

KOOPMAN, Hilda & Claire LEFEBVRE. 1981. "Haitian creole *pu*". Muysken 1981.201-221.

KORHONEN, Mikko. 1982. "Reductive Phonetic Developments as the Trigger to Typological Change: Two examples from the Finno-Ugrian languages". *Papers from the 5th International Conference on Historical Linguistics*, ed. by Anders Ahlqvist (Current Issues in Linguistic Theory, 21), 190-195. Amsterdam: John Benjamins.

KOROSTOVCEV, M. A. 1963. *Vvedenie v egipetskuju filologiju*. (Akademija Nauk SSSR, Institut Narodov Azii) Moscow: Izdatel'stvo Vostočnoj Literatury.

KOSTER, J. & E. REULAND. 1991. *Long Distance Anaphora*. Cambridge: Cambridge Univ. Press.

KOTEY, Paul F. A. & Haig DER-HOUSSIKIAN, eds. 1977. *Language and*

Linguistic problems in Africa: Proceedings of the VIIth Conference on African Linguistics. Columbia, S.C.: Hornbeam Press.

KOULOUGHLI, Djamal. 1988. "Renouvellement énonciatif et valeur aoristique". *Langues Orientales Anciennes, Philologie et Linguistique* (Paris & Louvain: Peeters) 1.49-72.

KUHN, Thomas S. 1970. *The Structure of Scientific Revolutions.* 2nd enl. ed. Chicago: Univ. of Chicago Press.

KUNO, Susumu. 1987. *Functional Syntax, Anaphora, Discourse and Empathy.* Chicago: Univ. of Chicago Press.

— & E. KABURAKI. 1977. "Empathy and Syntax". *Linguistic Inquiry* 8:4.627-672.

KUPERUS, Juliana. 1985. *The Londo Word: Its philological and morphological structure.* (Annuaire, 119) Tervuren: Musée royal de l'Afrique Centrale.

LAKOFF, George & Mark JOHNSON. 1980. *Metaphors We Live By.* Chicago: Univ. of Chicago Press.

LANGACKER, Ronald W. 1977. "Syntactic Reanalysis". Li 1977.57-139.

LAUNEY, Michel. 1979. "Le datif dans une langue sans cas (nahuatl classique)". *Relations prédicat-actant(s) dans des langues de types divers,* ed. by Catherine Paris, vol.II (LACITO-Documents; Eurasie, 3), 29-70. Paris: SELAF.

— 1988. *Catégories et opérations dans la grammaire nahuatl.* Doctoral dissertation, Paris: Univ. de Paris-Sorbonne-Paris IV.

LAWTON, David. 1985. "Code Shifting in Jamaican Creole". *Diversity and Development in English-Related Creoles,* ed. by Ian F. Hancock, 68-88. Ann Arbor, Mich.: Karoma.

LAZARD, Gilbert. 1982. "Le morphème *râ* en persan et les relations actancielles". *BSLP* 77:1.177-207.

LEHMANN, Christian. 1982a. "Universal and typological aspects of agreement". *Apprehension, Das Sprachliche Erfassen von Gegenständen* (Teil II: Die Techniken und ihr Zusammenhang in Einzelsprachen), ed. by Hansjakob Seiler and Franz-Josef Stachowiak, 201-267. Tübingen: Gunter Narr Verlag.

— 1982b. *Thoughts on Grammaticalization.* (AKUP, 48) Cologne: Institut für Sprachwissenschaft, Univ. zu Köln.

— 1985. "The Role of Grammaticalization in Linguistic Typology". *Language Invariants and Mental Operations,* ed. by Hansjakob Seiler & Gunter Brettschneider (Language Universals Series, 5), 41-52. Tübingen:

Gunter Narr.

— 1987a. "Sprachwandel und Typologie". *Beiträge zum 3. Essener Kolloquium über Sprachwandel und seine bestimmenden Faktoren*, ed. by Norbert Boretzky, Werner Enninger & Thomas Stolz, 201-225. Bochum: Norbert Brockmeyer.

— 1987b. "Theoretical Implications of Processes of Grammaticalization". Paper prepared for the Conference on The Role of Theory in Language Description, 1-25. Ocho Rios (Jamaica).

— 1990. "Towards Lexical Typology". *Studies in Typology and Diachrony for Joseph H. Greenberg*, ed. by William Croft, Keith Denning & Suzanne Kemmer (Typological Studies in Language, 20), 161-185. Amsterdam & Philadelphia: John Benjamins.

LEHMANN, Winfred P., ed. 1986. *Language Typology 1985: Papers from the Linguistic Typology Symposium, Moscow 9-13 December 1985*. (Current Issues in Linguistic Theory, 47) Amsterdam & Philadelphia: John Benjamins.

LEMARÉCHAL, Alain. 1989. *Les parties du discours: Sémantique et syntaxe*. Paris: Presses Universitaires de France.

LÉVY, Ernst H. 1915. "Judéo-allemand *Schnerīe*". *Mémoires de la Société de Linguistique de Paris* 8:5.317-342. Paris.

LI, Charles N., ed. 1976. *Subject and Topic*. New York: Academic Press.

—, ed. 1977. *Mechanisms of Syntactic Change*. Austin & London: Univ. of Texas Press.

— & Sandra A. THOMPSON. 1977. "A Mechanism for the Development of Copula Morphemes". Li 1977.419-444.

LI, Ying-Che. 1980. "The Historical Development of the Coverb and the Coverbial Phrase in Chinese". *Journal of Chinese Linguistics* 8:2. 273-293.

LIPKA, Leonhard. 1968. "Kugelsicher: A l'épreuve des balles". *Wortbildung, Syntax und Morphologie: Festschrift zum 60. Geburtstag von Hans Marchand*, ed. by H. E. Brekle & L. Lipka, 127-143. The Hague: Mouton.

LOMBARD, Alf. 1974. *La langue roumaine, une présentation*. (Bibliothèque française et romane, A 29) Paris: Klincksieck.

LONGACRE, Robert E. 1985. "Sentences as Combinations of Clauses". Shopen 1985 II. 235-286.

LORD, Carol. 1976. "Evidence for Syntactic Reanalysis: From verb to complementizer in Kwa". Steever, Walker & Mufwene 1976.179-191.

LÜDTKE, Helmut. 1977. "Die Mundart von Ripatransone: Ein sprach-typologisches Kuriosum". *Studies in Linguistic Typology*, ed. by M. Romportl, V. Skalička, J. Popela & B. Palek (Philologica 5; Linguistica generalia, 1), 173-177. Prague: Charles Univ. (Acta Universitatis Carolinae).

— 1986. "Esquisse d'une théorie du changement langagier". *La Linguistique* 22:1.1-50.

LUKAS, Johannes. 1937. *A Study of the Kanuri Language: Grammar and vocabulary*. London: Oxford Univ. Press.

MAKKAI, Adam. 1972. *Idiom Structure in English*. The Hague: Mouton.

MARCHESE, Lynell. 1984. "Tense Innovation in the Kru Language Family". *Studies in African Linguistics* 15:2.189-213.

MARTIN, Paul. 1982. "Le système verbal montagnais, 1: Le noyau lexical et les déterminants personnels". *Langues et Linguistique* 8:1.203-239. Québec: Univ. Laval.

MASICA, Colin P. 1976. *Defining a Linguistic Area: South-Asia*. Chicago: Univ. of Chicago Press.

MASSON, Michel. 1986. *Langue et idéologie: Les mots étrangers en hébreu moderne*. Paris: Éditions du CNRS.

MATISOFF, James A. 1973. *The Grammar of Lahu*. (Univ. of California Publications in Linguistics, 75) Berkeley: Univ. of California Press.

— 1989. "Grammaticalisation en Asie du Sud-Est: traits aréaux et caractères universels". Paper prepared for Workshop on Language and Linguistics, June 1989. Paris: École des Hautes Études en Sciences Sociales.

MAURER, Philippe. 1987. "La comparaison des morphèmes temporels du papiamento et du palenquero: Arguments contre la théorie monogénétique de la genèse des langues créoles". Maurer & Stolz 1987.27-70.

— & Thomas STOLZ, eds. 1987. *Varia Creolica*. (Bochum-Essener Beiträge zur Sprachwandelforschung, 1) Bochum: Norbert Brockmeyer.

McLENDON, Sally. 1978. "Ergativity, Case, and Transitivity in Eastern Pomo". *IJAL* 44:1.1-9.

MEILLET, Antoine. 1912. "L'évolution des formes grammaticales". *Scientia* 12:6. (Repr. in Meillet 1958.130-148).

— 1958. *Linguistique historique et linguistique générale*, vol.I. (Collection Linguistique publiée par la Société de Linguistique de Paris, 8) Paris: Honoré Champion.

MEL'ČUK, Igor A. 1982. *Towards a Language of Linguistics*. (International Library of General Linguistics, 44) Munich: Wilhelm Fink.

— 1988. *Dependency Syntax: Theory and practice.* Albany, N.Y.: State Univ. of New York Press.

MENOVŠČIKOV, G. A. 1969. *O nekotoryx social'nyx aspektax evoljucii jazyka.* Leningrad: Izd. "Nauka".

MERRIFIELD, William R. 1959. "The Kiowa Verb Prefix". *IJAL* 25:3.168-176.

MICHAILOVSKY,. Boyd. 1976. "Typological sketch: Hayu". Unpubl. paper.

— 1988. *La langue hayu.* (Sciences du langage) Paris: Éditions du CNRS.

MITHUN, Marianne. 1984. "The evolution of noun incorporation". *Language* 60.847-893.

— 1986. "On the nature of noun incorporation". *Language* 62.32-37.

MONTEIL, Vincent. 1960. *L'arabe moderne.* (Études Arabes et Islamiques; Études et documents, 3) Paris: Klincksieck.

MOSEL, Ulrike. 1980. *Tolai and Tok Pisin: The influence of the substratum on the development of New Guinea Pidgin.* (Pacific Linguistics, B 70) Canberra: Australian National Univ.

MÜHLHÄUSLER, Peter. 1979. *Growth and Structure of the Lexicon of New Guinea Pidgin.* (Pacific Linguistics, C 52) Canberra: Australian National Univ.

— 1981. "The Development of the Category of Number in Tok Pisin". Muysken 1981.35-84.

— 1989. "On the Causes of Accelerated Linguistic Change in the Pacific Area". Breivik & Jahr 1989.137-172.

MUNRO, Pamela. 1977. "From Existential to Copula: The history of Yuman BE". Li 1977.445-490.

MUYSKEN, Pieter, ed. 1981. *Generative Studies in Creole Languages.* (Studies in Generative Grammar, 6) Dordrecht, Holland & Cinnaminson, N.J.: Foris.

NARO, Anthony J. 1978. "A Study on the Origins of Pidginization". *Language* 54.314-347.

NEVIS, Joel A. 1985. "Language-External Evidence for Clitics as Words: Lappish particle clitics". *Papers from the General Session,* ed. by W. H. Eilfort, P. D. Kroeber & K. L. Peterson (CLS 21:2), 289-305. Chicago: Chicago Linguistic Society.

NGUYEN, Phu-Phong. 1992. "L'espace énonciatif en vietnamien: relations déictiques et personnelles". Danon-Boileau & Morel 1992.177-186.

NICHOLS, Johanna. 1986a. "Head-Marking and Dependent-Marking

Grammar". *Language* 62.56-119.
— 1986b. "On Form and Content in Typology". Lehmann 1986.141-162.
— & Anthony C. WOODBURY, eds. 1985. *Grammar Inside and Outside the Clause: Some approaches to theory from the field*. Cambridge: Cambridge Univ. Press.

OHALA, John J. 1981. "The Listener as a Source of Sound Change". *Papers from the Parasession on Language and Behavior*, ed. by Carrie S. Masek, Roberta A. Hendrick & Mary F. Miller, 178-203. Chicago: Chicago Linguistic Society.

OSTHOFF, Hermann & Karl BRUGMANN. 1878. "Vorwort". *Morphologische Untersuchungen* 1.iii-xx. Leipzig: Salomon Hirzel. (English transl. in *A Reader in Nineteenth-Century Historical-Comparative Indo-European Linguistics*, ed. by Winfred P. Lehmann, 198-209. Bloomington & London: Indiana Univ. Press, 1967).

OWEN, Michael G. 1973. "Semantic Aspects of Yucatec Dual-Object Constructions". *Meaning in Mayan Languages*, ed. by Munro S. Edmonson, 51-57. The Hague-Paris: Mouton.

OZANNE-RIVIERRE, Françoise. 1976. *Le iaai, langue mélanésienne d'Ouvéa (Nouvelle-Calédonie)*. (Langues et Civilisations à Tradition Orale, 20) Paris: SELAF.
— 1986. "Redoublement expressif et dédoublement des séries consonantiques dans les langues des Iles Loyauté (Nouvelle-Calédonie)". *Te Reo* (Auckland, N.Z.) 29.25-53.
— & C. MOYSE. 1978. "L'incorporation nominale dans les langues océaniennes". *LACITO-Informations* 9.28-29. Paris: SELAF.

PARIS, Marie-Claude. 1989. *Linguistique générale et linguistique chinoise: Quelques exemples d'argumentation*. Paris: Université de Paris VII.

PASCH, Helma & Robin THELWALL. 1987. "Losses and Innovations in Nubi". Maurer & Stolz 1987.91-165.

PAULIAN, Christiane. 1975. *Le kukuya, langue teke du Congo: Phonologie, classes nominales*. (Bibliothèque de la SELAF, 49-50) Paris: SELAF.

PAWLEY, Andrew. 1975. "Kalam Classification of Body and Mental Processes". Unpubl. paper, Univ. of Auckland, N.Z.
— 1985. "On Speech Formulas and Linguistic Competence". *Lenguas Modernas* (Universidad de Chile) 12.84-104.

PERROT, Jean, ed. 1981. *Les langues dans le monde ancien et moderne*. Paris: Éditions du CNRS.

PEYRAUBE, Alain. 1988. *Syntaxe diachronique du chinois: Évolution des constructions datives du XIVe siècle av. J.-C. au XVIIIe siècle.* (Mémoires de l'Institut des Hautes Études Chinoises, 29) Paris: Collège de France, Institut des Hautes Études Chinoises.

PIOU, Nanie. 1982. "Le clivage du prédicat". *Syntaxe de l'haïtien*, ed. by Claire Lefebvre, H. Magloire-Holly & N. Piou, 122-151. Ann Arbor, Mich.: Karoma.

PLANK, Frans, ed. 1979. *Ergativity: Towards a theory of grammatical relations.* New York: Academic Press.

POLOTSKY, Hans Jakob. 1944. *Études de syntaxe copte.* Le Caire: Société d'Archéologie Copte.

— 1960. "The Coptic Conjugation System". *Orientalia* 29.392-422.

— 1978. "A Point of Arabic Syntax: The indirect attribute". *Israel Oriental Studies* 8.159-173.

PURY-TOUMI, Sybille de. 1981. "L'espace des possibles: L'exemple du nahuatl". *BSLP* 76:1.359-379.

QVONJE, J. E. 1980. "Die Grammatikalisierung der Präposition *na* im Bulgarischen". *Folia Linguistica Historica* 1:2.317-351.

RAZTORGEVA, V. S. 1952. *Očerki po tadžikskoj dialektologii.* 2 vols. Moscow: Izd. "Nauka".

RENAUD, Francis & Shen-Yi LUO. 1987. "Étude lexicographique de *zài* (à nouveau)". *Cahiers de Linguistique Asie Orientale* 16:1.81-108.

RICE, Keren D. 1986. "Some Remarks on Direct and Indirect Discourse in Slave (Northern Athapaskan)". Coulmas 1986.47-76.

ROBERTSON, Ian E. 1979. *Berbice Dutch: A description.* Doctoral dissertation, Univ. of the West Indies.

ROSÉN, Haiim B. 1958. "Sur quelques catégories à expression adnominale en hébreu israélien". *BSLP* 53:1.316-344.

— 1965. "Quelques phénomènes d'absence et de présence de l'accord dans la structure de la phrase en hébreu". *GLECS* 10.78-94.

— 1966. "Composition adjectivale en hébreu israélien". *GLECS* 10. 126-135.

— 1980."Weiteres über die Entstehung der periphrastischen 'Perfekt' Formen in Lateinischen". Brettschneider & Lehmann 1980.311-316.

ROSS, John Robert. 1967. *Constraints on Variables in Syntax.* Bloomington: Indiana Univ. Linguistics Club.

SADOCK, Jerrold M. 1980. "Noun Incorporation in Greenlandic". *Language* 56. 300-319.

— 1986. "Some notes on noun incorporation". *Language* 62.19-31.
SAMARIN, William J. 1965. "Perspectives on African Ideophones".
African Studies 24.117-121.
SAPIR, Edward. 1911. "The Problem of Noun Incorporation in American
Languages". *American Anthropologist* 13.248-283.
SAUSSURE, Ferdinand de. 1916. *Cours de linguistique générale*. Lausanne
& Paris: Payot.
SAXENA, Anuradha. 1981. "Verb Agreement in Hindi". *Linguistics*
19.467-474.
— 1985. "Verb Agreement in Hindi, Part II: A critique of Comrie's
analysis". *Linguistics* 22.857-864.
SCHLEGEL, August Wilhelm. 1818. *Observations sur la langue et la
littérature provençales*. Paris: Librairie grecque-latine-allemande.
SCHLEGEL, Friedrich. 1808. *Über die Sprache und Weisheit der Indier*.
Heidelberg: Mohr & Zimmer. (New ed., with an Introd. by Sebastiano
Timpanaro, Amsterdam: John Benjamins, 1977).
SCHLEICHER, August. 1861-1862. *Compendium der vergleichenden
Grammatik der indogermanischen Sprachen*. 2 vols. Weimar: Hermann
Böhlau. (4th ed., 1876).
SCHMIDT, Wilhelm. 1926. *Die Sprachfamilien und Sprachenkreise der
Erde*. Heidelberg: Carl Winter.
SCHOGT, Henry. 1988. *Linguistics, Literary Analysis, and Literary
Translation*. Toronto: Univ. of Toronto Press.
SCHUCHARDT, Hugo. 1979. *The Ethnography of Variation: Selected
Writings on Pidgins and Creoles*. Ed. and transl. by Thomas L. Markey.
(Linguistica Extranea; Studia, 3) Ann Arbor, Mich.: Karoma.
SCOTT, Graham. 1978. *The Fore Language of Papua New Guinea*.
(Pacific Linguistics, B 47) Canberra: Australian National Univ.
SEGAL, Moses H. 1927. *A Grammar of Mischnaic Hebrew*. Oxford:
Clarendon Press.
SELLS, Peter. 1987. "Aspects of Logophoricity". *Linguistic Inquiry*
18:3.445-479.
SERBAT, Guy. 1988. *Linguistique latine et linguistique générale*.
(Bibliothèque des Cahiers de l'Institut de Linguistique de Louvain, 39)
Louvain-la-Neuve: Peeters.
SHAUMYAN, Sebastian K. 1985. "Ergativity and Applicative Universal
Grammar". Unpubl. paper, Yale Univ.
SHIBATANI, Masayoshi. 1985. "Passives and Related Constructions: A

prototype analysis". *Language* 61.821-848.

— 1990. *The Languages of Japan.* Cambridge: Cambridge Univ. Press.

— & Taro KAGEYAMA, 1988. "Word Formation in a Modular Theory of Grammar: Postsyntactic compounds in Japanese". *Language* 64. 451-484.

SHIPLEY, William F. 1964. *Maidu Grammar.* (Univ. of California Publications in Linguistics, 41) Berkeley & Los Angeles: Univ. of California Press.

SHOPEN, Timothy, ed. 1985. *Language Typology and Syntactic Description.* 3 vols. Cambridge: Cambridge Univ. Press.

SIEGEL, Jeff. 1987. *Language Contact in a Plantation Environment: A sociolinguistic history of Fiji.* (Studies in the Social and Cultural Foundations of Language, 5) Cambridge: Cambridge Univ. Press.

SILVERSTEIN, Michael. 1976. "Hierarchy of Features and Ergativity". *Grammatical Categories in Australian Languages*, ed. by Robert M. W. Dixon, 112-171. Canberra: Australian Institute of Aboriginal Studies.

SKORIK, Pjotr J. 1961. *Grammatika čukotskogo jazyka.* (2nd part, 1977) Moskow & Leningrad: Izd. "Nauka".

SMITH, Norval S. H., Ian E. ROBERTSON, Kay WILLIAMSON. 1987. "The Ijo-Element in Berbice Dutch". *Language in Society* 14.49-90.

SRIDHAR, S. N. 1976. "Dative Subjects". *Papers from the Twelfth Regional Meeting*, ed. by Salikoko S. Mufwene, Cynthia A. Walker, Sanford B. Steever, 582-593. Chicago: Chicago Linguistic Society.

STEEVER, Sanford B., Cynthia A. WALKER, Salikoko S. MUFWENE, eds. 1976. *Papers from the Parasession on Diachronic Syntax.* Chicago: Chicago Linguistic Society.

STOLZ, Thomas. 1986. *Gibt es das kreolische Sprachwandelmodell?* (Europäische Hochschulschriften, 21) Frankfurt am Main-Bern-New York: Peter Lang.

— 1987a. "Natürlichkeit und Interferenz". *Papiere zur Linguistik.* 36.17-44.

— 1987b. "Verbale Morphosyntax der portugiesisch-basierten Kreols". *Ibero-Americana* 30.35-59.

— 1987c. "The Development of the AUX-Category in Pidgins and Creoles: The case of the resultative-perfective and its relation to anteriority". *Historical Development of Auxiliaries*, ed. by Martin B. Harris & Paolo Ramat (Trends in Linguistics; Studies and Monographs, 35), 291-315. Berlin-New York-Amsterdam: Mouton de Gruyter.

— 1988. "Markiertheitshierarchie und Merkmalhaftigkeit in Numerussystemen: Über den Dual". *ZPSK* 41:4.476-487.

— 1989. "Kreolische Morphologie". *ZPSK* 42:1.48-55.

— 1990. "Afrikaans: Eine Fallstudie zur diachronen Kontinuität und/oder Diskontinuität". *ZPSK* 43:4.457-475.

SWADESH, Morris. 1939. "Nootka Internal Syntax". *IJAL* 9:2/4.77-102.

TALMY, Leonard. 1985. "Lexicalization Patterns: Semantic structure in lexical forms". Shopen 1985 III, 57-149.

TAMBA-MECZ, Irène. 1988. *La sémantique*. (Que sais-je?, 655) Paris: Presses Universitaires de France.

TAYLOR, Douglas. 1977. *Languages of the West Indies*. Baltimore, Md.: Johns Hopkins Univ. Press.

TAYLOR, John R. 1987. "Tense and Metaphorizations of Time in Zulu". *Perspectives on Language in Performance: To honour Werner Hüllen*, ed. by Wolfgang Lörscher & Rainer Schulze, Vol.I, 214-229. Tübingen: Gunter Narr.

TERSIS, Nicole & Alain KIHM, eds. 1988. *Temps et aspects*. (Numéro spécial, 19) Paris: Peeters-SELAF.

TESNIÈRE, Lucien, 1959. *Éléments de syntaxe structurale*. Paris: Klincksieck. (2nd ed., 1965).

THOMAS, Jacqueline M. C. 1988. "Temps et espace: Du vécu au linguistique". Tersis & Kihm 1988.55-81.

THOMASON, Sarah Gray. 1983. "Genetic Relationship and the Case of Ma'a (Mbugu)". *Studies in African Linguistics* 14.195-231.

— 1986. "Contact-induced language change : possibilities and probabilities". Boretzky, Enninger & Stolz 1986.261-284.

THOMPSON, Laurence C. 1965. *A Vietnamese Grammar*. Seattle: Univ. of Washington Press.

— & M. Terry THOMPSON. 1971. "Clallam: A preview". *Studies in American Indian Languages*, ed. by J. Sawyer (Univ. of California Publications in Linguistics, 65), 251-294. Berkeley & Los Angeles: Univ. of California Press.

TIMBERLAKE, Alan. 1977. "Reanalysis and Actualization in Syntactic Change". Li 1977.141-177.

TOURNADRE, Laurent. 1992. "La deixis en tibétain: Quelques faits remarquables". Danon-Boileau & Morel 1992.197-208.

TRAUGOTT, Elizabeth Closs. 1985. "Conditional Markers". Haiman 1985.-289-307.

— 1989. "On the Rise of Epistemic Meanings in English: An example of subjectification in semantic change". *Language* 65.31-55.

— & Bernd HEINE, eds. 1991. *Approaches to Grammaticalization.* (Typological Studies in Language, 19) 2 vol. Amsterdam & Philadelphia: John Benjamins.

TROIKE, Rudolph C. 1981. "Subject-Object Concord in Coahuilteco". *Language* 57.658-673.

TSCHENKELI, K. 1958. *Einführung in die georgische Sprache.* Zürich: Amirani.

TSE, Kwok-Keung. 1986. "Le suffixe verbal *mai* en chinois cantonais". *Aspects, modalité: Problèmes de catégorisation grammaticale* (Département de Recherches Linguistiques; Collection ERA, 642), 11-22. Paris: Univ. de Paris VII.

TURNER, Lorenzo Dow. 1949. *Africanisms in the Gullah Dialect.* Chicago: Univ. of Chicago Press.

VANDAME, Charles. 1963. *Le ngambay-moundou.* Dakar: Institut Français d'Afrique Noire.

VAN DEN EYNDE, Karel. 1960. *Fonologie en morfologie van het Cokwe.* Leuven: Institut Royal d'Études Congolaises.

— & Kutumisa B. KYOTA. 1984. "Procédés tonals de construction syntaxique en yaka". *Fifth International Phonology Meeting: Discussion Papers,* ed. by Wolfgang U. Dressler, Oskar E. Pfeiffer & John R. Rennison (Wiener Linguistische Gazette; Supplement 3), 68-72. Vienna: Institut für Sprachwissenschaft, Univ. Wien.

VAN SCHOOR, J. L. 1983. *Die Grammatika van Standaard-Afrikaans.* Johannesburg: Lex Patria.

VENDRYES, Joseph. 1923. *Le langage: Introduction linguistique à l'histoire.* Paris: La Renaissance du Livre.

VOGT, Hans. 1971. *Grammaire de la langue géorgienne.* (Instituttet for Sammenlignende Kulturforskning, B LVII) Oslo: Universitetsforlaget.

von RONCADOR, Manfred. 1988. *Zwischen direkter und indirekter Rede: Nichtwörtliche direkte Rede, erlebte Rede, logophorische Konstruktionen und Verwandtes.* (Linguistische Arbeiten, 192) Tübingen: Max Niemeyer.

VOORHOEVE, C. L. 1977. "Ta-poman: Metaphorical use of words and poetic vocabulary in Asmat songs". *Language, Culture, Society, and the Modern World,* fasc.1, ed. by Stephen A. Wurm (Pacific Linguistics, C 40: New Guinea Area Languages and Language Study, 3), 19-38. Canberra: Australian National Univ.

VOORHOEVE, Jan. 1980. "Le pronom logophorique et son importance pour la reconstruction du Proto-Bantou (PB)". *Sprache und Geschichte in Afrika* 2.173-187.

WASHABAUGH, William. 1975. "On the Development of Complementizers in Creolization". *Working Papers in Language Universals* 17.109-140. Stanford Univ.

WEBSTER's 1976. *New World Dictionary of the American Language.* 2nd College ed. Cleveland, Ohio & New York: William Collins & World Publishing Co.

WEINREICH, Uriel. 1964. *Languages in Contact: Findings and problems.* 2nd ed. The Hague: Mouton. (1st ed., New York: Linguistic Circle of New York, 1953).

WELMERS, William E. 1973. *African Language Structures.* Berkeley & Los Angeles: Univ. of California Press.

WESTERMANN, Diedrich. 1907. *Grammatik der Ewe-Sprache.* Berlin: Reimer.

WIERZBICKA, Anna. 1972. *Semantic Primitives.* Frankfurt: Athenäum.

WILTSHIRE, Caroline, Randolph GRACZYK & Bradley MUSIC, eds. 1989. *Papers from the 25th Annual Regional Meeting,* Part I: *The general session.* Chicago: Chicago Linguistic Society.

WINGERD, Judy. 1977. "Serial verbs in Haitian Creole". Kotey & Der-Houssikian 1977.452-466.

WINTER, Werner, ed. 1984. *Anredeverhalten.* (Ars Linguistica, 13) Tübingen: Gunter Narr.

WITKOWSKI, Stanley R. & Cecil H. BROWN. 1983. "Marking Reversals and Cultural Importance". *Language* 59.569-582.

WITTGENSTEIN, Ludwig. 1967. *Philosophische Untersuchungen.* Frankfurt: Suhrkamp (1st ed., 1945).

WOODBURY, Hanni. 1975. "Onondaga Noun Incorporation: Some notes on the interdependence of syntax and semantics". *IJAL* 41.10-20.

WOOLFORD, Ellen. 1981. "The Developing Complementizer System of Tok Pisin". Muysken 1981.125-139.

WUNDT, Wilhelm. 1900. *Völkerpsychologie: Eine Untersuchung der Entwicklungsgesetze von Sprache, Mythus und Sitte.* Tome I: *Die Sprache.* 2 vols. Leipzig: Wilhelm Engelmann.

YEN, Sian L. 1986. "The Origin of the Copula *shi* in Chinese". *Journal of Chinese Linguistics* 14:2.227-241.

YOON, Jeong-Me. 1989. "Long-Distance Anaphors in Korean and Their

Crosslinguistic Implications". Wiltshire, Graczyk & Music 1989.479-495.
ZOLOTOVA, Galina A. 1989. "Structure de la proposition et types communicatifs de texte". Breuillard 1989.325-335.

Index of Subjects

Note: Terms in bold-faced type are new coinages

Index of languages

Index of Names

In the CURRENT ISSUES IN LINGUISTIC THEORY (CILT) series (Series Editor: E.F. Konrad Koerner) the following volumes have been published thus far, and will be published during 1993:

1. KOERNER, E.F. Konrad (ed.): *The Transformational-Generative Paradigm and Modern Linguistic Theory*. Amsterdam, 1975.
2. WEIDERT, Alfons: *Componential Analysis of Lushai Phonology*. Amsterdam, 1975.
3. MAHER, J. Peter: *Papers on Language Theory and History I: Creation and Tradition in Language*. Foreword by Raimo Anttila. Amsterdam, 1977.
4. HOPPER, Paul J. (ed.): *Studies in Descriptive and Historical Linguistics: Festschrift for Winfred P. Lehmann*. Amsterdam, 1977. Out of print.
5. ITKONEN, Esa: *Grammatical Theory and Metascience: A critical investigation into the methodological and philosophical foundations of 'autonomous' linguistics*. Amsterdam, 1978.
6. ANTTILA, Raimo: *Historical and Comparative Linguistics*. Amsterdam/Philadelphia, 1989.
7. MEISEL, Jürgen M. & Martin D. PAM (eds): *Linear Order and Generative Theory*. Amsterdam, 1979.
8. WILBUR, Terence H.: *Prolegomena to a Grammar of Basque*. Amsterdam, 1979.
9. HOLLIEN, Harry & Patricia (eds): *Current Issues in the Phonetic Sciences, Proceedings of the IPS-77 Congress, Miami Beach, Fla., 17-19 December 1977*. Amsterdam, 1979. 2 vols.
10. PRIDEAUX, Gary (ed.): *Perspectives in Experimental Linguistics. Papers from the University of Alberta Conference on Experimental Linguistics, Edmonton, 13-14 Oct. 1978*. Amsterdam, 1979.
11. BROGYANYI, Bela (ed.): *Studies in Diachronic, Synchronic, and Typological Linguistics: Festschrift for Oswald Szemerényi on the Occasion of his 65th Birthday*. Amsterdam, 1980.
12. FISIAK, Jacek (ed.): *Theoretical Issues in Contrastive Linguistics*. Amsterdam, 1980.
13. MAHER, J. Peter with coll. of Allan R. Bomhard & E.F. Konrad Koerner (ed.): *Papers from the Third International Conference on Historical Linguistics, Hamburg, August 22-26, 1977*. Amsterdam, 1982.
14. TRAUGOTT, Elizabeth C., Rebecca LaBRUM, Susan SHEPHERD (eds): *Papers from the Fourth International Conference on Historical Linguistics, Stanford, March 26-30, 1980*. Amsterdam, 1980.
15. ANDERSON, John (ed.): *Language Form and Linguistic Variation. Papers dedicated to Angus McIntosh*. Amsterdam, 1982.
16. ARBEITMAN, Yoël & Allan R. BOMHARD (eds): *Bono Homini Donum: Essays in Historical Linguistics, in Memory of J. Alexander Kerns*. Amsterdam, 1981.
17. LIEB, Hans-Heinrich: *Integrational Linguistics*. 6 volumes. Amsterdam, 1984-1986. Vol. I available; Vol. 2-6 n.y.p.
18. IZZO, Herbert J. (ed.): *Italic and Romance. Linguistic Studies in Honor of Ernst Pulgram*. Amsterdam, 1980.
19. RAMAT, Paolo et al. (eds): *Linguistic Reconstruction and Indo-European Syntax. Proceedings of the Coll. of the 'Indogermanische Gesellschaft' Univ. of Pavia, 6-7 Sept. 1979*. Amsterdam, 1980.
20. NORRICK, Neal R.: *Semiotic Principles in Semantic Theory*. Amsterdam, 1981.
21. AHLQVIST, Anders (ed.): *Papers from the Fifth International Conference on Historical Linguistics, Galway, April 6-10, 1981*. Amsterdam, 1982.
22. UNTERMANN, Jürgen & Bela BROGYANYI (eds): *Das Germanische und die Rekonstruktion der Indogermanische Grundsprache*. Akten, Proceedings from the Colloquium of the Indogermanische Gesellschaft, Freiburg, 26-27 February 1981. Amsterdam, 1984.
23. DANIELSEN, Niels: *Papers in Theoretical Linguistics*. Edited by Per Baerentzen. Amsterdam/Philadelphia, 1992.
24. LEHMANN, Winfred P. & Yakov MALKIEL (eds): *Perspectives on Historical Linguistics. Papers from a conference held at the meeting of the Language Theory Division, Modern Language Ass., San Francisco, 27-30 December 1979*. Amsterdam, 1982.
25. ANDERSEN, Paul Kent: *Word Order Typology and Comparative Constructions*. Amsterdam, 1983.

26. BALDI, Philip (ed.) *Papers from the XIIth Linguistic Symposium on Romance Languages, University Park, April 1-3, 1982.* Amsterdam, 1984.

27. BOMHARD, Alan: *Toward Proto-Nostratic.* Amsterdam, 1984.

28. BYNON, James: *Current Progress in Afroasiatic Linguistics: Papers of the Third International Hamito-Semitic Congress, London, 1978.* Amsterdam, 1984.

29. PAPROTTÉ, Wolf & René DIRVEN (eds): *The Ubiquity of Metaphor: Metaphor in Language and Thought.* Amsterdam, 1985.

30. HALL, Robert A., Jr.: *Proto-Romance Morphology.* Amsterdam, 1984.

31. GUILLAUME, Gustave: *Foundations for a Science of Language.* Translated and with an introd. by Walter Hirtle and John Hewson. Amsterdam, 1984.

32. COPELAND, James E. (ed.): *New Directions in Linguistics and Semiotics.* Houston/Amsterdam, 1984. No rights for US/Can. *Customers from USA and Canada: please order from Rice University.*

33. VERSTEEGH, Kees: *Pidginization and Creolization: The Case of Arabic.* Amsterdam, 1984.

34. FISIAK, Jacek (ed.): *Papers from the VIth International Conference on Historical Linguistics, Poznan, 22-26 August 1983.* Amsterdam, 1985.

35. COLLINGE, N.E.: *The Laws of Indo-European.* Amsterdam, 1985.

36. KING, Larry D. & Catherine A. MALEY (eds): *Selected Papers from the XIIIth Linguistics Symposium on Romance Languages.* Amsterdam, 1985.

37. GRIFFEN, T.D.: *Aspects of Dynamic Phonology.* Amsterdam, 1985.

38. BROGYANYI, Bela & Thomas KRÖMMELBEIN (eds): *Germanic Dialects: Linguistic and Philological Investigations.* Amsterdam, 1986.

39. BENSON, James D., Michael J. CUMMINGS & William S. GREAVES (eds): *Linguistics in a Systemic Perspective.* Amsterdam, 1988.

40. FRIES, Peter Howard and Nancy (eds): *Toward an Understanding of Language: Charles C. Fries in Perspective.* Amsterdam, 1985.

41. EATON, Roger, et al. (eds): *Papers from the 4th International Conference on English Historical Linguistics.* Amsterdam, 1985.

42. MAKKAI, Adam & Alan K. MELBY (eds): *Linguistics and Philosophy. Essays in honor of Rulon S. Wells.* Amsterdam, 1985.

43. AKAMATSU, Tsutomu: *The Theory of Neutralization and the Archiphoneme in Functional Phonology.* Amsterdam, 1988.

44. JUNGRAITHMAYR, Herrmann & Walter W. MUELLER (eds): *Proceedings of the 4th International Hamito-Semitic Congress.* Amsterdam, 1987.

45. KOOPMAN, W.F., F.C. VAN DER LEEK, O. FISCHER & R. EATON (eds): *Explanation and Linguistic Change.* Amsterdam, 1987.

46. PRIDEAUX, Gary D., and William J. BAKER: *Strategies and Structures: The Processing of Relative Clauses.* Amsterdam, 1986.

47. LEHMANN, Winfred P.: *Language Typology 1985. Papers from the Linguistic Typology Symposium, Moscow, 9-13 Dec. 1985.* Amsterdam, 1986.

48. RAMAT, Anna Giacalone (ed.): *Proceedings of the VII International Conference on Historical Linguistics, Pavia 9-13 September 1985.* Amsterdam, 1987.

49. WAUGH, Linda R. & Stephen RUDY (eds): *New Vistas in Grammar: Invariance and Variation.* Amsterdam/Philadelphia, 1991.

50. RUDZKA-OSTYN, Brygida (ed.): *Topics in Cognitive Linguistics.* Amsterdam/Philadelphia, 1988.

51. CHATTERJEE, Ranjit: *Aspect and Meaning in Slavic and Indic.* Amsterdam/Philadelphia, 1988.

52. FASOLD, Ralph & Deborah SCHIFFRIN (eds): *Language Change and Variation.* Amsterdam/Philadelphia, 1989.

53. SANKOFF, David (ed.): *Diversity and Diachrony.* Amsterdam, 1986.

54. WEIDERT, Alfons: *Tibeto-Burman Tonology. A Comparative Analysis.* Amsterdam, 1987.

55. HALL, Robert A. Jr.: *Linguistics and Pseudo-Linguistics.* Amsterdam, 1987.

56. HOCKETT, Charles F.: *Refurbishing our Foundations. Elementary Linguistics from an Advanced Point of View.* Amsterdam, 1987.

57. BUBENIK, Vít: *Hellenistic and Roman Greece as a Sociolinguistic Area.* Amsterdam/Philadelphia, 1989.

58. ARBEITMAN, Yoël L.: *FUCUS. A Semitic/Afrasian Gathering in Remembrance of Albert Ehrman.* Amsterdam/Philadelphia, 1988.

59. VOORST, Jan van: *Event Structure.* Amsterdam/Philadelphia, 1988.

60. KIRSCHNER, Carl and Janet DECESARIS (eds): *Studies in Romance Linguistics.* Amsterdam/Philadelphia, 1989.

61. CORRIGAN, Roberta, Fred ECKMAN and Michael NOONAN (eds): *Linguistic Categorization.* Amsterdam/Philadelphia, 1989.

62. FRAJZYNGIER, Zygmunt (ed.): *Current Progress in Chadic Linguistics.* Amsterdam/Philadelphia, 1989.

63. EID, Mushira (ed.): *Perspectives on Arabic Linguistics I. Papers from the First Annual Symposium on Arabic Linguistics.* Amsterdam/Philadelphia, 1990.

64. BROGYANYI, Bela (ed.): *Prehistory, History, and Historiography of Language, Speech, and Linguistic Theory.* Amsterdam/Philadelphia, 1992.

65. ADAMSON, Sylvia, Vivien A. LAW, Nigel VINCENT and Susan WRIGHT (eds): *Papers from the 5th International Conference of English Historical Linguistics.* Amsterdam/Philadelphia, 1990.

66. ANDERSEN, Henning and Konrad KOERNER (eds): *Historical Linguistics 1987. Papers from the 8th International Conference on Historical Linguistics, Lille, August 30-September 4, 1987.* Amsterdam/Philadelphia, 1990.

67. LEHMANN, Winfred (ed.): *Language Typology 1987. Systematic Balance in Language. Papers from the Linguistic Typology Symposium, Berkeley, 1-3 December 1987.* Amsterdam/Philadelphia, 1990.

68. BALL, Martin, James FIFE, Erich POPPE and Jenny ROWLAND (eds): *Celtic Linguistics / Ieithyddiaeth Geltaidd. Readings in the Brythonic Languages. Festschrift for T. Arwyn Watkins.* Amsterdam/Philadelphia, 1990.

69. WANNER, Dieter and Douglas A. KIBBEE (eds): *New Analyses in Romance Linguistics. Papers from the XVIII Linguistic Symposium on Romance Languages, Urbana-Champaign, April 7-9, 1988.* Amsterdam/Philadelphia, 1991.

70. JENSEN, John T.: *Morphology. Word Structure in Generative Grammar.* Amsterdam/Philadelphia, 1990.

71. O'GRADY, WILLIAM: *Categories and Case. The sentence structure of Korean.* Amsterdam/Philadelphia, 1991.

72. EID, Mushira and John McCARTHY (eds): *Perspectives on Arabic Linguistics II Papers from the Second Annual Symposium on Arabic Linguistics.* Amsterdam/Philadelphia, 1990.

73. STAMENOV, Maxim (ed.): *Current Advances in Semantic Theory.* Amsterdam/Philadelphia, 1992.

74. LAEUFER, Christiane and Terrell A. MORGAN (eds): *Theoretical Analyses in Romance Linguistics.* Amsterdam/Philadelphia, 1992.

75. DROSTE, Flip G. and John E. JOSEPH (eds): *Linguistic Theory and Grammatical Description.* Amsterdam/Philadelphia, 1991.

76. WICKENS, Mark A.: *Grammatical Number in English Nouns.* Amsterdam/Philadelphia, 1992.

77. BOLTZ, William G. and Michael C. SHAPIRO (eds): *Studies in the Historical Phonology of Asian Languages.* Amsterdam/Philadelphia, 1991.

78. KAC, Michael B.: *Grammars and Grammaticality.* Amsterdam/Philadelphia, 1992.

79. ANTONSEN, Elmer H. and Hans Henrich HOCK (eds): *STÆFCRÆFT: Studies in Germanic Linguistics.* Amsterdam/Philadelphia, 1991.

80. COMRIE, Bernard and Mushira EID (eds): *Perspectives on Arabic Linguistics III.* Amsterdam/Philadelphia, 1991.

81. LEHMANN, Winfred P. & H.J. HEWITT (eds): *Language Typology 1988. Typological Models in Reconstruction*. Amsterdam/Philadelphia, 1991.
82. VAN VALIN, Robert D. (ed.): *Advances in Role and Reference Grammar*. Amsterdam/Philadelphia, 1993.
83. FIFE, James & Erich POPPE (eds): *Studies in Brythonic Word Order*. Amsterdam/Philadelphia, 1991.
84. DAVIS, Garry W. & Gregory K. IVERSON (eds): *Explanation in Historical Linguistics*. Amsterdam/Philadelphia, 1992.
85. BROSELOW, Ellen, Mushira EID & John McCARTHY (eds): *Perspectives on Arabic Linguistics IV*. Amsterdam/Philadelphia, 1992.
86. KESS, Joseph L.: *Psycholinguistics. Psychology, Linguistics, and the Study of Natural Language*. Amsterdam/Philadelphia, 1992.
87. BROGYANYI, Bela & Reiner LIPP (eds): *Historical Philology: Greek, Latin, and Romance Papers in Honor of Oswald Szemerényi II*. Amsterdam/Philadelphia, 1992.
88. SHIELDS, Kenneth.: *A History of Indo-European Verb Morphology*. Amsterdam/Philadelphia, 1992.
89. BURRIDGE, Kate: *Syntactic Change in Germanic. A study of some aspects of language change in Germanic with particular reference to Middle Dutch*. Amsterdam/Philadelphia, 1992.
90. KING, Larry D.: *The Semantic Structure of Spanish. Meaning and grammatical form*. Amsterdam/Philadelphia, 1992.
91. HIRSCHBÜHLER, Paul and Konrad KOERNER (eds): *Romance Languages and Modern Linguistic Theory. Selected papers from the XX Linguistic Symposium on Romance Languages*. Amsterdam/Philadelphia, 1992.
92. POYATOS, Fernando: *Paralanguage: A linguistic and interdisciplinary approach to interactive speech and sounds*. Amsterdam/Philadelphia, 1993.
93. LIPPI-GREEN, Rosina (ed.): *Recent Developments in Germanic Linguistics*. Amsterdam/Philadelphia, 1992.
94. HAGÈGE, Claude: *The Language Builder. An essay on the human signature in linguistic morphogenesis*. Amsterdam/Philadelphia, 1993.
95. MILLER, D. Gary: *Complex Verb Formation*. Amsterdam/Philadelphia, 1993.
96. LIEB, Hans-Heinrich (ed.): *Prospects for a New Structuralism*. Amsterdam/Philadelphia, 1992.
97. BROGYANYI, Bela and Reiner LIPP (eds): *Comparative-Historical Linguistics: Indo-European and Finno-Ugric. Papers in honor of Oswald Szemerényi III*. Amsterdam/Philadelphia, 1993.
98. EID, Mushira and Gregory K. IVERSON: *Principles and Prediction. The analysis of natural language*. Amsterdam/Philadelphia, 1993.
99. JENSEN, John T.: *English Phonology*. Amsterdam/Philadelphia, n.y.p.
101. EID, Mushira and Clive HOLES (eds): *Perspectives on Arabic Linguistics V. Papers from the Fifth Annual Symposium on Arabic Linguistics*. Amsterdam/Philadelphia, 1993.
102. GARGOV, George and Petko STAYNOV (eds): *Explorations in Language and Cognition*. Amsterdam/Philadelphia, 1993.